Introduce Calculation Method (page 245): Introduce a new method, typically a stored function, which implements a calculation that uses data stored within the database.

Introduce Cascading Delete (page 215): Ensure that the database automatically deletes the appropriate "child records" when a "parent record" is deleted.

Introduce Column Constraint (page 180): Introduce a column constraint in an existing table.

Introduce Common Format (page 183): Apply a consistent format to all the data values in an existing table column.

Introduce Default Value (page 186): Let the database provide a default value for an existing table column.

Introduce Hard Delete (page 219): Remove an existing column which indicates that a row has been deleted and instead actually delete the row.

Introduce Index (page 248): Introduce a new index of either unique or non-unique type.

Introduce New Column (page 301): Introduce a new column in an existing table.

Introduce New Table (page 304): Introduce a new table in an existing database.

Introduce Read-Only Table (page 251): Create a read-only data store based on existing tables in the database.

Introduce Soft Delete (page 222): Introduce a flag to an existing table which indicates that a row has been deleted instead of actually deleting the row.

Introduce Surrogate Key (page 85): Replace an existing natural key with a surrogate key.

Introduce Trigger For History (page 227): Introduce a new trigger to capture data changes for historical or audit purposes.

Introduce Variable (page 287): Put the result of the expression, or parts of the expression, in a temporary variable with a name that explains the purpose.

Introduce View (page 306): Create a view based on existing tables in the database.

Make Column Non-Nullable (page 189): Change an existing column so that it does not accept any null values.

Merge Columns (page 92): Merge two or more columns within a single table.

Merge Tables (page 96): Merge two or more tables into a single table.

Migrate Method From Database (page 257): Rehost an existing database method (a stored procedure, stored function, or trigger) in the application(s) which currently invoke it.

Migrate Method To Database (page 261): Rehost existing application logic in the database.

Move Column (page 103): Migrate a table column, with all of its data, to another existing table.

Move Data (page 192): Move the data contained within a table, either all or a subset of its columns, to another existing table.

Parameterize Method (page 278): Create one method that uses a parameter for the different values.

continued in back of book

Praise for *Refactoring Databases*

"This groundbreaking book finally reveals why database schemas need not be difficult to change, why data need not be difficult to migrate, and why database professionals need not be overburdened by change requests from customers and developers. Evolutionary design is at the heart of agility. Ambler and Sadalage have now shown the world how to evolve agile databases. Bravo!"
—Joshua Kerievsky, founder, Industrial Logic, Inc.; author, *Refactoring to Patterns*

"This book not only lays out the fundamentals for evolutionary database development, it provides many practical, detailed examples of database refactoring. It is a must read for database practitioners interested in agile development."
—Doug Barry, president, Barry & Associates, Inc.; author of *Web Services and Service-Oriented Architectures: The Savvy Manager's Guide*

"Ambler and Sadalage have taken the bold step of tackling an issue that other writers have found so daunting. Not only have they addressed the theory behind database refactoring, but they have also explained step-by-step processes for doing so in a controlled and thoughtful manner. But what really blew me away were the more than 200 pages of code samples and deep technical details illustrating how to overcome specific database refactoring hurdles. This is not just another introductory book convincing people that an idea is a good one—this is a tutorial and technical reference book that developers and DBAs alike will keep near their computers. Kudos to the brave duo for succeeding where others have failed to even try."
—Kevin Aguanno, senior project manager, IBM Canada Ltd.

"Anybody working on non-greenfield projects will recognize the value that Scott and Pramod bring to the software development life cycle with Refactoring Databases. *The realities of dealing with existing databases is one that is tough to crack. Though much of the challenge can be cultural and progress can be held in limbo by strong-armed DBA tactics, this book shows how technically the refactoring and evolutionary development of a database can indeed be handled in an agile manner. I look forward to dropping off a copy on the desk of the next ornery DBA I run into."*
—Jon Kern

"This book is excellent. It is perfect for the data professional who needs to produce results in the world of agile development and object technology. A well-organized book, it shows the what, why, and how of refactoring databases and associated code. Like the best cookbook, I will use it often when developing and improving databases."
—David R. Haertzen, editor, The Data Management Center, First Place Software, Inc.

"This excellent book brings the agile practice of refactoring into the world of data. It provides pragmatic guidance on both the methodology to refactoring databases within your organization and the details of how to implement individual refactorings. Refactoring Databases *also articulates the importance of developers and DBAs working side by side. It is a must have reference for developers and DBAs alike."*
—Per Kroll, development manager, RUP, IBM; project lead, Eclipse Process Framework

"Scott and Pramod have done for database refactoring what Martin Fowler did for code refactoring. They've put together a coherent set of procedures you can use to improve the quality of your database. If you deal with databases, this book is for you."
—Ken Pugh, author, *Prefactoring*

"It's past time for data people to join the agile ranks, and Ambler and Sadalage are the right persons to lead them. This book should be read by data modelers and administrators, as well as software teams. We have lived in different worlds for too long, and this book will help to remove the barriers dividing us."
—Gary K. Evans, Agile Process evangelist, Evanetics, Inc.

"Evolutionary design and refactoring are already exciting, and with Refactoring Databases *this gets even better. In this book, the authors share with us the techniques and strategies to refactor at the database level. Using these refactorings, database schemas can safely be evolved even after a database has been deployed into production. With this book, database is within reach of any developer."*
—Sven Gorts

"Database refactoring is an important new topic and this book is a pioneering contribution to the community."
—Floyd Marinescu, creator of InfoQ.com and TheServerSide.com; author of *EJB Design Patterns*

Refactoring Databases

The Addison-Wesley Signature Series 

The Addison-Wesley Signature Series provides readers with practical and authoritative information on the latest trends in modern technology for computer professionals. The series is based on one simple premise: great books come from great authors. Books in the series are personally chosen by expert advisors, world-class authors in their own right. These experts are proud to put their signatures on the covers, and their signatures ensure that these thought leaders have worked closely with authors to define topic coverage, book scope, critical content, and overall uniqueness. The expert signatures also symbolize a promise to our readers: you are reading a future classic.

The Addison-Wesley Signature Series

Signers: Kent Beck and Martin Fowler

Kent Beck has pioneered people-oriented technologies like JUnit, Extreme Programming, and patterns for software development. Kent is interested in helping teams do well by doing good — finding a style of software development that simultaneously satisfies economic, aesthetic, emotional, and practical constraints. His books focus on touching the lives of the creators and users of software.

Martin Fowler has been a pioneer of object technology in enterprise applications. His central concern is how to design software well. He focuses on getting to the heart of how to build enterprise software that will last well into the future. He is interested in looking behind the specifics of technologies to the patterns, practices, and principles that last for many years; these books should be usable a decade from now. Martin's criterion is that these are books he wished he could write.

Titles in the Series

A Kent Beck Signature Book

Test-Driven Development: By Example
Kent Beck, ISBN 0321146530

User Stories Applied: For Agile Software Development
Mike Cohn, ISBN 0321205685

A Martin Fowler Signature Book

Refactoring Databases: Evolutionary Database Design
Scott W. Ambler and Pramodkumar J. Sadalage, ISBN 0321293533

Patterns of Enterprise Application Architecture
Martin Fowler, ISBN 0321127420

Beyond Software Architecture: Creating and Sustaining Winning Solutions
Luke Hohmann, ISBN 0201775948

Enterprise Integration Patterns: Designing, Building, and Deploying Messaging Solutions
Gregor Hohpe and Bobby Woolf, ISBN 0321200683

Refactoring to Patterns
Joshua Kerievsky, ISBN 0321213351

For more information, check out the series web site at www.awprofessional.com

Refactoring Databases

Evolutionary Database Design

Scott W. Ambler
Pramod J. Sadalage

Addison-Wesley

Upper Saddle River, NJ • Boston • Indianapolis • San Francisco
New York • Toronto • Montreal • London • Munich • Paris • Madrid
Capetown • Sydney • Tokyo • Singapore • Mexico City

Library of Congress Cataloging-in-Publication Data

Ambler, Scott W., 1966-
Refactoring databases : evolutionary database design / Scott W. Ambler and Pramod J. Sadalage.
p. cm.
Includes index.
ISBN 0-321-29353-3 (hardback : alk. paper) 1. Database design. 2. Computer software—Development. 3. Evolutionary programming (Computer science) I. Sadalage, Pramod J. II. Title.

QA76.9.D26A52 2006
005.74—dc22

2005031959

ISBN 0-321-29353-3

Text printed in the United States on recycled paper at R. R. Donnelley in Crawfordsville, Indiana.

First printing, March 2006

Scott:
For Beverley, my lovely new bride.

Pramod:
To the women I love most, Rupali and our daughter, Arula.

Contents

About the Authors

Scott W. Ambler is a software process improvement (SPI) consultant living just north of Toronto. He is founder and practice leader of the Agile Modeling (AM) (www.agilemodeling.com), Agile Data (AD) (www.agiledata.org), Enterprise Unified Process (EUP) (www.enterpriseunifiedprocess.com), and Agile Unified Process (AUP) (www.ambysoft.com/unifiedprocess) methodologies. Scott is the (co-)author of several books, including *Agile Modeling* (John Wiley & Sons, 2002), *Agile Database Techniques* (John Wiley & Sons, 2003), *The Object Primer, Third Edition* (Cambridge University Press, 2004), *The Enterprise Unified Process* (Prentice Hall, 2005), and *The Elements of UML 2.0 Style* (Cambridge University Press, 2005). Scott is a contributing editor with *Software Development* magazine (www.sdmagazine.com) and has spoken and keynoted at a wide variety of international conferences, including Software Development, UML World, Object Expo, Java Expo, and Application Development. Scott graduated from the University of Toronto with a Master of Information Science. In his spare time Scott studies the Goju Ryu and Kobudo styles of karate.

Pramod J. Sadalage is a consultant for ThoughtWorks, an enterprise application development and integration company. He first pioneered the practices and processes of evolutionary database design and database refactoring in 1999 while working on a large J2EE application using the Extreme Programming (XP) methodology. Since then, Pramod has applied the practices and processes to many projects. Pramod writes and speaks about database administration on evolutionary projects, the adoption of evolutionary processes with regard to databases, and evolutionary practices' impact upon database administration, in order to make it easy for everyone to use evolutionary design in regards to databases. When he is not working, you can find him spending time with his wife and daughter and trying to improve his running.

Forewords

A decade ago *refactoring* was a word only known to a few people, mostly in the Smalltalk community. It's been wonderful to watch more and more people learn how to use refactoring to modify working code in a disciplined and effective manner. As a result many people now see code refactoring as an essential part of software development.

I live in the world of enterprise applications, and a big part of enterprise application development is working with databases. In my original book on refactoring, I picked out databases as a major problem area in refactoring because refactoring databases introduces a new set of problems. These problems are exacerbated by the sad division that's developed in the enterprise software world where database professionals and software developers are separated by a wall of mutual incomprehension and contempt.

One of the things I like about Scott and Pramod is that, in different ways, they have both worked hard to try and cross this division. Scott's writings on databases have been a consistent attempt to bridge the gap, and his work on object-relational mapping has been a great influence on my own writings on enterprise application architecture. Pramod may be less known, but his impact has been just as great on me. When he started work on a project with me at ThoughtWorks we were told that refactoring of databases was impossible. Pramod rejected that notion, taking some sketchy ideas and turning them into a disciplined program that kept the database schema in constant, but controlled, motion. This freed up the application developers to use evolutionary design in the code, too. Pramod has since taken these techniques to many of our clients, spreading them around our ThoughtWorks colleagues and, at least for us, forever banishing databases from the list of roadblocks to continual design.

This book assembles the lessons of two people who have lived in the no-mans land between applications and data, and presents a guide on how to use refactoring techniques for databases. If you're familiar with refactoring, you'll notice that the major change is that you have to manage continual migration of the data itself, not just change the program and data structures. This book tells you how to do that, backed by the project experience (and scars) that these two have accumulated.

Much though I'm delighted by the appearance of this book, I also hope it's only a first step. After my refactoring book appeared I was delighted to find sophisticated tools appear that automated many refactoring tasks. I hope the

same thing happens with databases, and we begin to see vendors offer tools that make continual migrations of schema and data easier for everyone. Before that happens, this book will help you build your own processes and tools to help; afterward this book will have lasting value as a foundation for using such tools successfully.
—Martin Fowler, series editor; chief scientist, ThoughtWorks

In the years since I first began my career in software development, many aspects of the industry and technology have changed dramatically. What hasn't changed, however, is the fundamental nature of software development. It has never been hard to create software—just get a computer and start churning out code. But it was hard to create good software, and exponentially harder to create great software. This situation hasn't changed today. Today it is easier to create larger and more complex software systems by cobbling together parts from a variety of sources, software development tools have advanced in bounds, and we know a lot more about what works and doesn't work for the process of creating software. Yet most software is still brittle and struggling to achieve acceptable quality levels. Perhaps this is because we are creating larger and more complex systems, or perhaps it is because there are fundamental gaps in the techniques still used. I believe that software development today remains as challenging as ever because of a combination of these two factors. Fortunately, from time to time new technologies and techniques appear that can help. Among these advances, a rare few are have the power to improve greatly our ability to realize the potential envisioned at the start of most projects. The techniques involved in refactoring, along with their associate Agile methodologies, were one of these rare advances. The work contained in this book extends this base in a very important direction.

Refactoring is a controlled technique for safely improving the design of code without changing its behavioral semantics. Anyone can take a chance at improving code, but refactoring brings a discipline of safely making changes (with tests) and leveraging the knowledge accumulated by the software development community (through refactorings). Since Fowler's seminal book on the subject, refactoring has been widely applied, and tools assisting with detection of refactoring candidates and application of refactorings to code have driven widespread adoption. At the data tier of applications, however, refactoring has proven much more difficult to apply. Part of this problem is no doubt cultural, as this book shows, but also there has not been a clear process and set of refactorings applicable to the data tier. This is really unfortunate, since poor design at the data level almost always translates into problems at the higher tiers, typically causing a chain of bad designs in a futile effort to stabilize the shaky foundation. Further, the inability to evolve the data tier, whether due to denial or fear of change, hampers the ability of all that rests on it to deliver the best software possible. These problems are exactly what make this work so important: we now have a process and catalog for enabling iterative design improvements on in this vital area.

I am very excited to see the publication of this book, and hope that it drives the creation of tools to support the techniques it describes. The software industry is currently in an interesting stage, with the rise of open-source software and the collaborative vehicles it brings. Projects such as the Eclipse Data Tools Platform are natural collection areas for those interested in bringing database refactoring to life in tools. I hope the open-source community will work hard to realize this vision, because the potential payoff is great. Software development will move to the next level of maturity when database refactoring is as common and widely applied as general refactoring itself.

—John Graham, Eclipse Data Tools Platform, Project Management, committee chair, senior staff engineer, Sybase, Inc.

In many ways the data community has missed the entire agile software development revolution. While application developers have embraced refactoring, test-driven development, and other such techniques that encourage iteration as a productive and advantageous approach to software development, data professionals have largely ignored and even insulated themselves from these trends.

This became clear to me early in my career as an application developer at a large financial services institution. At that time I had a cubicle situated right between the development and database teams. What I quickly learned was that although they were only a few feet apart, the culture, practices, and processes of each group were significantly different. A customer request to the development team meant some refactoring, a code check-in, and aggressive acceptance testing. A similar request to the database team meant a formal change request processed through many levels of approval before even the modification of a schema could begin. The burden of the process constantly led to frustrations for both developers and customers but persisted because the database team knew no other way.

But they must learn another way if their businesses are to thrive in today's ever-evolving competitive landscape. The data community must somehow adopt the agile techniques of their developer counterparts.

Refactoring Databases is an invaluable resource that shows data professionals just how they can leap ahead and confidently, safely embrace change. Scott and Pramod show how the improvement in design that results from small, iterative refactorings allow the agile DBA to avoid the mistake of big upfront design and evolve the schema along with the application as they gradually gain a better understanding of customer requirements.

Make no mistake, refactoring databases is hard. Even a simple change like renaming a column cascades throughout a schema, to its objects, persistence frameworks, and application tier, making it seem to the DBA like a very inaccessible technique.

Refactoring Databases outlines a set of prescriptive practices that show the professional DBA exactly how to bring this agile method into the design and development of databases. Scott's and Pramod's attention to the minute details of what it takes to actually implement every database refactoring technique proves that it can be done and paves the way for its widespread adoption.

Thus, I propose a call to action for all data professionals. Read on, embrace change, and spread the word. Database refactoring is key to improving the data community's agility.

—Sachin Rekhi, program manager, Microsoft Corporation

In the world of system development, there are two distinct cultures: the world dominated by object-oriented (OO) developers who live and breathe Java and agile software development, and the relational database world populated by people who appreciate careful engineering and solid relational database design. These two groups speak different languages, attend different conferences, and rarely seem to be on speaking terms with each other. This schism is reflected within IT departments in many organizations. OO developers complain that DBAs are stodgy conservatives, unable to keep up with the rapid pace of change. Database professionals bemoan the idiocy of Java developers who do not have a clue what to do with a database.

Scott Ambler and Pramod Sadalage belong to that rare group of people who straddle both worlds. *Refactoring Databases: Evolutionary Database Design* is about database design written from the perspective of an OO architect. As a result, the book provides value to both OO developers and relational database professionals. It will help OO developers to apply agile code refactoring techniques to the database arena as well as give relational database professionals insight into how OO architects think.

This book includes numerous tips and techniques for improving the quality of database design. It explicitly focuses on how to handle real-world situations where the database already exists but is poorly designed, or when the initial database design failed to produce a good model.

The book succeeds on a number of different levels. First, it can be used as a tactical guide for developers in the trenches. It is also a thought-provoking treatise about how to merge OO and relational thinking. I wish more system architects echoed the sentiments of Ambler and Sadalage in recognizing that a database is more than just a place to put persistent copies of classes.

—Dr. Paul Dorsey, president, Dulcian, Inc.; president, New York Oracle Users Group; chairperson, J2EE SIG

Preface

Evolutionary, and often agile, software development methodologies, such as Extreme Programming (XP), Scrum, the Rational Unified Process (RUP), the Agile Unified Process (AUP), and Feature-Driven Development (FDD), have taken the information technology (IT) industry by storm over the past few years. For the sake of definition, an evolutionary method is one that is both iterative and incremental in nature, and an agile method is evolutionary and highly collaborative in nature. Furthermore, agile techniques such as refactoring, pair programming, Test-Driven Development (TDD), and Agile Model-Driven Development (AMDD) are also making headway into IT organizations. These methods and techniques have been developed and have evolved in a grassroots manner over the years, being honed in the software trenches, as it were, instead of formulated in ivory towers. In short, this evolutionary and agile stuff seems to work incredibly well in practice.

In the seminal book *Refactoring*, Martin Fowler describes a refactoring as a small change to your source code that improves its design without changing its semantics. In other words, you improve the quality of your work without breaking or adding anything. In the book, Martin discusses the idea that just as it is possible to refactor your application source code, it is also possible to refactor your database schema. However, he states that database refactoring is quite hard because of the significant levels of coupling associated with databases, and therefore he chose to leave it out of his book.

Since 1999 when *Refactoring* was published, the two of us have found ways to refactor database schemas. Initially, we worked separately, running into each other at conferences such as Software Development (www.sdexpo.com) and on mailing lists (www.agiledata.org/feedback.html). We discussed ideas, attended each other's conference tutorials and presentations, and quickly discovered that our ideas and techniques overlapped and were highly compatible with one another. So we joined forces to write this book, to share our experiences and techniques at evolving database schemas via refactoring.

The examples throughout the book are written in Java, Hibernate, and Oracle code. Virtually every database refactoring description includes code to modify the database schema itself, and for some of the more interesting refactorings, we show the effects they would have on Java application code. Because all databases are not created alike, we include discussions of alternative implementation strategies when important nuances exist between database products.

In some instances we discuss alternative implementations of an aspect of a refactoring using Oracle-specific features such as the SE,T UNUSED or RENAME TO commands, and many of our code examples take advantage of Oracle's COMMENT ON feature. Other database products include other features that make database refactoring easier, and a good DBA will know how to take advantage of these things. Better yet, in the future database refactoring tools will do this for us. Furthermore, we have kept the Java code simple enough so that you should be able to convert it to C#, C++, or even Visual Basic with little problem at all.

Why Evolutionary Database Development?

Evolutionary database development is a concept whose time has come. Instead of trying to design your database schema up front early in the project, you instead build it up throughout the life of a project to reflect the changing requirements defined by your stakeholders. Like it or not, requirements change as your project progresses. Traditional approaches have denied this fundamental reality and have tried to "manage change," a euphemism for preventing change, through various means. Practitioners of modern development techniques instead choose to embrace change and follow techniques that enable them to evolve their work in step with evolving requirements. Programmers have adopted techniques such as TDD, refactoring, and AMDD and have built new development tools to make this easy. As we have done this, we have realized that we also need techniques and tools to support evolutionary database development.

Advantages to an evolutionary approach to database development include the following:

1. **You minimize waste.** An evolutionary, just-in-time (JIT) approach enables you to avoid the inevitable wastage inherent in serial techniques when requirements change. Any early investment in detailed requirements, architecture, and design artifacts is lost when a requirement is later found to be no longer needed. If you have the skills to do the work up front, clearly you must have the skills to do the same work JIT.

2. **You avoid significant rework.** As you will see in Chapter 1, "Evolutionary Database Development," you should still do some initial modeling up front to think major issues through, issues that could potentially lead to significant rework if identified late in the project; you just do not need to investigate the details early.

3. **You always know that your system works.** With an evolutionary approach, you regularly produce working software, even if it is just deployed into a demo environment, which works. When you have a new, working version of the system every week or two, you dramatically reduce your project's risk.

4. **You always know that your database design is the highest quality possible.** This is exactly what database refactoring is all about: improving your schema design a little bit at a time.

5. **You work in a compatible manner with developers.** Developers work in an evolutionary manner, and if data professionals want to be effective members of modern development teams, they also need to choose to work in an evolutionary manner.

6. **You reduce the overall effort.** By working in an evolutionary manner, you only do the work that you actually need today and no more.

There are also several disadvantages to evolutionary database development:

1. **Cultural impediments exist.** Many data professionals prefer to follow a serial approach to software development, often insisting that some form of detailed logical and physical data models be created and baselined before programming begins. Modern methodologies have abandoned this approach as being too inefficient and risky, thereby leaving many data professionals in the cold. Worse yet, many of the "thought leaders" in the data community are people who cut their teeth in the 1970s and 1980s but who missed the object revolution of the 1990s, and thereby missed gaining experience in evolutionary development. The world changed, but they did not seem to change with it. As you will learn in this book, it is not only possible for data professionals to work in an evolutionary, if not agile, manner, it is in fact a preferable way to work.

2. **Learning curve.** It takes time to learn these new techniques, and even longer if you also need to change a serial mindset into an evolutionary one.

3. **Tool support is still evolving.** When *Refactoring* was published in 1999, no tools supported the technique. Just a few years later, every single integrated development environment (IDE) has code-refactoring features built right in to it. At the time of this writing, there are no database refactoring tools in existence, although we do include all the code that you need to implement the refactorings by hand. Luckily, the Eclipse Data Tools Project (DTP) has indicated in their project prospectus the need to develop database-refactoring functionality in Eclipse, so it is only a matter of time before the tool vendors catch up.

Agility in a Nutshell

Although this is not specifically a book about agile software development, the fact is that database refactoring is a primary technique for agile developers. A process is considered agile when it conforms to the four values of the Agile Alliance (www.agilealliance.org). The values define preferences, not alternatives, encouraging a focus on certain areas but not eliminating others. In other words, whereas you should value the concepts on the right side, you should value the things on the left side even more. For example, processes and tools are important, but individuals and interactions are more important. The four agile values are as follows:

1. **Individuals and interactions OVER processes and tools.** The most important factors that you need to consider are the people and how they work together; if you do not get that right, the best tools and processes will not be of any use.

2. **Working software OVER comprehensive documentation.** The primary goal of software development is to create working software that meets the needs of its stakeholders. Documentation still has its place; written properly, it describes how and why a system is built, and how to work with the system.

3. **Customer collaboration OVER contract negotiation.** Only your customer can tell you what they want. Unfortunately, they are not good at this—they likely do not have the skills to exactly specify the system, nor will they get it right at first, and worse yet they will likely change their minds as time goes on. Having a contract with your customers is important, but a contract is not a substitute for effective communication. Successful IT professionals work closely with their customers, they invest the effort to discover what their customers need, and they educate their customers along the way.

4. **Responding to change OVER following a plan.** As work progresses on your system, your stakeholders' understanding of what they want changes, the business environment changes, and so does the underlying technology. Change is a reality of software development, and as a result, your project plan and overall approach must reflect your changing environment if it is to be effective.

How to Read This Book

The majority of this book, Chapters 6 through 11, consists of reference material that describes each refactoring in detail. The first five chapters describe the fundamental ideas and techniques of evolutionary database development, and in particular, database refactoring. You should read these chapters in order:

- Chapter 1, "Evolutionary Database Development," overviews the fundamentals of evolutionary development and the techniques that support it. It summarizes refactoring, database refactoring, database regression testing, evolutionary data modeling via an AMDD approach, configuration management of database assets, and the need for separate developer sandboxes.
- Chapter 2, "Database Refactoring," explores in detail the concepts behind database refactoring and why it can be so hard to do in practice. It also works through a database-refactoring example in both a "simple" single-application environment as well as in a complex, multi-application environment.
- Chapter 3, "The Process of Database Refactoring," describes in detail the steps required to refactor your database schema in both simple and complex environments. With single-application databases, you have much greater control over your environment, and as a result need to do far less work to refactor your schema. In multi-application environments, you need to support a transition period in which your database supports both the old and new schemas in parallel, enabling the application teams to update and deploy their code into production.
- Chapter 4, "Deploying into Production," describes the process behind deploying database refactorings into production. This can prove particularly challenging in a multi-application environment because the changes of several teams must be merged and tested.
- Chapter 5, "Database Refactoring Strategies," summarizes some of the "best practices" that we have discovered over the years when it comes to refactoring database schemas. We also float a couple of ideas that we have been meaning to try out but have not yet been able to do so.

About the Cover

Each book in the Martin Fowler Signature Series has a picture of a bridge on the front cover. This tradition reflects the fact that Martin's wife is a civil engineer, who at the time the book series started worked on horizontal projects such as bridges and tunnels. This bridge is the Burlington Bay James N. Allan Skyway in Southern Ontario, which crosses the mouth of Hamilton Harbor. At this site are three bridges: the two in the picture and the Eastport Drive lift bridge, not shown. This bridge system is significant for two reasons. Most importantly it shows an incremental approach to delivery. The lift bridge originally bore the traffic through the area, as did another bridge that collapsed in 1952 after being hit by a ship. The first span of the Skyway, the portion in the front with the metal supports above the roadway, opened in 1958 to replace the lost bridge. Because the Skyway is a major thoroughfare between Toronto to the north and Niagara Falls to the south, traffic soon exceeded capacity. The second span, the one without metal supports, opened in 1985 to support the new load. Incremental delivery makes good economic sense in both civil engineering and in software development. The second reason we used this picture is that Scott was raised in Burlington Ontario—in fact, he was born in Joseph Brant hospital, which is near the northern footing of the Skyway. Scott took the cover picture with a Nikon D70S.

Acknowledgments

We want to thank the following people for their input into the development of this book: Doug Barry, Gary Evans, Martin Fowler, Bernard Goodwin, Joshua Graham, Sven Gorts, David Hay, David Haertzen, Michelle Housely, Sriram Narayan, Paul Petralia, Sachin Rekhi, Andy Slocum, Brian Smith, Michael Thurston, Michael Vizdos, and Greg Warren.

In addition, Pramod wants to thank Irfan Shah, Narayan Raman, Anishek Agarwal, and my other teammates who constantly challenged my opinions and taught me a lot about software development. I also want to thank Martin for getting me to write, talk, and generally be active outside of ThoughtWorks; Kent Beck for his encouragement; my colleagues at ThoughtWorks who have helped me in numerous ways and make working fun; my parents Jinappa and Shobha who put a lot of effort in raising me; and Praveen, my brother, who since my childhood days has critiqued and improved the way I write.

Chapter 1

Evolutionary Database Development

Waterfalls are wonderful tourist attractions. They are spectacularly bad strategies for organizing software development projects.

—Scott Ambler

Modern software processes, also called methodologies, are all evolutionary in nature, requiring you to work both iteratively and incrementally. Examples of such processes include Rational Unified Process (RUP), Extreme Programming (XP), Scrum, Dynamic System Development Method (DSDM), the Crystal family, Team Software Process (TSP), Agile Unified Process (AUP), Enterprise Unified Process (EUP), Feature-Driven Development (FDD), and Rapid Application Development (RAD), to name a few. Working iteratively, you do a little bit of an activity such as modeling, testing, coding, or deployment at a time, and then do another little bit, then another, and so on. This process differs from a serial approach in which you identify all the requirements that you are going to implement, then create a detailed design, then implement to that design, then test, and finally deploy your system. With an incremental approach, you organize your system into a series of releases rather than one big one.

Furthermore, many of the modern processes are agile, which for the sake of simplicity we will characterize as both evolutionary and highly collaborative in nature. When a team takes a collaborative approach, they actively strive to find ways to work together effectively; you should even try to ensure that project stakeholders such as business customers are active team members. Cockburn (2002) advises that you should strive to adopt the "hottest" communication technique applicable to your situation: Prefer face-to-face conversation around a whiteboard over a telephone call, prefer a telephone call over sending someone an e-mail, and prefer an e-mail over sending someone a detailed document. The better the communication and collaboration within a software development team, the greater your chance of success.

Although both evolutionary and agile ways of working have been readily adopted within the development community, the same cannot be said within the data community. Most data-oriented techniques are serial in nature, requiring the creation of fairly detailed models before implementation is "allowed" to begin. Worse yet, these models are often baselined and put under change management control to minimize changes. (If you consider the end results, this should really be called a change prevention process.) Therein lies the rub: Common database development techniques do not reflect the realities of modern software development processes. It does not have to be this way.

Our premise is that data professionals need to adopt the evolutionary techniques similar to those of developers. Although you could argue that developers should return to the "tried-and-true" traditional approaches common within the data community, it is becoming more and more apparent that the traditional ways just do not work well. In Chapter 5 of *Agile & Iterative Development,* Craig Larman (2004) summarizes the research evidence, as well as the overwhelming support among the thought leaders within the information technology (IT) community, in support of evolutionary approaches. The bottom line is that the evolutionary and agile techniques prevalent within the development community work much better than the traditional techniques prevalent within the data community.

It is possible for data professionals to adopt evolutionary approaches to all aspects of their work, if they choose to do so. The first step is to rethink the "data culture" of your IT organization to reflect the needs of modern IT project teams. The Agile Data (AD) method (Ambler 2003) does exactly that, describing a collection of philosophies and roles for modern data-oriented activities. The philosophies reflect how data is one of many important aspects of business software, implying that developers need to become more adept at data techniques and that data professionals need to learn modern development technologies and skills. The AD method recognizes that each project team is unique and needs to follow a process tailored for their situation. The importance of looking beyond your current project to address enterprise issues is also stressed, as is the need for enterprise professionals such as operational database administrators and data architects to be flexible enough to work with project teams in an agile manner.

The second step is for data professionals, in particular database administrators, to adopt new techniques that enable them to work in an evolutionary manner. In this chapter, we briefly overview these critical techniques, and in our opinion the most important technique is database refactoring, which is the focus of this book. The evolutionary database development techniques are as follows:

1. **Database refactoring.** Evolve an existing database schema a small bit at a time to improve the quality of its design without changing its semantics.

2. **Evolutionary data modeling.** Model the data aspects of a system iteratively and incrementally, just like all other aspects of a system, to ensure that the database schema evolves in step with the application code.
3. **Database regression testing.** Ensure that the database schema actually works.
4. **Configuration management of database artifacts.** Your data models, database tests, test data, and so on are important project artifacts that should be managed just like any other artifact.
5. **Developer sandboxes.** Developers need their own working environments in which they can modify the portion of the system that they are building and get it working before they integrate their work with that of their teammates.

Let's consider each evolutionary database technique in detail.

1.1 Database Refactoring

Refactoring (Fowler 1999) is a disciplined way to make small changes to your source code to improve its design, making it easier to work with. A critical aspect of a refactoring is that it retains the behavioral semantics of your code—you neither add nor remove anything when you refactor; you merely improve its quality. An example refactoring would be to rename the *getPersons()* operation to *getPeople()*. To implement this refactoring, you must change the operation definition, and then change every single invocation of this operation throughout your application code. A refactoring is not complete until your code runs again as before.

Similarly, a database refactoring is a simple change to a database schema that improves its design while retaining both its behavioral and informational semantics. You could refactor either structural aspects of your database schema such as table and view definitions or functional aspects such as stored procedures and triggers. When you refactor your database schema, not only must you rework the schema itself, but also the external systems, such as business applications or data extracts, which are coupled to your schema. Database refactorings are clearly more difficult to implement than code refactorings; therefore, you need to be careful. Database refactoring is described in detail in Chapter 2, and the process of performing a database refactoring in Chapter 3.

1.2 Evolutionary Data Modeling

Regardless of what you may have heard, evolutionary and agile techniques are not simply "code and fix" with a new name. You still need to explore requirements and to think through your architecture and design before you build it, and one good way of doing so is to model before you code. Figure 1.1 reviews the life cycle for Agile Mobile Driven Development (AMDD) (Ambler 2004; Ambler 2002). With AMDD, you create initial, high-level models at the beginning of a project, models that overview the scope of the problem domain that you are addressing as well as a potential architecture to build to. One of the models that you typically create is a "slim" conceptual/domain model that depicts the main business entities and the relationships between them (Fowler and Sadalage 2003). Figure 1.2 depicts an example for a simple financial institution. The amount of detail shown in this example is all that you need at the

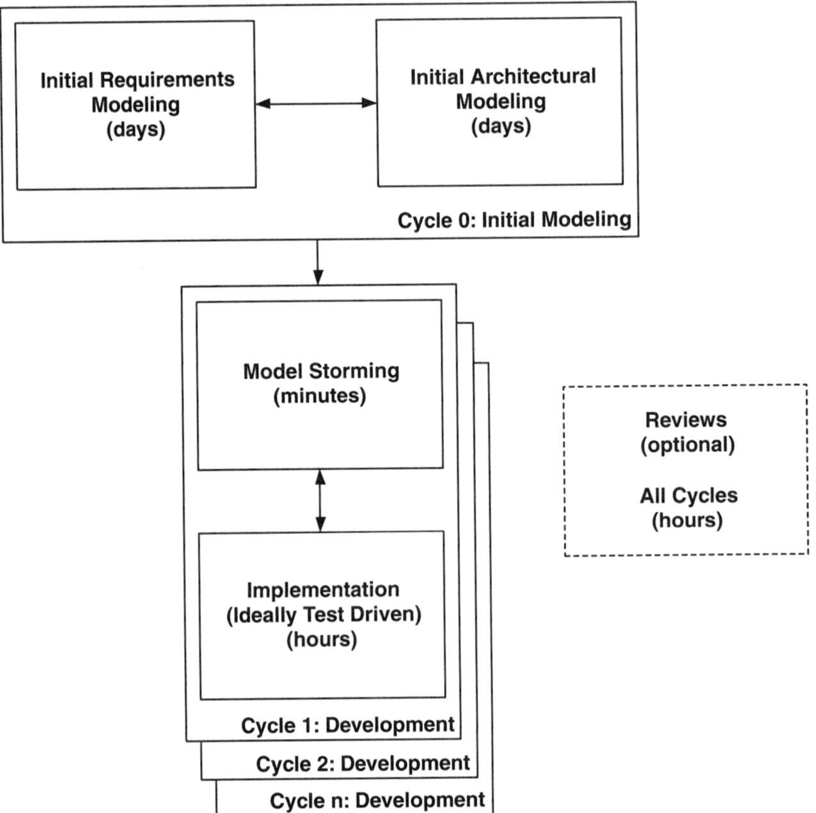

Figure 1.1 The Agile Model-Driven Development (AMDD) life cycle.

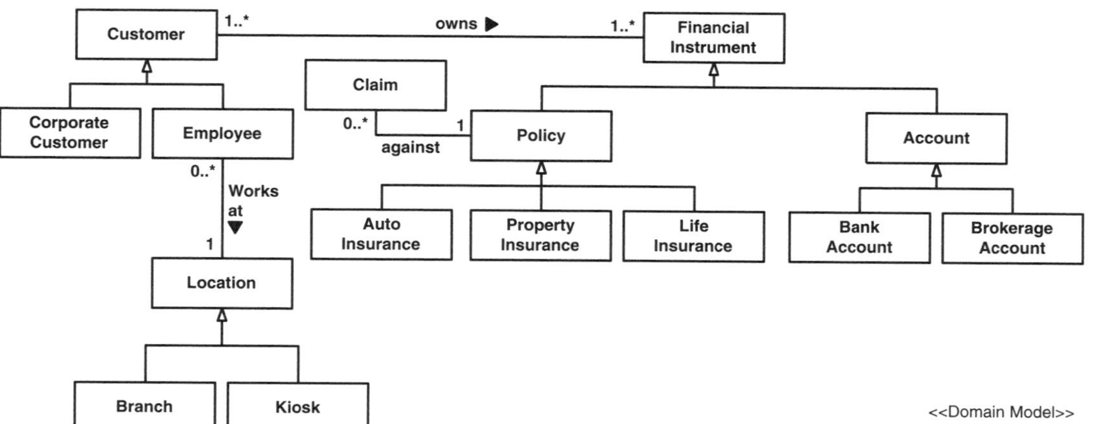

Figure 1.2 Conceptual/domain model for a fictional financial institution using UML.

beginning of a project; your goal is to think through major issues early in your project without investing in needless details right away—you can work through the details later on a just-in-time (JIT) basis.

Your conceptual model will naturally evolve as your understanding of the domain grows, but the level of detail will remain the same. Details are captured within your object model (which could be your source code) and your physical data model. These models are guided by your conceptual domain model and are developed in parallel along with other artifacts to ensure consistency. Figure 1.3 depicts a detailed physical data model (PDM) that represents the extent of the model at the end of the third development cycle. If "cycle 0" was one week in length, a period of time typical for projects of less than one year, and development cycles are two weeks in length, this is the PDM that exists at the end of the seventh week on the project. The PDM reflects the data requirements, and any legacy constraints, of the project up until this point. The data requirements for future development cycles are modeled during those cycles on a JIT basis.

Evolutionary data modeling is not easy. You need to take legacy data constraints into account, and as we all know, legacy data sources are often nasty beasts that will maim an unwary software development project. Luckily, good data professionals understand the nuances of their organization's data sources, and this expertise can be applied on a JIT basis as easily as it could on a serial basis. You still need to apply intelligent data modeling conventions, just as Agile Modeling's *Apply Modeling Standards* practice suggests. A detailed example of evolutionary/agile data modeling is posted at www.agiledata.org/essays/agileDataModeling.html.

1.3 Database Regression Testing

To safely change existing software, either to refactor it or to add new functionality, you need to be able to verify that you have not broken anything after you have made the change. In other words, you need to be able to run a full regression test on your system. If you discover that you have broken something, you must either fix it or roll back your changes. Within the development community, it has become increasingly common for programmers to develop a full unit test suite in parallel with their domain code, and in fact agilists prefer to write their test code before they write their "real" code. Just like you test your application source code, shouldn't you also test your database? Important business logic is implemented within your database in the form of stored procedures, data validation rules, and referential integrity (RI) rules, business logic that clearly should be tested thoroughly.

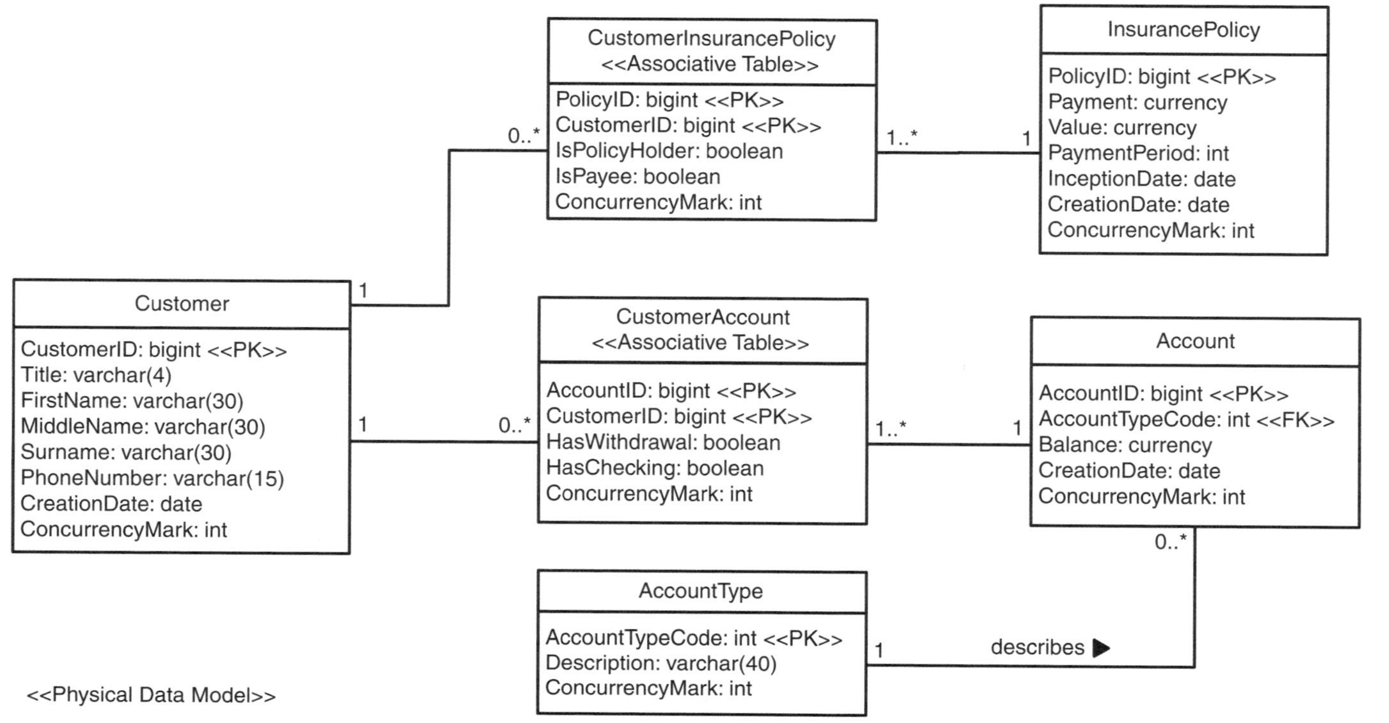

Figure 1.3 Detailed physical data model (PDM) using UML.

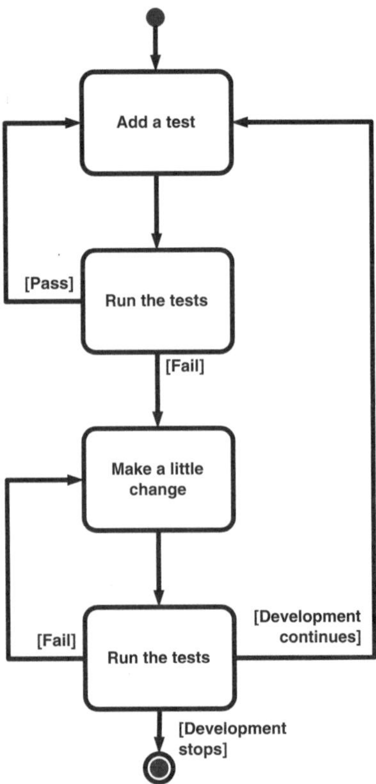

Figure 1.4 A test-first approach to development.

Test-First Development (TFD), also known as Test-First Programming, is an evolutionary approach to development; you must first write a test that fails before you write new functional code. As depicted by the UML activity diagram of Figure 1.4, the steps of TFD are as follows:

1. Quickly add a test, basically just enough code so that your tests now fail.
2. Run your tests—often the complete test suite, although for the sake of speed you may decide to run only a subset—to ensure that the new test does in fact fail.
3. Update your functional code so that it passes the new test.
4. Run your tests again. If the tests fail, return to Step 3; otherwise, start over again.

The primary advantages of TFD are that it forces you to think through new functionality before you implement it (you're effectively doing detailed design), it ensures that you have testing code available to validate your work, and it gives you the courage to know that you can evolve your system because you know that you can detect whether you have "broken" anything as the result of the change. Just like having a full regression test suite for your application source code enables code refactoring, having a full regression test suite for your database enables database refactoring (Meszaros 2006).

Test-Driven Development (TDD) (Astels 2003; Beck 2003) is the combination of TFD and refactoring. You first write your code taking a TFD approach; then after it is working, you ensure that your design remains of high quality by refactoring it as needed. As you refactor, you must rerun your regression tests to verify that you have not broken anything.

An important implication is that you will likely need several unit testing tools, at least one for your database and one for each programming language used in external programs. The XUnit family of tools (for example, JUnit for Java, VBUnit for Visual Basic, NUnit for .NET, and OUnit for Oracle) luckily are free and fairly consistent with one another.

1.4 Configuration Management of Database Artifacts

Sometimes a change to your system proves to be a bad idea and you need to roll back that change to the previous state. For example, renaming the *Customer.FName* column to *Customer.FirstName* might break 50 external programs, and the cost to update those programs may prove to be too great for now. To enable database refactoring, you need to put the following items under configuration management control:

- Data definition language (DDL) scripts to create the database schema
- Data load/extract/migration scripts
- Data model files
- Object/relational mapping meta data
- Reference data
- Stored procedure and trigger definitions
- View definitions

- Referential integrity constraints
- Other database objects like sequences, indexes, and so on
- Test data
- Test data generation scripts
- Test scripts

1.5 Developer Sandboxes

A "sandbox" is a fully functioning environment in which a system may be built, tested, and/or run. You want to keep your various sandboxes separated for safety reasons—developers should be able to work within their own sandbox without fear of harming other efforts, your quality assurance/test group should be able to run their system integration tests safely, and your end users should be able to run their systems without having to worry about developers corrupting their source data and/or system functionality. Figure 1.5 depicts a logical organization for your sandboxes—we say that it is logical because a large/complex environment may have seven or eight physical sandboxes, whereas a small/simple environment may only have two or three physical sandboxes.

To successfully refactor your database schema, developers need to have their own physical sandboxes to work in, a copy of the source code to evolve, and a copy of the database to work with and evolve. By having their own environment, they can safely make changes, test them, and either adopt or back out of them. When they are satisfied that a database refactoring is viable, they promote it into their shared project environment, test it, and put it under change management control so that the rest of the team gets it. Eventually, the team promotes their work, including all database refactorings, into any demo and/or preproduction testing environments. This promotion often occurs once a development cycle, but could occur more or less often depending on your environment. (The more often you promote your system, the greater the chance of receiving valuable feedback.) Finally, after your system passes acceptance and system testing, it will be deployed into production. Chapter 4, "Deploying into Production," covers this promotion/deployment process in greater detail.

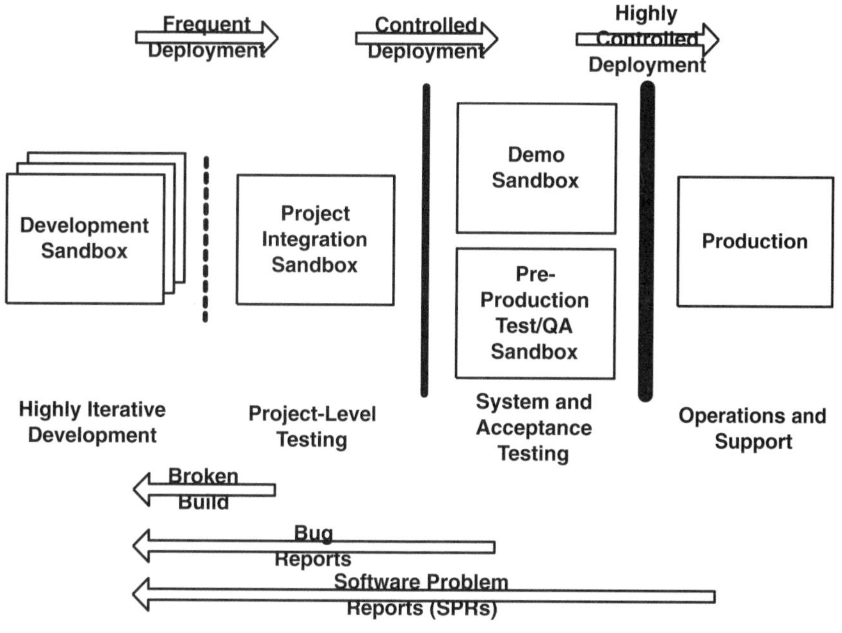

Figure 1.5 Logical sandboxes to provide developers with safety.

1.6 Impediments to Evolutionary Database Development Techniques

We would be remiss if we did not discuss the common impediments to adopting the techniques described in this book. The first impediment, and the hardest one to overcome, is cultural. Many of today's data professionals began their careers in the 1970s and early 1980s when "code-and-fix" approaches to development were common. The IT community recognized that this approach resulted in low-quality, difficult-to-maintain code and adopted the heavy, structured development techniques that many still follow today. Because of these experiences, the majority of data professionals believed that the evolutionary techniques introduced by the object technology revolution of the 1990s were just a rehash of the code-and-fix approaches of the 1970s; to be fair, many object practitioners did in fact choose to work that way. They have chosen to equate evolutionary approaches with low quality; but as the agile community has shown, this does not have to be the case. The end result is that the majority of data-oriented literature appears to be mired in the traditional, serial thought processes of the past and has mostly missed agile approaches. The data community has a lot of catching up to do, and that is going to take time.

The second impediment is a lack of tooling, although open source efforts (at least within the Java community) are quickly filling in the gaps. Although a lot of effort has been put into the development of object/relational (O/R) mapping tools, and some into database testing tools, there is still a lot of work to be done. Just like it took several years for programming tool vendors to implement refactoring functionality within their tools—in fact, now you would be hard pressed to find a modern integrated development environment (IDE) that does not offer such features—it will take several years for database tool vendors to do the same. Clearly, a need exists for usable, flexible tools that enable evolutionary development of a database schema—the open source community is clearly starting to fill that gap, and we suspect that the commercial tool vendors will eventually do the same.

1.7 What You Have Learned

Evolutionary approaches to development that are iterative and incremental in nature are the de facto standard for modern software development. When a project team decides to take this approach to development, everyone on that team must work in an evolutionary manner, including the data professionals. Luckily, evolutionary techniques exist that enable data professionals to work in an evolutionary manner. These techniques include database refactoring, evolutionary data modeling, database regression testing, configuration management of data-oriented artifacts, and separate developer sandboxes.

Chapter 2

Database Refactoring

As soon as one freezes a design, it becomes obsolete.

—Fred Brooks

This chapter overviews the fundamental concepts behind database refactoring, explaining what it is, how it fits into your development efforts, and why it is often hard to do successfully. In the following chapters, we describe in detail the actual process of refactoring your database schema.

2.1 Code Refactoring

In *Refactoring*, Martin Fowler (1999) describes the programming technique called refactoring, which is a disciplined way to restructure code in small steps. Refactoring enables you to evolve your code slowly over time, to take an evolutionary (iterative and incremental) approach to programming. A critical aspect of a refactoring is that it retains the behavioral semantics of your code. You do not add functionality when you are refactoring, nor do you take it away. A refactoring merely improves the design of your code—nothing more and nothing less. For example, in Figure 2.1 we apply the *Push Down Method* refactoring to move the *calculateTotal()* operation from *Offering* into its subclass *Invoice*. This change looks easy on the surface, but you may also need to change the code that invokes this operation to work with *Invoice* objects rather than *Offering* objects. After you have made these changes, you can say you have truly refactored your code because it works again as before.

Clearly, you need a systematic way to refactor your code, including good tools and techniques to do so. Most modern integrated development environments (IDEs) now support code refactoring to some extent, which is a good start. However, to make refactoring work in practice, you also need to develop

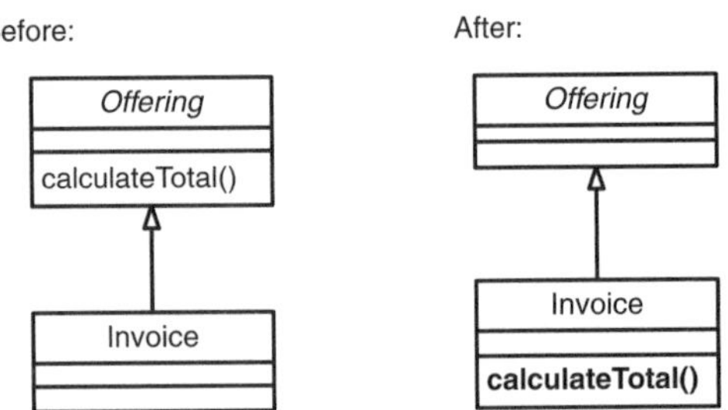

Figure 2.1 Pushing a method down into a subclass.

an up-to-date regression-testing suite that validates that your code still works—you will not have the confidence to refactor your code if you cannot be reasonably assured that you have not broken it.

Many agile developers, and in particular Extreme Programmers (XPers), consider refactoring to be a primary development practice. It is just as common to refactor a bit of code as it is to introduce an *if* statement or a loop. You should refactor your code mercilessly because you are most productive when you are working on high-quality source code. When you have a new feature to add to your code, the first question that you should ask is "Is this code the best design possible that enables me to add this feature?" If the answer is yes, add the feature. If the answer is no, first refactor your code to make it the best design possible, and then add the feature. On the surface, this sounds like a lot of work; in practice, however, if you start with high-quality source code, and then refactor it to keep it so, you will find that this approach works incredibly well.

2.2 Database Refactoring

A database refactoring (Ambler 2003) is a simple change to a database schema that improves its design while retaining both its behavioral and informational semantics—in other words, you cannot add new functionality or break existing functionality, nor can you add new data or change the meaning of existing data. From our point of view, a database schema includes both structural aspects, such as table and view definitions, and functional aspects, such as stored procedures and triggers. From this point forward, we use the terms *code refactoring* to refer to traditional refactoring as described by Martin Fowler and *database refactoring* to refer to the refactoring of database schemas. The *process of database refactoring*, described in detail in Chapter 3, is the act of making these simple changes to your database schema.

Database refactorings are conceptually more difficult than code refactorings: Code refactorings only need to maintain behavioral semantics, whereas database refactorings must also maintain informational semantics. Worse yet, database refactorings can become more complicated by the amount of coupling resulting from your database architecture, overviewed in Figure 2.2. Coupling is a measure of the dependence between two items; the more highly coupled two things are, the greater the chance that a change in one will require a change in another. The single-application database architecture is the simplest situation—your application is the only one interacting with your database, enabling you to refactor both in parallel and deploy both simultaneously. These situations do exist and are often referred to as standalone applications or stovepipe systems. The second architecture is much more complicated because you have many external programs interacting with your database, some of which are beyond the scope of your control. In this situation, you cannot assume that all the external programs will be deployed at once, and must therefore support a transition period (also referred to as a deprecation period) during which both the old schema and the new schema are supported in parallel. More on this later.

Although we discuss the single-application environment throughout the book, we focus more on the multi-application environment, in which your database currently exists in production and is accessed by many other external programs over which you have little or no control. Don't worry. In Chapter 3, we describe strategies for working in this sort of situation.

To put database refactoring into context, let's step through a quick example. You have been working on a banking application for a few weeks and have noticed something strange about the *Customer* and *Account* tables depicted in Figure 2.3. Does it really make sense that the *Balance* column be part of the *Customer* table? No, so let's apply the *Move Column* (page 103) refactoring to improve our database design.

2.2.1 Single-Application Database Environments

Let's start by working through an example of moving a column from one table to another within a single-application database environment. This is the simplest situation that you will ever be in, because you have complete control over both the database schema and the application source code that accesses it. The implication is that you can refactor both your database schema and your application code simultaneously—you do not need to support both the original

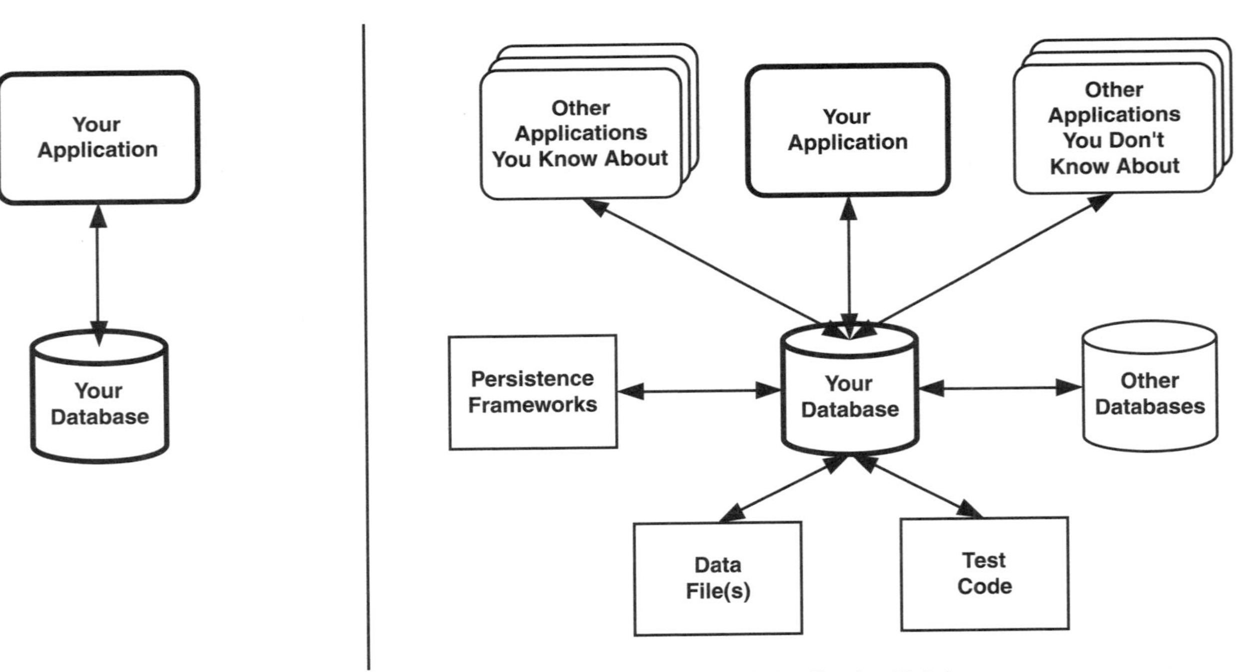

Figure 2.2 The two categories of database architecture.

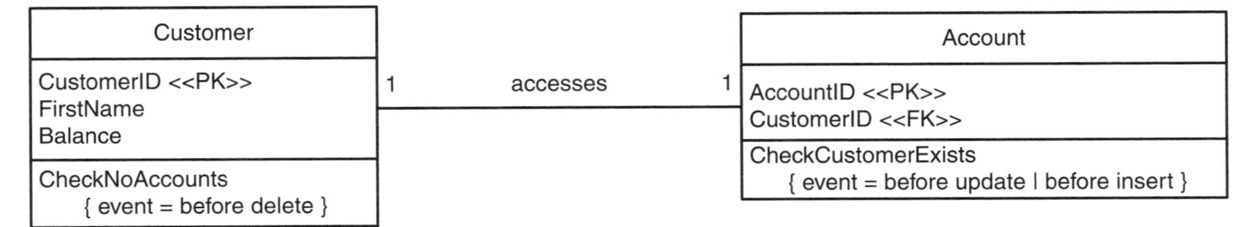

Figure 2.3 The initial database schema for Customer and Account.

and new database schemas in parallel because only the one application accesses your database.

In this scenario, we suggest that two people work together as a pair; one person should have application programming skills, and the other database development skills, and ideally both people have both sets of skills. This pair begins by determining whether the database schema needs to be refactored. Perhaps the programmer is mistaken about the need to evolve the schema, and how best to go about the refactoring. The refactoring is first developed and tested within the developer's sandbox. When it is finished, the changes are promoted into the project-integration environment, and the system is rebuilt, tested, and fixed as needed.

To apply the *Move Column* (page 103) refactoring in the development sandbox, the pair first runs all the tests to see that they pass. Next, they write a test because they are taking a Test-Driven Development (TDD) approach. A likely test is to access a value in the *Account.Balance* column. After running the tests and seeing them fail, they introduce the *Account.Balance* column, as you see in Figure 2.4. They rerun the tests and see that the tests now pass. They then refactor the existing tests, which verify that customer deposits work properly with the *Account.Balance* column rather than the *Customer.Balance* column. They see that these tests fail, and therefore rework the deposit functionality to work with *Account.Balance*. They make similar changes to other code within the tests suite and the application, such as withdrawal logic, that currently works with *Customer.Balance*.

After the application is running again, they then back up the data in *Customer.Balance*, for safety purposes, and then copy the data from *Customer.Balance* into the appropriate row of *Account.Balance*. They rerun their tests to verify that the data migration has safely occurred. To complete the schema changes, the final step is to drop the *Customer.Balance* column and then rerun all tests and fix anything as necessary. When they finish doing so, they promote their changes into the project-integration environment as described earlier.

2.2.2 Multi-Application Database Environments

This situation is more difficult because the individual applications have new releases deployed at different times over the next year and a half. To implement this database refactoring, you do the same sort of work that you did for the single-application database environment, except that you do not delete the *Customer.Balance* column right away. Instead, you run both columns in parallel during a "transition period" of at least 1.5 years to give the development teams time to update and redeploy all of their applications. This portion of the database schema during the transition period is shown in Figure 2.5. Notice

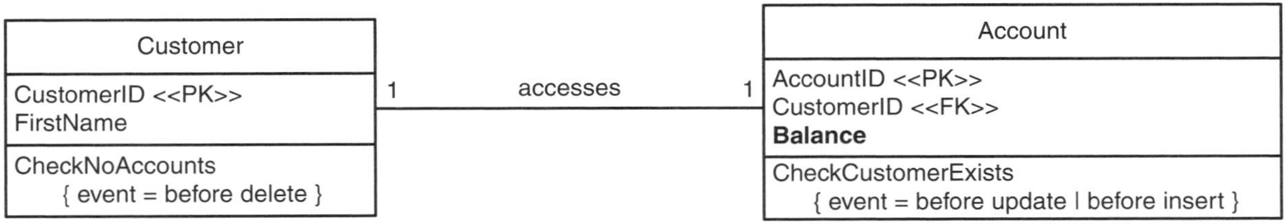

Customer
CustomerID <<PK>>
FirstName
CheckNoAccounts
{ event = before delete }

1 accesses 1

Account
AccountID <<PK>>
CustomerID <<FK>>
Balance
CheckCustomerExists
{ event = before update | before insert }

Figure 2.4 The final database schema for Customer and Account.

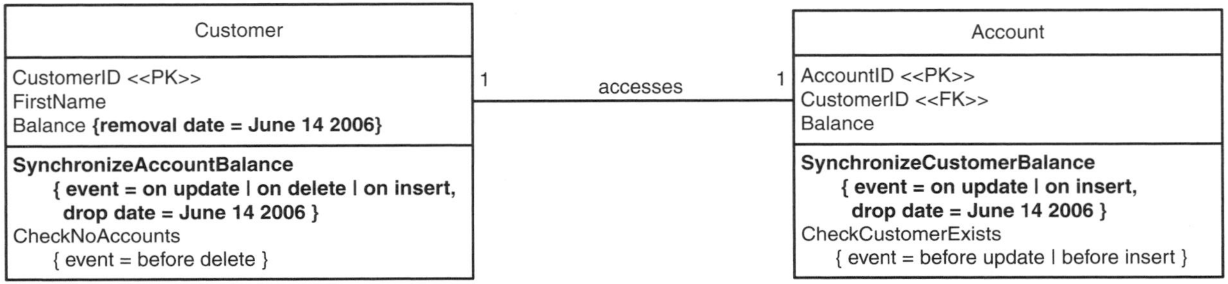

Customer
CustomerID <<PK>>
FirstName
Balance **{removal date = June 14 2006}**
SynchronizeAccountBalance
{ event = on update | on delete | on insert,
drop date = June 14 2006 }
CheckNoAccounts
{ event = before delete }

1 accesses 1

Account
AccountID <<PK>>
CustomerID <<FK>>
Balance
SynchronizeCustomerBalance
{ event = on update | on insert,
drop date = June 14 2006 }
CheckCustomerExists
{ event = before update | before insert }

Figure 2.5 The database schema during the transition period.

how there are two triggers, *SynchronizeCustomerBalance* and *SynchronizeAccountBalance*, which are run in production during the transition period to keep the two columns in sync.

Why such a long period of time for the transition period? Because some applications currently are not being worked on, whereas other applications are following a traditional development life cycle and only release every year or so—your transition period must take into account the slow teams as well as the fast ones. Furthermore, because you cannot count on the individual applications to update both columns, you need to provide a mechanism such as triggers to keep their values synchronized. There are other options to do this, such as views or synchronization after the fact, but as we discuss in Chapter 5, "Database Refactoring Strategies," we find that triggers work best.

After the transition period, you remove the original column plus the trigger(s), resulting in the final database schema of Figure 2.4. You remove these things only after sufficient testing to ensure that it is safe to do so. At this point, your refactoring is complete. In Chapter 3, we work through implementing this example in detail.

2.2.3 Maintaining Semantics

When you refactor a database schema, you must maintain both the informational and behavioral semantics—you should neither add anything nor take anything away. Informational semantics refers to the meaning of the information within the database from the point of view of the users of that information. Preserving the informational semantics implies that if you change the values of the data stored in a column, the clients of that information should not be affected by the change—for example, if you apply the *Introduce Common Format* (page 183) database refactoring to a character-based phone number column to transform data such as (416) 555-1234 and 905.555.1212 into 4165551234 and 9055551212, respectively. Although the format has been improved, requiring simpler code to work with the data, from a practical point of view the true information content has not. Note that you would still choose to display phone numbers in (XXX) XXX-XXXX format; you just would not store the information in that manner.

Focusing on practicality is a critical issue when it comes to database refactoring. Martin Fowler likes to talk about the issue of "observable behavior" when it comes to code refactoring, his point being that with many refactorings you cannot be completely sure that you have not changed the semantics in some small way, that all you can hope for is to think it through as best you can, to write what you believe to be sufficient tests, and then run those tests to verify that the semantics have not changed. In our experience, a similar issue exists when it comes to preserving information semantics when refactoring a database schema—changing (416) 555-1234 to 4165551234 may in fact have changed the semantics of that information for an application in some slightly nuanced way that we do not know about. For example, perhaps a report exists that somehow only works with data rows that have phone numbers in the (XXX) XXX-XXXX format, and the report relies on that fact. Now the report is outputting numbers in the XXXXXXXXXX format, making it harder to read, even though from a practical sense the same information is still being output. When the problem is eventually discovered, the report may need to be updated to reflect the new format.

Similarly, with respect to behavioral semantics, the goal is to keep the black-box functionality the same—any source code that works with the changed aspects of your database schema must be reworked to accomplish the same functionality as before. For example, if you apply *Introduce Calculation Method* (page 245), you may want to rework other existing stored procedures to invoke that method rather than implement the same logic for that calculation. Overall, your database still implements the same logic, but now the calculation logic is just in one place.

It is important to recognize that database refactorings are a subset of database transformations. A database transformation may or may not change the semantics; a database refactoring does not. We describe several common database transformations in Chapter 11, "Non-Refactoring Transitions," because they are not only important to understand, they can often be a step within a database refactoring. For example, when applying the *Move Column* earlier to move the *Balance* column from *Customer to Account*, you needed to apply the *Introduce Column* transformation (page 180) as one of the steps.

On the surface, the *Introduce Column* sounds like a perfectly fine refactoring; adding an empty column to a table does not change the semantics of that table until new functionality begins to use it. We still consider it a transformation (but not a refactoring) because it could inadvertently change the behavior of an application. For example, if we introduce the column in the middle of the table, any program logic using positional access (for example, code that refers to column 17 rather than the column's name) will break. Furthermore, COBOL code bound to a DB2 table will break if it is not rebound to the new schema, even if the column is added at the end of the table. In the end, practicality should be your guide. If we were to label *Introduce Column* as a refactoring, or as a "Yabba Dabba Do" for all that matter, would it affect the way that you use it? We hope not.

Why Not Just Get It Right Up Front?

We are often told by existing data professionals that the real solution is to model everything up front, and then you would not need to refactor your database schema. Although that is an interesting vision, and we have seen it work in a few situations, experience from the past three decades has shown that this approach does not seem to be working well in practice for the overall IT community. The traditional approach to data modeling does not reflect the evolutionary approach of modern methods such as the RUP and XP, nor does it reflect the fact that business customers are demanding new features and changes to existing functionality at an accelerating rate. The old ways are simply no longer sufficient.

As discussed in Chapter 1, "Evolutionary Database Development," we suggest that you take an Agile Model-Driven Development (AMDD) approach, in which you do some high-level modeling to identify the overall "landscape" of your system, and then model storm the details on a just-in-time (JIT) basis. Take advantage of the benefits of modeling without suffering from the costs of overmodeling, overdocumentation, and the resulting bureaucracy of trying to keep too many artifacts up-to-date and synchronized with one another. Your application code and your database schema evolve as your understanding of the problem domain evolves, and you maintain quality through refactoring both.

2.3 Categories of Database Refactorings

We also distinguish six different categories of database refactorings, as described in Table 2.1. This categorization strategy was introduced to help organize this book, and hopefully to help organize future database refactoring tools. Our categorization strategy is not perfect; for example, the *Replace Method With View* refactoring (page 265) arguably fits into both the Architectural and Method categories. (We have put it into the Architectural category.)

2.4 Database Smells

Fowler (1997) introduced the concept of a "code smell," a common category of problem in your code that indicates the need to refactor it. Common code smells

Table 2.1 *Database Refactoring Categories*

Database Refactoring Category	Description	Example(s)
Structural (Chapter 6)	A change to the definition of one or more tables or views.	Moving a column from one table to another or splitting a multipurpose column into several separate columns, one for each purpose.
Data Quality (Chapter 7)	A change that improves the quality of the information contained within a database.	Making a column non-nullable to ensure that it always contains a value or applying a common format to a column to ensure consistency.
Referential Integrity (Chapter 8)	A change that ensures that a referenced row exists within another table and/or that ensures that a row that is no longer needed is removed appropriately.	Adding a trigger to enable a cascading delete between two entities, code that was formerly implemented outside of the database.
Architectural (Chapter 9)	A change that improves the overall manner in which external programs interact with a database.	Replacing an existing Java operation in a shared code library with a stored procedure in the database. Having it as a stored procedure makes it available to non-Java applications.
Method (Chapter 10)	A change to a method (a stored procedure, stored function, or trigger) that improves its quality. Many code refactorings are applicable to database methods.	Renaming a stored procedure to make it easier to understand.
Non-Refactoring Transformation (Chapter 11)	A change to your database schema that changes its semantics.	Adding a new column to an existing table.

include switch statements, long methods, duplicated code, and feature envy. Similarly, there are common database smells that indicate the potential need to refactor it (Ambler 2003). These smells include the following:

Database Smells

- **Multipurpose column.** If a column is being used for several purposes, it is likely that extra code exists to ensure that the source data is being used the "right way," often by checking the values of one or more other columns. An example is a column used to store either someone's birth date if he or she is a customer or the start date if that person is an employee. Worse yet, you are likely constrained in the functionality that you can now support—for example, how would you store the birth date of an employee?
- **Multipurpose table.** Similarly, when a table is being used to store several types of entities, there is likely a design flaw. An example is a generic *Customer* table that is used to store information about both people and corporations. The problem with this approach is that data structures for people and corporations differ—people have a first, middle, and last name, for example; whereas a corporation simply has a legal name. A generic *Customer* table would have columns that are NULL for some kinds of customers but not others.
- **Redundant data.** Redundant data is a serious problem in operational databases because when data is stored in several places, the opportunity for inconsistency occurs. For example, it is quite common to discover that customer information is stored in many different places within your organization. In fact, many companies are unable to put together an accurate list of who their customers actually are. The problem is that in one table John Smith lives at 123 Main Street, and in another table at 456 Elm Street. In this case, this is actually one person who used to live at 123 Main Street but who moved last year; unfortunately, John did not submit two change of address forms to your company, one for each application that knows about him.
- **Tables with too many columns.** When a table has many columns, it is indicative that the table lacks cohesion—that it is trying to store data from several entities. Perhaps your *Customer* table contains columns to store three different addresses (shipping, billing, seasonal) or several phone numbers (home, work, cell, and so on). You likely need to normalize this structure by adding *Address* and *PhoneNumber* tables.
- **Tables with too many rows.** Large tables are indicative of performance problems. For example, it is time-consuming to search a table with millions of rows. You may want to split the table vertically by moving some columns into another table, or split it horizontally by moving some rows

into another table. Both strategies reduce the size of the table, potentially improving performance.

- **"Smart" columns.** A smart column is one in which different positions within the data represent different concepts. For example, if the first four digits of the client ID indicate the client's home branch, then client ID is a smart column because you can parse it to discover more granular information (for example, home branch ID). Another example includes a text column used to store XML data structures; clearly, you can parse the XML data structure for smaller data fields. Smart columns often need to be reorganized into their constituent data fields at some point so that the database can easily deal with them as separate elements.
- **Fear of change.** If you are afraid to change your database schema because you are afraid to break something—for example, the 50 applications that access it—that is the surest sign that you need to refactor your schema. Fear of change is a good indication that you have a serious technical risk on your hands, one that will only get worse over time.

It is important to understand that just because something smells, it does not mean that it is bad—limburger cheese smells even when it is perfectly fine. However, when milk smells bad, you know that you have a problem. If something smells, look at it, think about it, and refactor it if it makes sense.

2.5 How Database Refactoring Fits In

Modern software development processes, including the Rational Unified Process (RUP), Extreme Programming (XP), Agile Unified Process (AUP), Scrum, and Dynamic System Development Method (DSDM), are all evolutionary in nature. Craig Larman (2004) summarizes the research evidence, as well as the overwhelming support among the thought leaders within the IT community, in support of evolutionary approaches. Unfortunately, most data-oriented techniques are serial in nature, relying on specialists performing relatively narrow tasks, such as logical data modeling or physical data modeling. Therein lies the rub—the two groups need to work together, but both want to do so in different manners.

Our position is that data professionals can benefit from adopting modern evolutionary techniques similar to those of developers, and that database refactoring is one of several important skills that data professionals require. Unfortunately, the data community missed the object revolution of the 1990s, which means they missed out on opportunities to learn the evolutionary techniques that application programmers now take for granted. In many ways, the data community is also missing out on the agile revolution, which is taking evolutionary development one step further to make it highly collaborative and cooperative.

How Database Refactoring Fits In

Database refactoring is a database implementation technique, just like code refactoring is an application implementation technique. You refactor your database schema to ease additions to it. You often find that you have to add a new feature to a database, such as a new column or stored procedure, but the existing design is not the best one possible to easily support that new feature. You start by refactoring your database schema to make it easier to add the feature, and after the refactoring has been successfully applied, you then add the feature. The advantage of this approach is that you are slowly, but constantly, improving the quality of your database design. This process not only makes your database easier to understand and use, it also makes it easier to evolve over time; in other words, you improve your overall development productivity.

Figure 2.6 provides a high-level overview of the critical development activities that occur on a modern project working with both object and relational database technologies. Notice how all the arrows are bidirectional. You iterate back and forth between activities as needed. Also notice how there is neither a defined starting point nor a defined ending point—this clearly is not a traditional, serial process.

Database refactoring is only part of the evolutionary database development picture. You still need to take an evolutionary/agile approach to data modeling. You still need to test your database schema and put it under configuration management control. And, you still need to tune it appropriately. These are topics better left to other books.

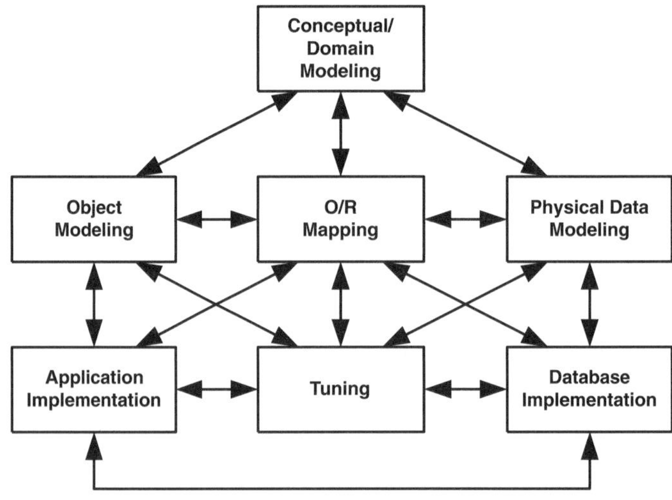

Figure 2.6 Potential development activities on an evolutionary development project.

2.6 Making It Easier to Refactor Your Database Schema

The greater the coupling, the harder it is to refactor something. This is true of code refactoring, and it is certainly true of database refactoring. Our experience is that coupling becomes a serious issue when you start to consider behavioral issues (for example, code), something that many database books choose not to address. The easiest scenario is clearly the single-application database because your database schema will only be coupled to itself and to your application. With the multi-application database architecture depicted in Figure 2.7, your database schema is potentially coupled to application source code, persistence frameworks and Object-Relational Mapping (ORM) tools, other databases (via replication, data extracts/loads, and so on), data file schemas, testing code, and even to itself.

An effective way to decrease the coupling that your database is involved with is to encapsulate access to it. You do this by having external programs access your database via persistence layers, as depicted in Figure 2.8. A persistence layer can be implemented in several ways—via data access objects (DAOs), which implement the necessary SQL code; by frameworks; via stored procedures; or even via Web services. As you see in the diagram, you can never get the coupling down to zero, but you can definitely reduce it to something manageable.

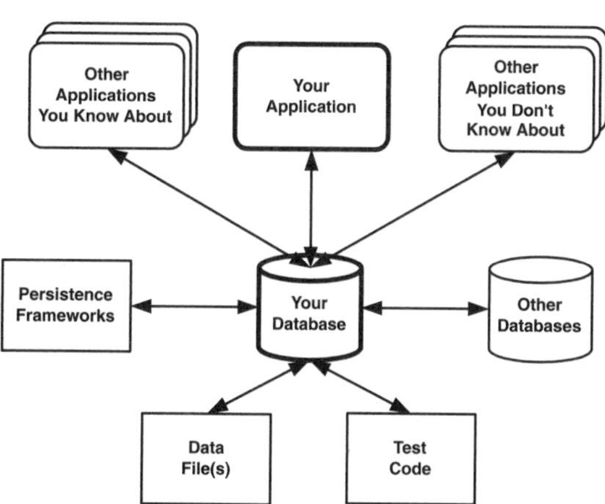

Figure 2.7 Databases are highly coupled to external programs.

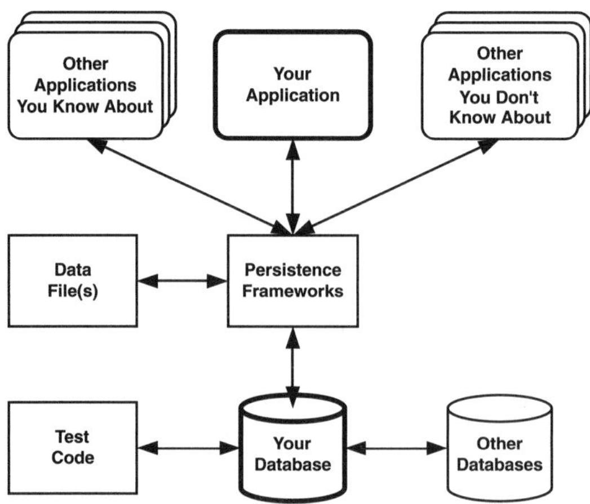

Figure 2.8 Reducing coupling via encapsulating access.

2.7 What You Have Learned

Code refactoring is a disciplined way to restructure code in small, evolutionary steps to improve the quality of its design. A code refactoring retains the behavioral semantics of your code; it neither adds functionality nor takes functionality away. Similarly, a database refactoring is a simple change to a database schema that improves its design while retaining both its behavioral and informational semantics. Database refactoring is one of the core techniques that enable data professionals to take an evolutionary approach to database development. The greater the coupling that your database is involved with, the harder it will be to refactor.

Chapter 3

The Process of Database Refactoring

A new scientific truth does not triumph by convincing its opponents and making them see the light, but rather because its opponents eventually die, and a new generation grows up that is familiar with it.

—Max Planck

This chapter describes how to implement a single refactoring within your database. We work through an example of applying the *Move Column* (page 103), a structural refactoring. Although this seems like a simple refactoring, and it is, you will see it can be quite complex to safely implement it within a production environment. Figure 3.1 overviews how we will move the *Customer.Balance* column to the *Account* table, a straightforward change to improve the database design.

In Chapter 1, "Evolutionary Database Development," we overviewed the concept of logical working sandboxes—development sandboxes in which developers have their own copy of the source code and database to work with; a project-integration environment where team members promote and then test their changes; preproduction environments for system, integration, and user acceptance testing; and production. The hard work of database refactoring is done within your development sandbox—it is considered, implemented, and tested before it is promoted into other environments. The focus of this chapter is on the work that is performed within your development sandbox. Chapter 4, "Deploying into Production," covers the promotion and eventual deployment of your refactorings.

Because we are describing what occurs within your development sandbox, this process applies to both the single-application database as well as the

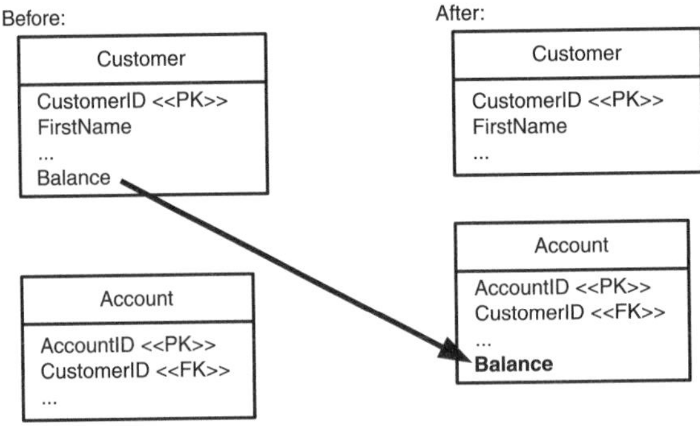

Figure 3.1 Moving the Customer.Balance column to Account.

multi-application database environments. The only real difference between the two situations is the need for a longer transition period (more on this later) in the multi-application scenario.

Figure 3.2 depicts a UML 2 Activity diagram that overviews the database refactoring process. The process begins with a developer who is trying to implement a new requirement to fix a defect. The developer realizes that the database schema may need to be refactored. In this example, Eddy, a developer, is adding a new type of financial transaction to his application and realizes that the *Balance* column actually describes Account entities, not Customer entities. Because Eddy follows common agile practices such as pair programming (Williams & Kessler 2002) and modeling with others (Ambler 2002), he decides to enlist the help of Beverley, the team's database administrator (DBA), to help him to apply the refactoring. Together they iteratively work through the following activities:

- Verify that a database refactoring is appropriate.
- Choose the most appropriate database refactoring.
- Deprecate the original database schema.
- Test before, during, and after.
- Modify the database schema.
- Migrate the source data.
- Modify external access program(s).

- Run regression tests.
- Version control your work.
- Announce the refactoring.

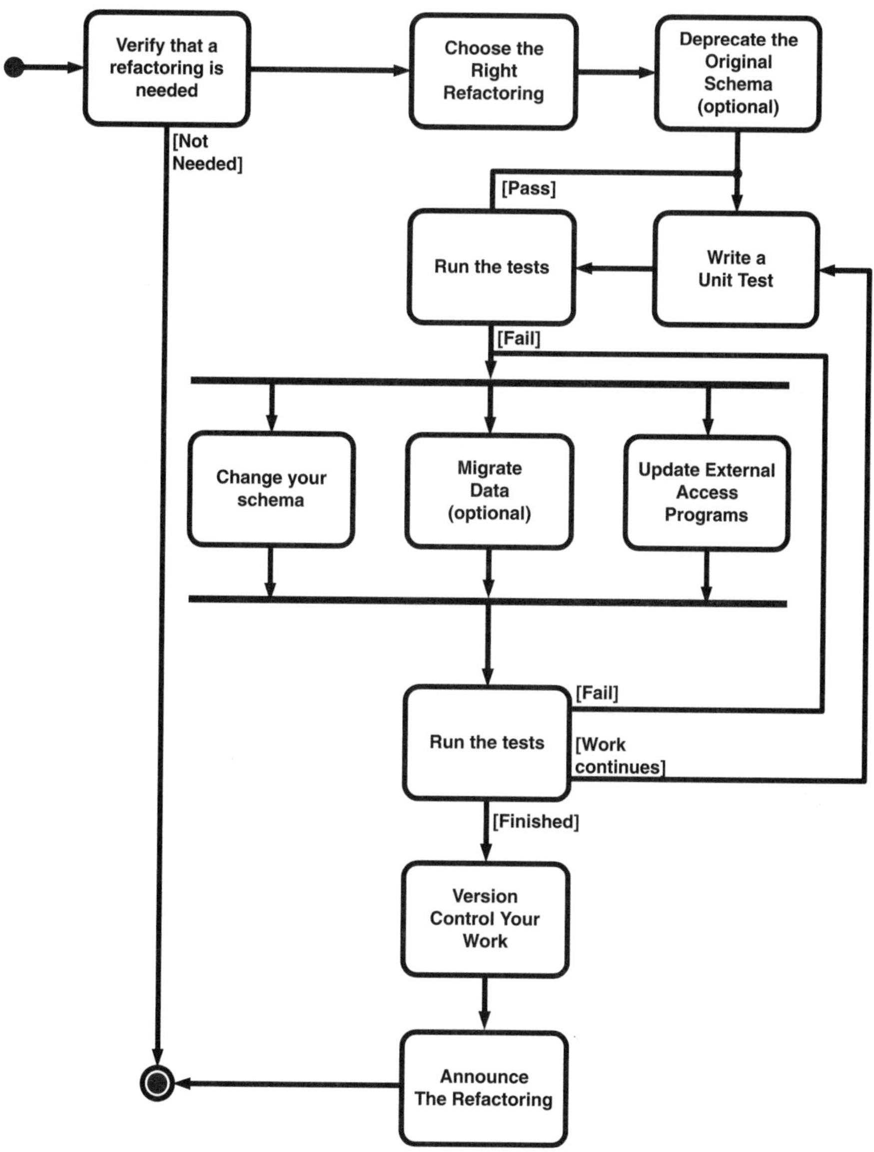

Figure 3.2 The database refactoring process.

3.1 Verify That a Database Refactoring Is Appropriate

First, Beverley determines whether the suggested refactoring needs to occur. There are three issues to consider:

1. Does the refactoring make sense?

   Perhaps the existing table structure is correct. It is common for developers to either disagree with, or to simply misunderstand, the existing design of a database. This misunderstanding could lead them to believe that the design needs to change when it really does not. The DBA should have a good knowledge of the project team's database, other corporate databases, and will know whom to contact about issues such as this. Therefore, they will be in a better position to determine whether the existing schema is the best one. Furthermore, the DBA often understands the bigger picture of the overall enterprise, providing important insight that may not be apparent when you look at it from the point of view of the single project. However, in our example, it appears that the schema needs to change.

2. Is the change actually needed now?

   This is usually a "gut call" based on her previous experience with the application developer. Does Eddy have a good reason for making the schema change? Can Eddy explain the business requirement that the change supports? Does the requirement feel right? Has Eddy suggested good changes in the past? Has Eddy changed his mind several days later, requiring Beverley to back out of the change? Depending on this assessment, Beverley may suggest that Eddy think the change through some more or may decide to continue working with him, but will wait for a longer period of time before they actually apply the change in the project-integration environment (Chapter 4) if they believe the change will need to be reversed.

3. Is it worth the effort?

   The next thing that Beverley does is to assess the overall impact of the refactoring. To do this, Beverley should have an understanding of how the external program(s) are coupled to this part of the database. This is knowledge that Beverley has built up over time by working with the enterprise architects, operational database administrators, application developers, and other DBAs. When Beverley is not sure of the impact,

Take Small Steps

Database refactoring changes the schema in small steps; each refactoring should be made one at a time. For example, assume you realize that you need to move an existing column, rename it, and apply a common format to it. Instead of trying this all at once, you should instead successfully implement *Move Column* (page 103), then successfully implement *Rename Column* (page 109), and then apply *Introduce Common Format* (page 183) one step at a time. The advantage is that if you make a mistake, it is easy to find the bug because it will likely be in the part of the schema that you just changed.

she needs to make a decision at the time and go with her gut feeling or decide to advise the application developer to wait while she talks to the right people. Her goal is to ensure that she implements database refactorings that will succeed—if you are going to need to update, test, and redeploy 50 other applications to support this refactoring, it may not be viable for her to continue. Even when there is only one application accessing the database, it may be so highly coupled to the portion of the schema that you want to change that the database refactoring simply is not worth it. In our example, the design problem is so clearly severe that she decides to implement it even though many applications will be affected.

3.2 Choose the Most Appropriate Database Refactoring

As you can see in this book, you could potentially apply a large number of refactorings to your database schema. To determine which is the most appropriate refactoring for your situation, you must first analyze and understand the problem you face. When Eddy first approached Beverley, he may or may not have done this analysis. For example, he may have just gone to her and said that the *Account* table needs to store the current balance; therefore, we need to add a new column (via the *Introduce Column* transformation on page 180). However, what he did not realize was that the column already exists in the *Customer* table, which is arguably the wrong place for it to be—Eddy had identified the problem correctly, but had misidentified the solution. Based on her

Sometimes the Data Is Elsewhere

Your database is likely not the only source of data within your organization. A good DBA should at least know about, if not understand, the various data sources within your enterprise to determine the best source of data. In our example, another database could potentially be the official repository of Account information. If that is the case, moving the column may not make sense because the true refactoring would be *Use Official Data Source* (page 271).

knowledge of the existing database schema, and her understanding of the problem identified by Eddy, Beverley instead suggests that they apply the *Move Column* (page 103) refactoring.

3.3 Deprecate the Original Database Schema

If multiple applications access your database, you likely need to work under the assumption that you cannot refactor and then deploy all of these programs simultaneously. Instead, you need a transition period, also called a deprecation period, for the original portion of the schema that you are changing (Sadalage & Schuh 2002; Ambler 2003). During the transition period, you support both the original and new schemas in parallel to provide time for the other application teams to refactor and redeploy their systems. Typical transition periods last for several quarters, if not years. The potentially long time to fully implement a refactoring underscores the need to automate as much of the process as possible. Over a several-year period, people within your department will change, putting you at risk if parts of the process are manual. Having said that, even in the case of a single-application database, your team may still require a transition period of a few days within your project-integration sandbox—your teammates need to refactor and retest their code to work with the updated database schema.

Figure 3.3 depicts the life cycle of a database refactoring within a multi-application scenario. You first implement it within the scope of your project, and if successful, you eventually deploy it into production. During the transition period, both the original schema and the new schema exist, with sufficient scaffolding code to ensure that any updates are correctly supported.

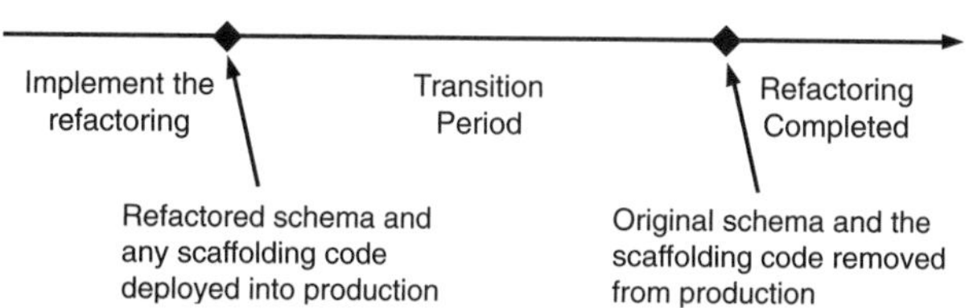

Figure 3.3 The life cycle of a database refactoring in a multi-application scenario.

During the transition period, you need to assume two things: first, that some applications will use the original schema whereas others will use the new schema; and second, that applications should only have to work with one but not both versions of the schema. In our example, some applications will work with *Customer.Balance* and others with *Account.Balance*, but not both simultaneously. Regardless of which column they work with, the applications should all run properly. When the transition period has expired, the original schema plus any scaffolding code is removed and the database retested. At this point, the assumption is that all applications work with *Account.Balance.*

Figure 3.4 depicts the original database schema, and Figure 3.5 shows what the database schema would look like during the transition period for when we apply the *Move Column* database refactoring to *Customer.Balance*. In Figure 3.5, the changes are shown in bold, a style that we use throughout the book. Notice how both versions of the schema are supported during this period. *Account.Balance* has been added as a column, and *Customer.Balance* has been marked for removal on or after June 14, 2006. A trigger was also introduced to keep the values contained in the two columns synchronized, the assumption being that new application code will work with *Account.Balance* but will not keep *Customer.Balance* up-to-date. Similarly, we assume that older application code that has not been refactored to use the new schema will not know to keep *Account.Balance* up-to-date. This trigger is an example of database scaffolding code, simple and common code that is required to keep your database "glued together." This code has been assigned the same removal date as *Customer.Balance.*

Not all database refactorings require a transition period. For example, neither *Introduce Column Constraint* (page 180) nor *Apply Standard Codes* (page 157) database refactorings require a transition period because they simply improve the data quality by narrowing the acceptable values within a column. A narrower value may break existing applications, so beware of the refactorings.

Chapter 5, "Database Refactoring Strategies," discusses strategies for choosing an appropriate transition period.

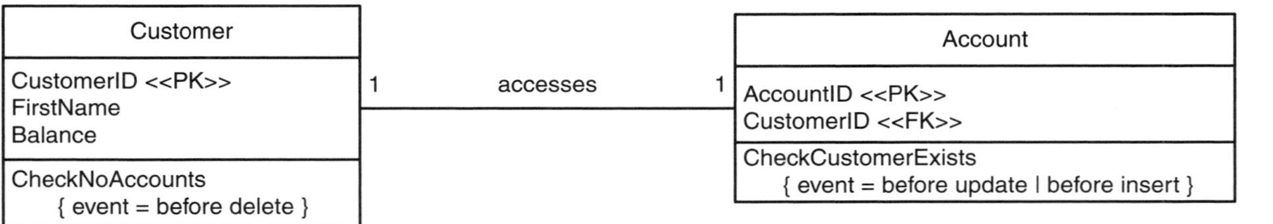

Figure 3.4 The original Customer/Account schema.

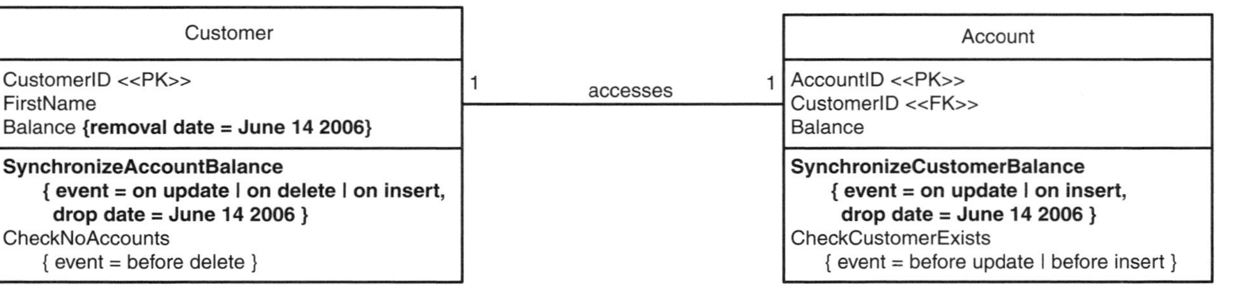

Figure 3.5 Supporting both versions of the schema.

3.4 Test Before, During, and After

You can have the confidence to change your database schema if you can easily validate that the database still works with your application after the change, and the only way to do that is to take a Test-Driven Development (TDD) approach, as suggested in Chapter 1. With a TDD-based approach, you write a test and then you write just enough code, often data definition language (DDL), to fulfill the test. You continue in this manner until the database refactoring has been implemented fully. You will potentially need to write tests that do the following:

- Test your database schema.
- Test the way your application uses the database schema.
- Validate your data migration.
- Test your external program code.

3.4.1 Testing Your Database Schema

Because a database refactoring will affect your database schema, you need to write database-oriented tests. Although this may sound strange at first, you can validate many aspects of a database schema:

- **Stored procedures and triggers.** Stored procedures and triggers should be tested just like your application code would be.
- **Referential integrity (RI).** RI rules, in particular cascading deletes in which highly coupled "child" rows are deleted when a parent row is deleted, should also be validated. Existence rules, such as a customer row corresponding to an account row, must exist before the row can be inserted into the *Account* table, and can be easily tested, too.
- **View definitions.** Views often implement interesting business logic. Things to look out for include: Does the filtering/select logic work properly? Do you get back the right number of rows? Are you returning the right columns? Are the columns, and rows, in the right order?
- **Default values.** Columns often have default values defined for them. Are the default values actually being assigned? (Someone could have accidentally removed this part of the table definition.)
- **Data invariants.** Columns often have invariants, implemented in the forms of constraints, defined for them. For example, a number column may be

restricted to containing the values 1 through 7. These invariants should be tested.

Database testing is new to many people, and as a result you are likely to face several challenges when adopting database refactoring as a development technique:

Test Before, During, and After

- **Insufficient testing skills.** This problem can be overcome through training, through pairing with someone with good testing skills (pairing a DBA without testing skills and a tester without DBA skills still works), or simply through trial and error. The important thing is that you recognize that you need to pick up these skills.
- **Insufficient unit tests for your database.** Few organizations have yet to adopt the practice of database testing, so it is likely that you will not have a sufficient test suite for your existing schema. Although this is unfortunate, there is no better time than the present to start writing your test suite.
- **Insufficient database testing tools.** Luckily, tools such as DBUnit (dbunit.sourceforge.net) for managing test data and SQLUnit (sqlunit .sourceforge.net) for testing stored procedures are available as open source software (OSS). In addition, several commercial tools are available for database testing. However, at the time of this writing, there is still significant opportunity for tool vendors to improve their database testing offerings.

So how would we test the changes to the database schema? As you can see in Figure 3.5, there are two changes to the schema during the transition period that we must validate. The first one is the addition of the *Balance* column to the *Account* table. This change is covered by our data migration and external program testing efforts, discussed in the following sections. The second change is the addition of the two triggers, *SynchronizeAccountBalance* and *SynchronizeCustomerBalance*, which, as their names imply, keep the two data columns synchronized. We need tests to ensure that if *Customer.Balance* is updated that *Account.Balance* is similarly updated, and vice versa.

3.4.2 Validating Your Data Migration

Many database refactorings require you to migrate and sometimes even cleanse the source data. In our example, we must copy the data values from *Customer.Balance* to *Account.Balance* as part of implementing the refactoring. In this case, we want to validate that the correct balance was in fact copied over for individual customers.

In refactorings such as *Apply Standard Codes* (page 157) and *Consolidate Key Strategy* (page 168), you actually "cleanse" data values. This cleansing

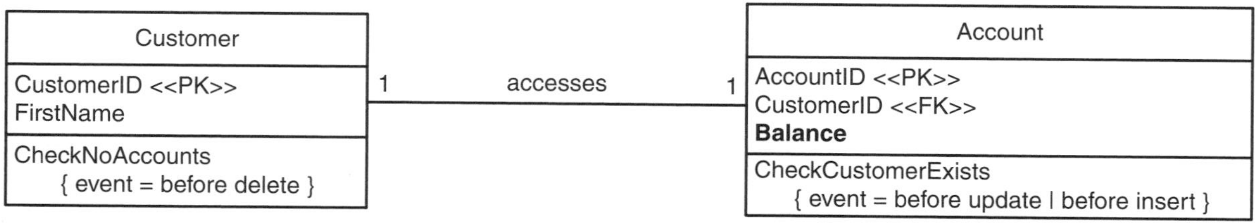

Figure 3.6 The final version of the database schema.

logic must be validated. With the first refactoring, you may convert code values such as USA and U.S. all to the standard value of US throughout your database. You would want to write tests to validate that the older codes were no longer being used and that they were converted properly to the official value. With the second refactoring, you might discover that customers are identified via their customer ID in some tables, by their social security number (SSN) in other tables, and by their phone number in other tables. You would want to choose one way to identify customers, perhaps by their customer ID, and then refactor the other tables to use this type of column instead. In this case, you would want to write tests to verify that the relationship between the various rows was still being maintained properly. (For example, if the telephone number 555-1234 referenced the Sally Jones customer record, the Sally Jones record should still be getting referenced when you replace it with customer ID 987654321.)

3.4.3 Testing Your External Access Programs

Your database is accessed by one or more programs, including the application that you are working on. These programs should be validated just like any other IT asset within your organization. To successfully refactor your database, you need to be able to introduce the final schema, shown in Figure 3.6, and see what breaks in your external access programs. The only way that you can have the confidence to refactor your database schema is if you have a full regression test suite for these programs—yes, we realize that you likely do not have these test suites. Once again, there is no better time than the present to start building up your test suite. We suggest that you write all the testing code you require to support each individual database refactoring for all external access programs. (Actually, the owners of these systems need to write those tests, not you.) If you work this way, over time you will build up the test suite that you require.

3.5 Modify the Database Schema

Eddy and Beverley work together to make the changes within their development sandbox. As you see in Figure 3.5, they need to add the *Account.Balance* column as well as the two triggers, *SynchronizeAccountBalance* and *SynchronizeCustomerBalance*. The DDL code to do this is shown here:

```
ALTER TABLE Account ADD Balance Numeric;
COMMENT ON Account.Balance 'Move of Customer.Balance column, finaldate = 2006-06-14';

CREATE OR REPLACE TRIGGER SynchronizeCustomerBalance
 BEFORE INSERT OR UPDATE
 ON Account
 REFERENCING OLD AS OLD NEW AS NEW
 FOR EACH ROW
 DECLARE
 BEGIN
  IF :NEW.Balance IS NOT NULL THEN
   UpdateCustomerBalance;
  END IF;
 END;
/
COMMENT ON SynchronizeCustomerBalance 'Move of Customer.Balance column to Account,
dropdate = 2006-06-14';

CREATE OR REPLACE TRIGGER SynchronizeAccountBalance
 BEFORE INSERT OR UPDATE OR DELETE
 ON Customer
 REFERENCING OLD AS OLD NEW AS NEW
 FOR EACH ROW
 DECLARE
 BEGIN
  IF DELETING THEN
   DeleteCustomerIfAccountNotFound;
  END IF;
  IF (UPDATING OR INSERTING) THEN
   IF :NEW.Balance IS NOT NULL THEN
    UpdateAccountBalanceForCustomer;
   END IF;
  END IF;
 END;
/
COMMENT ON SynchronizeAccountBalance 'Move of Customer.Balance column to Account,
dropdate = 2006-06-14'
```


At the time of this writing, no automated database refactoring tools are available—therefore, you need to code everything by hand for now. Do not worry. This will change in time. For now, you want to write a single script containing the preceding code that you can apply against the database schema. We suggest assigning a unique, incremental number to each script. The easiest way to do so is just to start at the number one and increment a counter each time you define a new database refactoring—the easiest way to do that is to use the build number of your application. However, to make this strategy work within a multiple team environment, you need a way to either assign unique numbers across all teams or to add a unique team identifier to the individual refactorings. Fundamentally, you need to be able to differentiate between Team A's refactoring number 1701 and Team B's refactoring number 1701. Another option, discussed in more detail in Chapter 5, is to assign timestamps to the refactoring.

There are several reasons why you want to work with small scripts for individual refactorings:

- **Simplicity**. Small, focused change scripts are easier to maintain than scripts comprising many steps. If you discover that a refactoring should not be performed because of unforeseen problems (perhaps you cannot update a major application that accesses the changed portion of the schema), for example, you want to be able to easily not perform that refactoring.
- **Correctness**. You want to be able to apply each refactoring, in the appropriate order, to your database schema so as to evolve it in a defined manner. Refactorings can build upon each other. For example, you might rename a column and then a few weeks later move it to another table. The second refactoring would depend on the first refactoring because its code would refer to the new name of the column.
- **Versioning**. Different database instances will have different versions of your database schema. For example, Eddy's development sandbox may have version 163, the project-integration sandbox version 161, the QA/Test sandbox version 155, and the production database version 134. To migrate the project-integration sandbox schema to version 163, you should merely have to apply database refactoring 162 and 163. To keep track of the version number, you need to introduce a common table, such as *DatabaseConfiguration*, that stores the current version number among other things. This table is discussed in further detail in Chapter 5.

The following DDL code must be run against your database after the transition period has ended (discussed in Chapter 4). Similarly, this code should be captured in a single script file, along with the identifier of 163 in this case, and run in sequential order against your database schema as appropriate.

```
ALTER TABLE Customer DROP COLUMN Balance;
DROP TRIGGER SynchronizeAccountBalance;
DROP TRIGGER SynchronizeCustomerBalance;
```

Follow Your Database Design Conventions

An important part of implementing a refactoring is ensuring that the changed portion of your database schema follows your corporate database development guidelines. These guidelines should be provided and supported by your Database Administration group, and at a minimum should address naming and documentation guidelines.

3.6 Migrate the Source Data

Many database refactorings require you to manipulate the source data in some way. Sometimes, you just need to move data from one location to another, something we need to do with *Move Data* (page 192). Other times, you need to cleanse the values of the data itself; this is common with the data quality refactorings (Chapter 7, "Data Quality Refactorings") such as *Apply Standard Type* (page 162) and *Introduce Common Format* (page 183).

Similar to modifying your database schema, you will potentially need to create a script to perform the required data migration. This script should have the same identification number as your other script to make them easy to manage. In our example of moving the *Customer.Balance* column to *Account*, the data migration script would contain the following data manipulation language (DML) code:

```
/*
One time migration of data from Customer.Balance to Account.Balance.
*/

UPDATE Account SET Balance =
 (SELECT Balance FROM Customer
  WHERE CustomerID = Account.CustomerID);
```

Depending on the quality of the existing data, you may quickly discover the need to further cleanse the source data. This would require the application of one or more data quality database refactorings. It is good practice to keep your eye out for data quality problems when you are working through structural and architectural database refactorings. Data quality problems are quite common with legacy database designs that have been allowed to degrade over time.

The Need to Document Reflects a Need to Refactor

When you find that you need to write supporting documentation to describe a table, column, or stored procedure, that is a good indication that you need to refactor that portion of your schema to make it easier to understand. Perhaps a simple renaming can avoid several paragraphs of documentation. The cleaner your design, the less documentation you require.

3.7 Refactor External Access Program(s)

When your database schema changes, you will often need to refactor any existing external programs that access the changed portion of the schema. As you learned in Chapter 2, "Database Refactoring," this includes legacy applications, persistence frameworks, data replication code, and reporting systems, to name a few.

Several good books provide guidance for effective refactoring of external access programs:

- *Refactoring: Improving the Design of Existing Code* (Fowler 1999) is the classic text on the subject.
- *Working Effectively with Legacy Code* (Feathers 2004) describes how to refactor legacy systems that have existed within your organization for many years.
- *Refactoring to Patterns* (Kerievsky 2004) describes how to methodically refactor your code to implement common design and architectural patterns.

When many programs access your database, you run the risk that some of them will not be updated by the development teams responsible for them, or worse yet they may not even be assigned to a team at the present moment. The implication is that someone will need to be assigned responsibility for updating the application(s), as well as the responsibility to burden the cost. Hopefully, other teams are responsible for these external programs; otherwise, your team will need to accept responsibility for making the required changes. It is frustrating to discover that the political challenges surrounding the need to update other systems often far outweigh the technical challenges of doing so.

Aim for Continuous Development

Ideally, your organization would continuously work on all of their applications, evolving them over time and deploying them on a regular basis. Although this sounds complicated, and it can be, shouldn't your IT department actively strive to ensure that the systems within your organization meet its changing needs? In these environments, you can have a relatively short transition period because you know that all the applications accessing your database evolve on a regular basis and therefore can be updated to work with the changed schema.

So what do you do when there is no funding to update the external programs? You have two basic strategies from which to choose. First, make the database refactoring and assign it a transition period of several decades. This way the external programs that you cannot change still work; however, other applications can access the improved design. This strategy has the unfortunate disadvantage that the scaffolding code to support both schemas will exist for a long time, reducing database performance and cluttering your database. The second strategy is to not do the refactoring.

3.8 Run Your Regression Tests

Part of implementing your refactoring is to test it to ensure that it works. As indicated earlier, you will test a little, change a little, test a little, and so on until the refactoring is complete. Your testing activities should be automated as much as possible. A significant advantage of database refactoring is that because the refactorings represent small changes, when a test breaks you have a pretty good idea where the problem lies—where you just made the change.

3.9 Version Control Your Work

When your database refactoring is successful, you should put all your work under configuration management (CM) control by checking it into a version control tool. If you treat your database-oriented artifacts the exact same way that you treat your source code, you should be okay. Artifacts to version control include the following:

- Any scripts that you have created
- Test data and/or generation code
- Test cases
- Documentation
- Models

3.10 Announce the Refactoring

A database is a shared resource. Minimally, it is shared within your application development team, if not by several application teams. Therefore, you need to communicate to interested parties that the database refactoring has been made. Early in the life cycle of the refactoring, you need to communicate the changes within your team, something that could be as simple as announcing the change at your team's next standup meeting. In a multi-application database environment, you must communicate the changes to other teams, particularly when you decide to promote the refactoring into your preproduction test environments. This communication might be a simple e-mail on an internal mailing list specifically used to announce database changes, it could be a line item in your regular project status report, or it could be a formal report to your operational database administration group.

An important aspect of your announcement efforts will be the update of any relevant documentation. This documentation will be critical during your promotion and deployment efforts (see Chapter 4) because the other teams need to know how the database schema has evolved. A simple approach is to develop database release notes that summarize the changes that you have made, listing each database refactoring in order. Our example refactoring would appear in this list as "163: Move the *Customer.Balance* column into the *Account* table." These release notes will likely be required by enterprise administrators so that they can update the relevant meta data. (Better yet, your team should update this meta data as part of their refactoring efforts.)

You will want to update the physical data model (PDM) for your database. Your PDM is the primary model describing your database schema and is often one of the few "keeper" models created on application development projects, and therefore should be kept up-to-date as much as possible.

Do Not Publish Data Models Prematurely

Your object and database schemas are likely to fluctuate initially because with an evolutionary approach to development your design emerges over time. Because of this initial flux, you should wait until new portions of your schema have stabilized before publishing updates to your physical data model. This will reduce your documentation effort as well as minimize the impact to other application teams that rely on your database schema.

3.11 What You Have Learned

The hard work of database refactoring is done within your development sandbox, hopefully by a developer paired with a DBA. The first step is to verify that a database refactoring is even appropriate—perhaps the cost of performing the refactoring currently outweighs the benefit, or perhaps the current schema is the best design for that specific issue. If a refactoring is required, you must choose the most appropriate one to get the job done. In a multi-application environment, many refactorings require you to run both the original and new versions of the schema in parallel during a transition period that is long enough to allow any applications accessing that portion of the schema time to be redeployed.

To implement the refactoring, you should take a Test-First approach to increase the chance that you detect any breakages introduced by the refactoring. You must modify the database schema, potentially migrate any relevant source data, and then modify any external programs that access the schema. All of your work should be version controlled, and after the refactoring has been implemented within your development environment, it should be announced to your teammates and then eventually to appropriate external teams that might need to know about the schema change.

Chapter 4

Deploying into Production

If we do not change direction soon we will end up where we are going.

—Dr. Irwin Corey

It is not enough just to refactor your database schemas within your development and integration sandboxes. You must also deploy the changes into production. The way that you do so must reflect your organization's existing deployment process—you may need to improve this existing process to reflect the evolutionary approach described in this book. You will likely discover that your organization already has experience at deploying database changes, but because schema changes are often feared in many environments, you will also discover that your experiences have not been all that good. Time to change that.

The good news is that deploying database refactorings is much safer than deploying traditional database schema changes, assuming, of course, you are following the advice presented in this book. This is true for several reasons. First, individual database refactorings are less risky to deploy than traditional database schema changes because they are small and simple. However, collections of database refactorings, what you actually deploy, can become complex if you do not manage them well. This chapter provides advice for doing exactly that. Second, when you take a Test-Driven Development (TDD) approach, you have a full regression test suite in place that validates your refactorings. Knowing that the refactorings actually work enables you to deploy them with greater confidence. Third, by having a transition period during which both the old and new schemas exist in parallel, you are not required to also deploy a slew of application changes that reflect the schema changes.

To successfully deploy database refactorings into production, you need to adopt strategies for the following:

- Effectively deploying between sandboxes
- Applying bundles of database refactorings

- Scheduling deployment windows
- Deploying your system
- Removing deprecated schema

4.1 Effectively Deploying Between Sandboxes

Effectively Deploying Between Sandboxes

Chapter 1, "Evolutionary Database Development," described the idea that you need a series of sandboxes in which to implement, test, and run your systems. As you see in Figure 4.1, each project team has a collection of developer sandboxes and possibly even their own corresponding demo sandbox. The preproduction test sandbox is shared between teams, as is the production environment. You can also see that there are deployment gates between the various sandboxes. It should be relatively easy to deploy database refactorings from a developer's workstation into your shared project-integration sandbox because the impact of a mistake is fairly low: You only affect the team. It should be a little more difficult to deploy into your preproduction testing environment(s) because the impact of a mistake is much greater: Not only could your system be unavailable to the testers, it could also cause other systems within these environments to crash, thereby affecting other teams. Deploying into your production environment is often a rigorous process because the potential cost of a mistake is quite high because you could easily impact your customers.

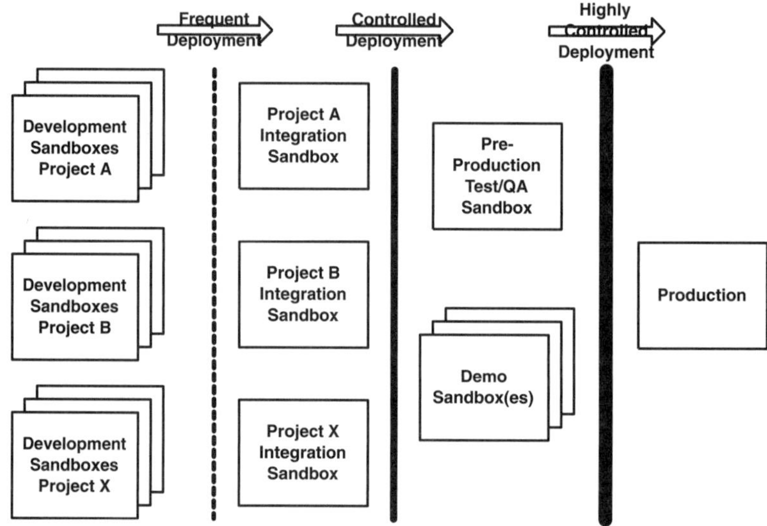

Figure 4.1 Deploying between sandboxes.

To deploy into each sandbox, you will need to both build your application and run your database management scripts (the change log, the update log, and the data migration log, or equivalent, described in Chapter 3, "The Process of Database Refactoring"). The next step is to rerun your regression tests to ensure that your system still works—if it does not, you must fix it in your development sandbox, redeploy, and retest. The goal in your project-integration sandbox is to validate that the changes made by the individual developer (pairs) work together, whereas your goal in the preproduction test/QA sandbox is to validate that your system works well with the other systems within your organization.

It is quite common to see developers promote changes from their development sandboxes into the project-integration sandbox several times a day. As a team, you should strive to deploy your system into at least your demo environment at least once an iteration so that you can share your current working software with appropriate internal project stakeholders. Better yet, you should also deploy your system into your preproduction test environments so that it can be acceptance tested and system tested, ideally at least once an iteration. You want to deploy regularly into your preproduction environment for two reasons. First, you get concrete feedback as to how well your system actually works. Second, because you deploy regularly, you discover ways to get better at deployment—by running your installation scripts on a regular basis, including the tests that validate the installation scripts, you will quickly get them to the point where they are robust enough to deploy your system successfully into production.

4.2 Applying Bundles of Database Refactorings

Modern development teams work in short iterations; within an agile team, iterations of one or two weeks in length are quite common. But just because a team is developing working software each week, it does not mean that they are going to deploy a new version of the system into production each week. Typically, they will deploy into production once every few months. The implication is that the team will need to bundle up all the database refactorings that they performed since the last time they deployed into production so that they can be applied appropriately.

As you saw in Chapter 3, the easiest way to do this is just to treat each database refactoring as its own transaction that is implemented as a combination of data definition language (DDL) scripts to change the database schema and to migrate any data as appropriate, as well as changes to your program source code that accesses that portion of the schema. This transaction should be assigned a unique ID, a number or date/timestamp suffices, which enables you

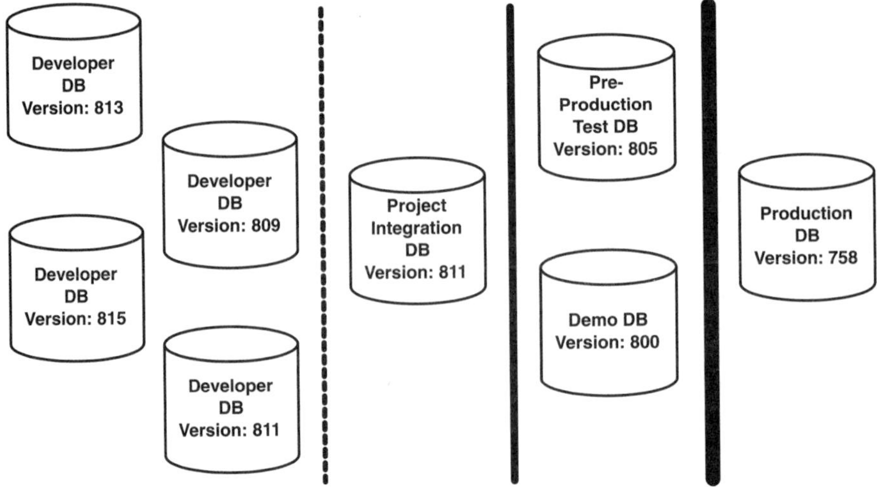

Figure 4.2 Different databases, different versions.

to put the refactorings in order. This allows you to apply the refactorings in order, either with a handwritten script or some sort of generic tool, in any of your sandboxes as you need.

Because you cannot assume that all database schemas will be identical to one another, you need some way to safely apply different combinations of refactorings to each schema. For example, consider the number-based scheme depicted in Figure 4.2. The various developer databases are each at different versions. Your database is at version 813, another at 811, and another at 815. Because your project-integration database is at version 811, we can tell that your database schema has been changed since the last time you synced up with the project-integration environment, that the second developer has not changed his version of the schema and has not yet obtained the most recent version (809 is less than 811), and that the third developer has made changes in parallel to yours. The changes must have been made in parallel because neither of you have promoted your changes to the integration environment yet (otherwise, that environment would have the same number as one of the two databases). To update the project-integration database, you need to run it for changes starting at 812; to update the preproduction test database, you start at change script 806; to update the demo environment, you start at change script 801; and to update the production database, you start at change number 758. Furthermore, you might not want to apply all changes to all versions—for example, you may only bring production up to version 794 for the next release.

One way to think about this is that at the beginning of development for a new release of your system, you start a new stack of database refactorings.

Throughout your development efforts, you keep adding new schema changes to the stack, and sometimes remove some of them that you decide to back out of. At the end of the development of that release, you baseline the stack, accepting it as the bundle of schema changes for the current release.

4.3 Scheduling Deployment Windows

A deployment window, often called a release window, is a specific point in time in which it is permissible to deploy a system into production. Your operations staff will likely have strict rules regarding when application teams may deploy systems. It is quite common to have rules such as application teams only being allowed to deploy new releases on Saturday evening between 2 a.m. and 6 a.m., and bug fixes between 4 a.m. and 6 a.m. on other evenings. These deployment windows are typically defined to coincide with periods of reduced system activity. Furthermore, they may have rules about when database schema changes are allowed to be made—for example, only on the third Saturday of each month. Smaller organizations, particularly those without many development projects underway, may choose to have deployment windows once every few months.

The implication is that your team will not be allowed to deploy your system into production whenever you want, but instead it must schedule deployment into a predefined deployment window. Figure 4.3 captures this concept, showing how two project teams schedule the deployment of their changes (including database refactorings) into available deployment windows. Sometimes there is nothing to deploy, sometimes one team has changes, and other times both teams have schema changes to deploy. The deployment windows in Figure 4.3 coincide with the final deployment from your preproduction test environment into your production environment in Figure 4.1.

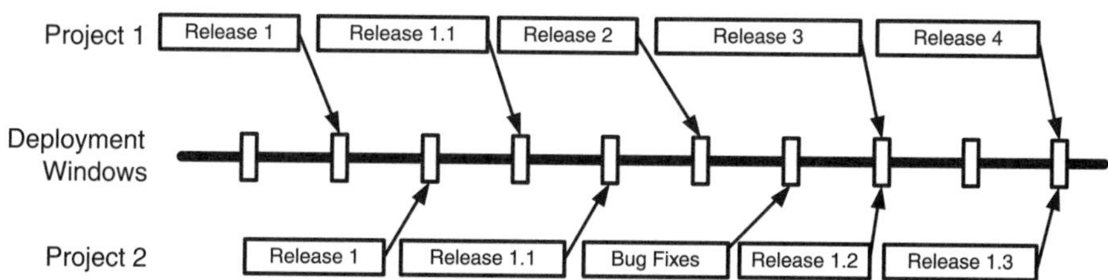

Figure 4.3 Deploy schema changes into production at predefined points in time.

You will naturally need to coordinate with any other teams that are deploying during the same deployment window. This coordination will occur long before you go to deploy, and frankly, the primary reason why your preproduction test environment exists is to provide a sandbox in which you can resolve multisystem issues. Regardless of how many database refactorings are to be applied to your production database, or how many teams those refactorings were developed by, they will have first been tested within your preproduction testing environment before being applied in production.

The primary benefit of defined deployment windows is that it provides a control mechanism over what goes into production when. This helps your operations staff to organize their time, it provides development teams with target dates to aim for, and sets the expectations of your end users as to when they might receive new functionality.

4.4 Deploying Your System

You generally will not deploy database refactorings on their own. Instead, you will deploy them as part of the overall deployment of one or more systems. Deployment is easiest when you have one application and one database to update, and this situation does occur in practice. Realistically, however, you must consider the situation in which you are deploying several systems and several data sources simultaneously. Figure 4.4 depicts a UML activity diagram overviewing the deployment process. You will need to do the following:

1. **Back up your database.** Although this is often difficult at best with large production databases, whenever possible you want to be able to back out to a known state if your deployment does not go well. One advantage of database refactorings is that they are small, so they are easy to back out of on an individual basis, an advantage that gets lost the longer you wait to deploy the refactorings because there is a greater chance that other refactorings will depend on it.

2. **Run your previous regression tests.** You first want to ensure that the existing production system(s) are in fact up and running properly. Although it should not have happened, someone may have inadvertently changed something that you do not know about. If the test suite corresponding to the previous deployment fails, your best bet is to abort and then investigate the problem. Note that you also need to ensure that your regression tests do not have any inadvertent side effects within your production environment. The implication is that you will need to be careful with your testing efforts.

3. **Deploy your changed application(s).** Follow your existing procedures to do this.

4. **Deploy your database refactorings.** You need to run the appropriate schema change scripts and data migration scripts to your data sources.

5. **Run your current regression tests.** After the application(s) and database refactorings have been deployed, you must run the current version of your test suite to verify that the deployed system(s) work in production. Once again, beware of side effects from your tests.

6. **Back out if necessary.** If your regression tests reveal serious defects, you must back out your applications and database schemas to the previous versions, in addition to restoring the database based on the backup from Step 1. If the deployment is complex, you may want to deploy in

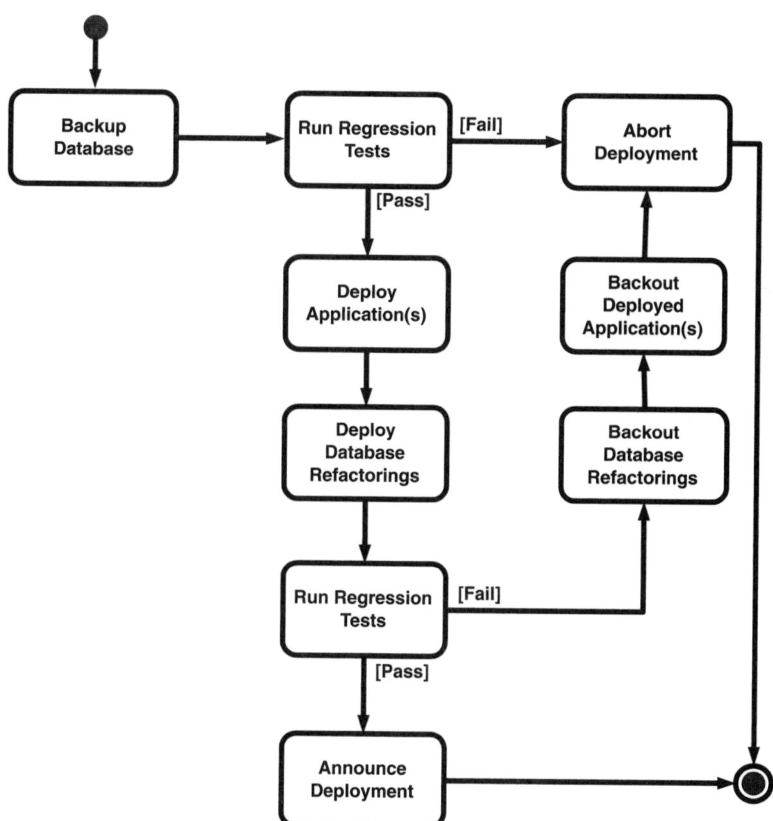

Figure 4.4 The deployment process.

increments, testing each increment one at a time. An incremental deployment approach is more complex to implement but has the advantage that the entire deployment does not fail just because one portion of it is problematic.

7. **Announce the deployment results.** When systems are successfully deployed, you should let your stakeholders know immediately. Even if you have to abort the deployment, you should still announce what happened and when you will attempt to deploy again. You need to manage your stakeholders' expectations—they are hoping for the successful deployment of one or more systems that they have been waiting for, so they are likely interested to hear how things have gone.

4.5 Removing Deprecated Schema

A database refactoring has not been truly deployed until you have removed the deprecated schema from production. When the transition period has ended, the deprecated schema and any scaffolding code, such as triggers to keep different versions of the schema synchronized, must be removed. Because the transition period may be several years, because that is how long it will take to update all the programs accessing the database, you need to have a process in place to manage these changes. The easiest approach, as described in Chapter 3, is to simply have specified dates (perhaps once a quarter) on which a transition period can end. The implication is that not only will you bundle up database schema improvements to apply them all at one time, you will also bundle up the removal of deprecated schema and apply those changes all at once.

We cannot say this enough: You must test thoroughly. Before removing the deprecated portions of the schema from production, you should first remove it from your preproduction test/QA environment and retest everything to ensure that it all still works. After you have done that, apply the changes in production, run your test suite there, and either back out or continue as appropriate.

4.6 What You Have Learned

Not only do you need to implement database refactorings, you also need to deploy them into production; otherwise, why do them at all? By having separate sandboxes, you can safely implement and test your refactorings to get them ready to be deployed. By deploying development versions of your system into your preproduction test environment on a regular basis, you improve and validate your deployment scripts long before you need to apply them within a production environment. Although you may develop working software on a regular basis, sometimes weekly, you generally will not release it into production that often. Instead, you will bundle up your database refactorings and deploy a collection of them all at one time during a predefined deployment window. Your application may not be the only one deploying into production during a given deployment window; therefore, you may need to coordinate with other teams to deploy successfully.

Chapter 5

Database Refactoring Strategies

Knowing more today than yesterday is good news about today, not bad news about yesterday.

—Ron Jeffries

This chapter describes some of our experiences with database refactoring on actual projects, and suggests a few potential strategies that you may want to consider. In many ways, this chapter summarizes a collection of "lessons learned" that we hope will help your adoption efforts. These lessons include the following:

- Smaller changes are easier to apply.
- Uniquely identify individual refactorings.
- Implement a large change by many small ones.
- Have a database configuration table.
- Prefer triggers over views or batch synchronization.
- Choose a sufficient deprecation period.
- Simplify your database change control board (CCB) strategy.
- Simplify negotiations with other teams.
- Encapsulate database access.
- Be able to easily set up a database environment.
- Do not duplicate SQL.
- Put database assets under change control.
- Beware of politics.

5.1 Smaller Changes Are Easier to Apply

It is tempting to try to make several changes to your database at once. For example, what is stopping you from moving a column from one table to another, renaming it, and applying a standard type to it all at the same time? Absolutely nothing, other than the knowledge that doing this all at once is harder, and therefore riskier, than doing it one step at a time. If you make a small change and discover that something is broken, you pretty much know which change caused the problem.

Small Changes Decrease Project Risk

It is safer to proceed in small steps, one at time. The larger the change, the greater the chance that you will introduce a defect, and the greater the difficulty in finding any defects that you do inject.

5.2 Uniquely Identify Individual Refactorings

During a software development project, you are likely to apply hundreds of refactorings and/or transformations to your database schema. Because these refactorings often build upon each other—for example, you may rename a column and then a few weeks later move it to another table—you need to ensure that the refactorings are applied in the right order. To do this, you need to identify each refactoring somehow and identify any dependencies between them. Table 5.1 compares and contrasts the three basic strategies for doing so. The strategies in Table 5.1 assume that you are working in a single-application single-database environment.

When you are in a multi-application environment in which several project teams may be applying refactorings to the same database schema, you also need to find a way to identify which team produced a refactoring. The easiest way to do this is to assign a unique identifier to each team and then include that value as part of the refactoring identifier. Therefore, with a build number strategy, team 1 might have refactorings with IDs 1-7, 1-12, 1-15, and so on; and team 7 could have refactorings with IDs 7-3, 7-7, 7-13, and so on.

Our experience is that when a single team is responsible for a database, the build number strategy works best. However, when several teams can evolve the

Table 5.1 *Version Identification Strategies*

Approach	Advantages	Disadvantages
Build number. The application build number, typically an integer number that is assigned by your build tool (for example, CruiseControl), whenever your application compiles and all your unit tests run successfully after a change (even if that change is a database refactoring).	Simple strategy. Refactorings can be treated as a First In, First Out (FIFO) queue to be applied in order by the build number. Database version directly linked to application version.	Assumes that your database refactoring tool is integrated with your build tool, or that each refactoring is one or more scripts kept under configuration management control. Many builds do not involve database changes. Therefore, the version identifiers are not contiguous for the database. (For example, they may go 1, 7, 11, 12, ... rather than 1, 2, 3, 4, ...) Difficult to manage when you have multiple applications being developed against the same database, because each team will have the same build numbers.
Date/timestamp. The current date/time is assigned to the refactoring.	Simple strategy. Refactorings managed as a FIFO queue.	With a script-based approach to implementing refactorings, using a date/timestamp for a filename can be awkward. You need a strategy to associate the refactorings with the appropriate application build.
Unique identifier. A unique identifier, such as a GUID or an incremental value, is assigned to the refactoring.	Existing strategies for generating unique values. (For example, a globally unique identifier (GUID) generator can be used.)	GUIDs are awkward filenames. With GUIDs, you still need to identify the order in which to apply the refactorings. You need a strategy to associate the refactorings with the appropriate application build.

same database, a date/timestamp approach works best because you can readily tell in which order the refactorings were applied from the date/timestamp. With a build number approach, you cannot—for example, determine which refactoring comes first, refactoring 1-7 or 7-7?

It is not, however, as simple as applying refactorings in order. Scott worked in an organization in which four separate teams could evolve the same database schema. There were two database administrators (DBAs)—we will call them Fred and Barney—to support the teams that worked closely together. Although we tried to coordinate their efforts, and most of the time succeeded, mistakes would happen. One time Fred applied the refactoring *Apply Standard Codes* (page 157) to a column, and a few days later Barney applied the same refactoring on a different team, but used a different set of "standard" values. As it turned out, Barney's "standard" values was the right set, but we did not find that out until the two teams promoted their changes into the preproduction testing environment and effectively clobbered one another. The point to be made is that in a multiple-team environment, you need a coordination strategy. (Several are discussed later in this chapter.)

5.3 Implement a Large Change by Many Small Ones

Large changes to your database, such as implementing a common surrogate key strategy across all tables or applying a consistent naming strategy throughout your database, should be implemented as a collection of small refactorings. This strategy follows the old adage, "How do you eat an elephant? One bite at a time."

Consider splitting an existing table in two. Although we have a single refactoring called *Split Table* (page 145), the reality is that in practice you need to apply many refactorings to get this done. For example, you need to apply the *Introduce New Table* (page 304) transformation to add the new table, the *Move Column* (page 103) refactoring several times (one for each column) to move, and potentially the *Introduce Index* (page 248) refactoring to implement the primary key of the new table. To implement each of the *Move Column* refactorings, you must apply the *Introduce New Column* (page 301) transformation and the *Move Data* (page 192) transformation. When doing this, you may discover that you need to apply one or more data quality refactorings (Chapter 7, "Data Quality Refactorings") to improve the source data in the individual columns.

5.4 Have a Database Configuration Table

Chapter 3, "The Process of Database Refactoring," discussed the need to identify the current schema version of the database to enable you to update the schema appropriately. This schema version should reflect your database refactoring strategy; for example, if you identify refactorings using a date/timestamp strategy, you should identify the current schema version with a date/timestamp, too. The easiest way to do that is to have a table that maintains this information. In the following code, we create a single-row, single-column table called *DatabaseConfiguration* that reflects a build number strategy:

```
CREATE TABLE DatabaseConfiguration
 (SchemaVersion NUMBER NOT NULL);

INSERT INTO DatabaseConfiguration
 ( SchemaVersion ) VALUES (0);
```

This table is updated with the identifier value of a database refactoring whenever the refactoring is applied to the database. For example, when you apply refactoring number 17 to the schema, *DatabaseConfiguration.SchemaVersion*, would be updated to 17, as shown in the following code:


```
UPDATE DatabaseConfiguration
 SET SchemaVersion = 17;
```

5.5 Prefer Triggers over Views or Batch Synchronization

In Chapter 2, "Database Refactoring," you learned that when several applications access the same database schema, you often require a transition period during which both the original and new schemas exist in production. You need a way to ensure that regardless of which version of the schema an application accesses, it accesses consistent data. Table 5.2 compares and contrasts the three strategies that you may use to keep the data synchronized. Our experience is that triggers are the best approach for the vast majority of situations. We have used views a couple of times and have taken a batch approach rarely. All of the examples throughout this book assume a trigger-based synchronization approach.

Table 5.2 *Schema Synchronization Strategies*

Strategy	Advantages	Disadvantages
Trigger. One or more triggers are implemented that make the appropriate update to the other version of the schema.	Real-time update.	Potential performance bottleneck. Potential for trigger cycles. Potential for deadlocks. Often introduces duplicate data. (Data is stored in both the original and new schema.)
Views. View(s) representing the original table(s) are introduced; see *Encapsulate Table With View* (page 243), which updates both the original and new schemas appropriately.	Real-time update. No need to move physical data between tables/columns.	Updateable views are not supported by some databases, or the database does not support joins within an updateable view. Additional complexity of introducing and eventually removing the view(s).
Batch updates. A batch job that processes and updates the data accordingly is run on a regular basis (for example, daily).	Performance impact from data synchronization is absorbed during nonpeak loads.	Huge potential for referential integrity problems. You need to keep track of previous versions of data to determine which changes were made to the record. When multiple changes are made during the batch period—for example, someone updates data contained in both the original and new schemas—it can be difficult to determine which change(s) to accept. Often introduces duplicate data. (Data is stored in both the original and new schema.)

Prefer Triggers over Views or Batch Synchronization

5.6 Choose a Sufficient Transition Period

The DBA must assign a realistic transition period to the refactoring that is sufficient for all the other application teams. We have found that the easiest approach is to agree on a common transition period for the various categories of refactoring and then apply that transition period consistently. For example, structural refactorings may have a two-year transition period, whereas architecture refactorings may have a three-year transition period. The primary disadvantage is that this approach requires you to adopt the longest transition periods, even when you are refactoring schema that is accessed by a handful of applications that are deployed frequently. You can mitigate this problem by actively removing schema within your production databases that are no longer required, even though the transition period may not have expired yet, or by negotiating a shorter transition period via a database change control board or through direct negotiation with the other teams.

5.7 Simplify Your Database Change Control Board (CCB) Strategy

Scott worked with one company in which they had a database CCB comprised of the operational DBAs, people who understood the enterprise data assets well. This CCB met once a week, and at their meetings the project DBAs would bring a list of suggested changes that their teams wanted to make to existing production data sources. (The teams were free to change data sources not yet in production.) The CCB would determine whether the change would be allowed and if so what the deprecation period would be. The advantage is that there is the perception of tighter control on the part of the CCB. (Of course, this strategy completely falls apart if a development team chooses to go around them.) It has the disadvantage that it slows down the development efforts of the teams. Even when you can get a decision within a few hours or days, that is still time during which the development team has to tolerate the original schema. Our suggestion is to either give the project DBA the authority to make the changes to the database schema as needed, with the understanding that the CCB may later decide to override the change, or to have the CCB meet daily to discuss changes.

5.8 Simplify Negotiations with Other Teams

An alternative strategy for defining the transition period is to negotiate individual refactorings with the owners of any system that might be affected by the database refactoring. You could do this one time for each refactoring, or in batch during a regular database schema change negotiation meeting. This approach has the advantages that it will help to communicate the potential changes to everyone affected and will likely result in the most accurate transition period (assuming that everyone at the meeting can accurately predict when they can deploy their required changes). The primary disadvantage is that this approach might be slow and arduous. We have never seen this tried in practice. If you do try it, however, we suggest that you keep things as simple as possible.

5.9 Encapsulate Database Access

In Chapter 2, we argued that the more database access is encapsulated, the easier it is to refactor. Minimally, even if your application contains hard-coded SQL, you should at least strive to put that SQL code in one place so that you can easily find and update it when you need to. You could implement the SQL logic in a consistent manner, such as having save(), delete(), retrieve(), and find() operations for each business class. Or you could implement data access objects (DAOs), classes that implement the data access logic separately from business classes. For example, your *Customer* and *Account* business classes would have *CustomerDAO* and *AccountDAO* classes respectively. Better yet, you could forego SQL code completely by generating your database access logic from mapping meta data (Ambler 2003).

5.10 Be Able to Easily Set Up a Database Environment

People join, and eventually leave, your project throughout its life cycle. As you see in Figure 5.1, your team(s) will need to be able to create instances of your database, often with different versions of the schema on a range of machines, as you learned in Chapter 4, "Deploying into Production." The most effective way to do this is with an installation script that applies the initial DDL to create the database schema and any applicable change scripts, and then runs your regression test suite to ensure that the installation was successful.

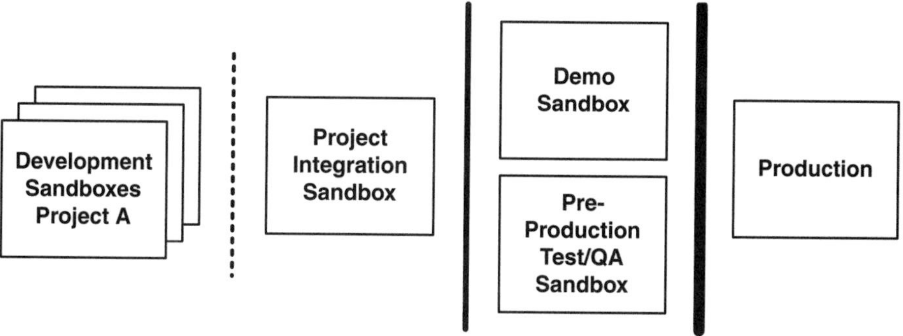

Figure 5.1 Sandboxes.

5.11 Do Not Duplicate SQL

One of the great things about SQL is that it is fairly easy to write. Unfortunately, because it is fairly easy to write, we have found that SQL code is often duplicated throughout an application, and even throughout a database within its views, stored procedures, and triggers. The more SQL code you have, the harder it is to refactor your database schema, because there will potentially be more code coupled to whatever you are refactoring. It is best if you write SQL in a single package or class, have the SQL generated from meta data, or store the SQL code in XML files that is accessed at runtime.

5.12 Put Database Assets Under Change Control

Chapter 1, "Evolutionary Database Development," described how important it is to put all database assets, such as data models and database scripts, under change control management. Both of us have been involved with project teams where the DBAs, and sometimes even the developers, did not do this. As you would expect, these teams often struggled to identify the proper version of the data model, or of a change script, when it came time to deploy their applications into preproduction testing and sometimes even into production. Your database assets, just like the rest of your critical project assets, should be managed effectively. We have found it most helpful when database assets are co-located in the same repository as the application, enabling us to see who made changes and supporting rollback capabilities.

5.13 Beware of Politics

Introducing evolutionary database techniques, and in particular database refactoring, is likely to be a major change within your organization. As Manns and Rising (2005) point out in *Fearless Change*, politics is likely to rear its ugly head as you try to make these improvements to the way that you work. Although many IT professionals prefer to ignore politics, naively believing that they are above it, they do so at their peril. The techniques that we describe in this book work; we know this because we have done it. We also know that many traditional data professionals are threatened by these techniques, and rightfully so, because these techniques force them to make significant changes to the way that they will work in the future. You will likely need to "play the political game" if you want to adopt database refactoring within your organization.

What You Have Learned

5.14 What You Have Learned

Database refactoring is a relatively new development technique, but you can still learn from the experiences of other people. In this chapter, we shared some of our experiences and suggested a few new strategies that you may want to try.

Online Resources

We administer the Agile Databases mailing list at Yahoo Groups. The URL for the group is groups.yahoo.com/group/agileDatabases/. We invite you to get involved with the discussions and share your experiences.

We also maintain both www.databaserefactoring.com and www.agiledata.org where up-to-date lists of database refactorings are maintained. New refactorings will be added as they are discovered.

Chapter 6

Structural Refactorings

Structural refactorings, as the name implies, change the table structure of your database schema. The structural refactorings are as follows:

- Drop Column
- Drop Table
- Drop View
- Introduce Calculated Column
- Introduce Surrogate Key
- Merge Columns
- Merge Tables
- Move Column
- Rename Column
- Rename Table
- Rename View
- Replace Large Object (LOB) With Table
- Replace Column
- Replace One-to-Many With Associative Table
- Replace Surrogate Key With Natural Key
- Split Column
- Split Table

Common Issues When Implementing Structural Refactorings

When implementing structural refactorings, you need to consider several common issues when updating the database schema, including the following:

1. **Avoid trigger cycles.** You need to implement the trigger so that cycles do not occur—if the value in one of the original columns changes, *Table.NewColumn1..N* should be updated, but that update should not trigger the same update to the original columns and so on. The following code shows an example of keeping the value of two columns synchronized:

```
CREATE OR REPLACE TRIGGER SynchronizeFirstName
 BEFORE INSERT OR UPDATE
 ON Customer
 REFERENCING OLD AS OLD NEW AS NEW
 FOR EACH ROW
 DECLARE
 BEGIN
 IF INSERTING THEN
        IF :NEW.FirstName IS NULL THEN
         :NEW.FirstName := :NEW.FName;
        END IF;
        IF :NEW.Fname IS NULL THEN
         :NEW.FName := :NEW.FirstName;
        END IF;
       END IF;
       IF UPDATING THEN
         IF NOT(:NEW.FirstName=:OLD.FirstName) THEN
          :NEW.FName:=:NEW.FirstName;
         END IF;
         IF NOT(:NEW.FName=:OLD.FName) THEN
          :NEW.FirstName:=:NEW.FName;
         END IF;
        END IF;
       END;
    /
```

2. **Fix broken views.** Views are coupled to other portions of your database; so when you apply a structural refactoring, you may inadvertently break a view. View definitions are typically coupled to other views and table definitions. For example, the *VCustomerBalance* view is defined by joining the *Customer* and *Account* table together to obtain by *CustomerNumber* the total balance across all accounts for each individual customer. If you rename *Customer.CustomerNumber*, this view will effectively be broken.

3. **Fix broken triggers.** Triggers are coupled to table definitions; therefore, structural changes such as a renamed or moved column could potentially break a trigger. For example, an insert trigger may validate the data stored in a specific column; and if that column has been changed, the trigger will potentially be broken. The following code finds broken triggers in Oracle, something that you should add to your test suite. You still need other tests to find business logic defects:

```
SELECT Object_Name, Status
        FROM User_Objects
WHERE Object_Type='TRIGGER'
AND Status='INVALID';
```

4. **Fix broken stored procedures.** Stored procedures invoke other stored procedures and access tables, views, and columns. Therefore, any structural refactoring has the potential to break an existing stored procedure. The following code finds broken stored procedures in Oracle, something that you should add to your test suite. You still need other tests to find business logic defects:

```
SELECT Object_Name, Status
        FROM User_Objects
        WHERE Object_Type='PROCEDURE'
AND Status='INVALID';
```

5. **Fix broken tables.** Tables are indirectly coupled to the columns of other tables via naming conventions. For example, if you rename the *Customer .CustomerNumber* column, you should similarly rename *Account.CustomerNumber* and *Policy.CustomerNumber*. The following code finds all the tables with column names containing the text CUSTOMERNUMBER in Oracle:

```
SELECT Table_Name,Column_Name
        FROM User_Tab_Columns
WHERE Column_Name LIKE '%CUSTOMERNUMBER%';
```

6. **Define the transition period.** Structural refactorings require a transition period when you implement them in a multi-application environment. You must assign the same drop dates to the original schema that is being refactored as well as any columns and the trigger. This drop date must take into account the time required to update the external programs accessing that portion of the database.

Drop Column

Remove a column from an existing table.

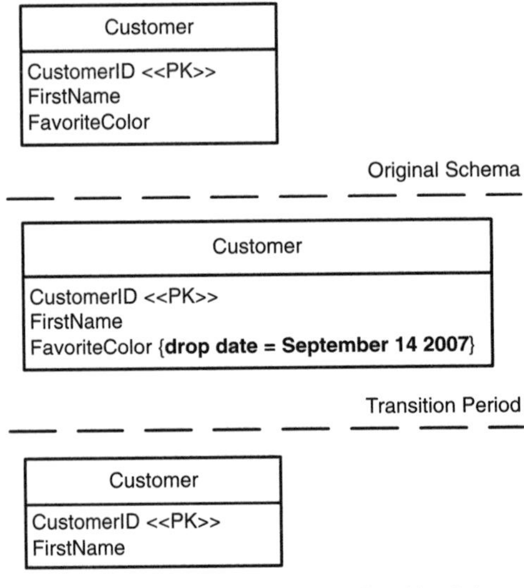

Figure 6.1 Drop the Customer.FavoriteColor column.

Motivation

The primary reason to apply *Drop Column* is to refactor a database table design or as the result of the refactoring of external applications, such that the column is no longer used. *Drop Column* is often applied as a step of the *Move Column* (page 103) database refactoring because the column is removed from the source table. Or, sometimes you discover that some of the columns are not really used. Usually, it is better to remove these columns before someone starts using them by mistake.

Potential Tradeoffs

The column being dropped may contain valuable data; in that case, the data may need to be preserved. You can use *Move Data* (page 192) to move the data to some other table so that it is preserved. On tables containing many rows, the dropping of a column may run for a long time, making your table unavailable for update during the execution of *Drop Column*.

Schema Update Mechanics

To update the schema to remove a column, you must do the following:

1. **Choose a remove strategy.** Some database products may not allow for a column to be removed, forcing you to create a temporary table, move all the data into a temporary table, drop the original table, re-create the original table without the column, move the data from the temporary table, and then drop the temporary table. If your database provides a way to remove columns, you just have to remove the column using the **DROP COLUMN** option of the **ALTER TABLE** command.

2. **Drop the column.** Sometimes, when the amount of data is large, we have to make sure that the *Drop Column* runs in a reasonable amount of time. To minimize the disruption, schedule the physical removal of the column to a time when the table is least used. Another strategy is to mark the database column as unused; this can be achieved by using the **SET UNUSED** option of the **ALTER TABLE** command. The **SET UNUSED** command runs much faster, thus minimizing disruption. You can then remove the unused columns during scheduled downtimes. When this option is used, the database does not physically remove the column but hides the column from everyone.

3. **Rework foreign keys.** If *FavoriteColor* is part of a primary key, you must also remove the corresponding columns from the other tables that use it as (part of) the foreign key to *Customer*. You will have to re-create the foreign key constraints on these other tables. In this situation, you may want to consider applying refactorings such as *Introduce Surrogate Key* (page 85) or *Replace Surrogate Key with Natural Key* (page 135) before applying *Drop Column* to simplify this refactoring.

   An alternative strategy to physically removing the column is masking its existence by introducing a table view that does not reference *FavoriteColor* via the refactoring *Encapsulate Table With View* (page 243).

   During the transition period, you just associate a comment with *Customer.FavoriteColor* to indicate that it will soon be dropped. After the transition period, you remove the column from the *Customer* table via the **ALTER TABLE** command, as you see here:

```
COMMENT ON Customer.FavoriteColor 'Drop date = September 14 2007';

–On September 14 2004
ALTER TABLE Customer DROP COLUMN FavoriteColor;
```

If you are using the **SET UNUSED** option, you can use the following command to make the *Customer.FavoriteColor* unused so that it is not really physically removed from the *Customer* table, but is made unavailable and invisible to all the clients:

```
ALTER TABLE Customer SET UNUSED FavoriteColor;
```

Data-Migration Mechanics

To support the removal of a column from a table, you may discover that you need to preserve existing data or you may need to plan for the performance of the *Drop Column* (because removing a column from a table will disallow data modifications on the table). The primary issue here is to preserve the data before you drop the column. When you are going to remove an existing column from a table that has been in production, you will likely be required by the business to preserve the existing data "just in case" they need it again at some point in the future. The simplest approach is to create a temporary table with the primary key of the source table and the column that is being removed and then move the appropriate data into this new temporary table. You can choose other methods of preserving the data such as archiving data to external files.

The following code depicts the steps to remove the *Customer.FavoriteColor* column. To preserve the data, you create a temporary table called *CustomerFavoriteColor*, which includes the primary key from the *Customer* table and the *FavoriteColor* column.

```
CREATE TABLE CustomerFavoriteColor
  AS SELECT CustomerID, FavoriteColor FROM Customer;
```

Access Program Update Mechanics

You must identify and then update any external programs that reference *Customer.FavoriteColor*. Issues to consider include the following:

1. **Refactor code to use alternate data sources.** Some external programs may include code that still uses the data currently contained within *Customer.FavoriteColor*. When this is the case, alternate data sources must be found, and the code reworked to use them; otherwise, the refactoring must be abandoned.

2. **Slim down** SELECT **statements.** Some external programs may include queries that read in the data but then ignore the retrieved value.

3. **Refactor database inserts and updates.** Some external programs may include code that puts a "fake value" into this column for inserts of new data, code that must be removed. Or the programs may include code to not write over *FavoriteColor* during an insert or update into the database. In other cases, you may have **SELECT * FROM Customer** where the application expects a certain number of columns and gets the columns from the result set using positional reference. This application code is likely to break now because the result set of the **SELECT** statement now returns one less column. Generally, it is not a good idea to use **SELECT *** from any table in your application. Granted, the real problem here is the fact that the application is using positional references, something you should consider refactoring, too.

The following code shows how you have to remove the reference to *FavoriteColor*:

```
//Before code
public Customer findByCustomerID(Long customerID) {
  stmt = DB.prepare("SELECT CustomerId, FirstName, "+
    "FavoriteColor FROM Customer WHERE CustomerId = ?");
  stmt.setLong(1, customerID.longValue());
  stmt.execute();
  ResultSet rs = stmt.executeQuery();
  if (rs.next()) {
    customer.setCustomerId(rs.getLong("CustomerId"));
    customer.setFirstName(rs.getString("FirstName"));
    customer.setFavoriteColor(rs.getString
    ("FavoriteColor"));
  }
  return customer;
}

public void insert(long customerId,String firstName, String favoriteColor) {
  stmt = DB.prepare("INSERT into customer" +
    "(Customerid, FirstName, FavoriteColor)" +
    "values (?, ?, ?)");
  stmt.setLong(1, customerId);
  stmt.setString(2, firstName);
  stmt.setString(3, favoriteColor);
  stmt.execute();
}

public void update(long customerId, String firstName, String color) {
  stmt = DB.prepare("UPDATE Customer "+
  "SET FirstName = ?, FavoriteColor=? " +
  "WHERE Customerid = ?");
  stmt.setString(1, firstName);
  stmt.setString(2, color);
```

```
  stmt.setLong(3, customerId);
  stmt.executeUpdate();
}

//After code

public Customer findByCustomerID(Long customerID) {
  stmt = DB.prepare("SELECT CustomerId, FirstName " +
    "FROM Customer WHERE CustomerId = ?");
  stmt.setLong(1, customerID.longValue());
  stmt.execute();
  ResultSet rs = stmt.executeQuery();
  if (rs.next()) {
    customer.setCustomerId(rs.getLong("CustomerId"));
    customer.setFirstName(rs.getString("FirstName"));
  }
  return customer;
}

public void insert(long customerId,String firstName) {
  stmt = DB.prepare("INSERT into customer" +
    "(Customerid, FirstName) " +
    "values (?, ?)");
  stmt.setLong(1, customerId);
  stmt.setString(2, firstName);
  stmt.execute();
}

public void update(long customerId, String firstName, String color) {
  stmt = DB.prepare("UPDATE Customer "+
  "SET FirstName = ? " +
  "WHERE Customerid = ?");
  stmt.setString(1, firstName);
  stmt.setLong(2, customerId);
  stmt.executeUpdate();
}
```

Drop Table

Remove an existing table from the database.

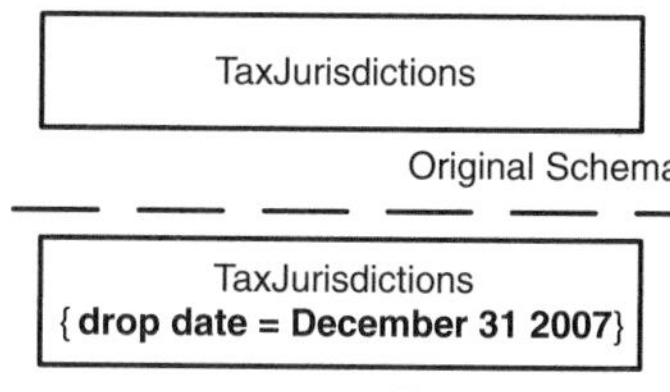

Figure 6.2 Dropping the TaxJurisdictions table.

Motivation

Apply *Drop Table* when a table is no longer required and/or used. This occurs when the table has been replaced by another similar data source, such as another table or a view, or simply when there is no longer need for that specific data source.

Potential Tradeoffs

Dropping a table deletes that specific data from your database, so you may need to preserve some or all of the data. If this is the case, the required data must be stored within another data source, especially when you are normalizing a database design and find that some of the data exists in other tables(s). You can replace the table with a view or a query to the data source. In this scenario, you cannot write back to the same view or data source query.

Schema Update Mechanics

To perform *Drop Table*, you must resolve data-integrity issues. If *TaxJurisdictions* is being referenced by any other tables, you have to either remove the foreign key constraint or point the foreign key constraint to another table. Figure 6.2 depicts an example of how to go about removing the *TaxJurisdictions* table—you just mark the table as deprecated and then remove it after the transition date. The following code depicts the DDL to remove the table:

```
– drop date = June 14 2007
DROP TABLE TaxJurisdictions;
```

You can also choose to just rename the table, as shown below. When doing this, some database products automatically change all references from *TaxJurisdictions* to *TaxJurisdictionsRemoved* automatically. You want to delete those referential integrity constraints by using *Drop Foreign Key* (page 213) because you may not want to have referential integrity constraints to a table that is going to be dropped:

```
- rename date = June 14 2007
ALTER TABLE TaxJurisdictions RENAME TO
TaxJurisdictionsRemoved;
```

Data-Migration Mechanics

The only data-migration issue with this refactoring is the potential need to archive the existing data so that it can be restored if needed at a later date. You can do this by using the **CREATE TABLE AS SELECT** command. The following code depicts the DDL to optionally preserve data in the *TaxJurisdictions* table:

```
-copy data before drop
CREATE TABLE TaxJurisdictionsRemoved AS
        SELECT * FROM TaxJurisdictions;

- drop date = June 14 2007
DROP TABLE TaxJurisdictions;
```


Access Program Update Mechanics

Any external programs referencing *TaxJurisdictions* must be refactored to access the alternative data source(s) that have replaced *TaxJurisdictions*. If there are no alternatives, and the data is still required, you must not remove the table until the alternative(s) exist.

Drop View

Remove an existing view.

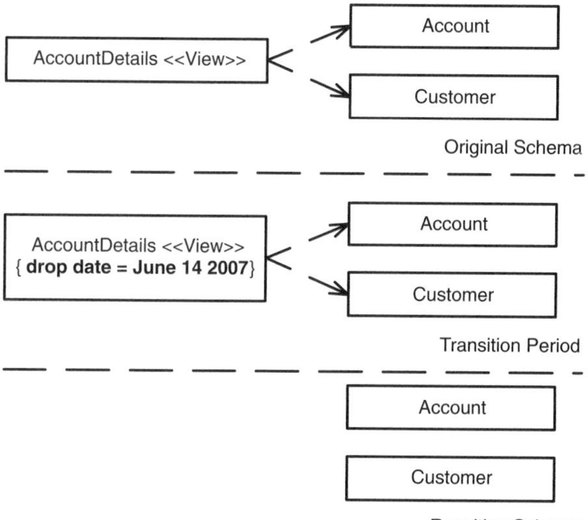

Figure 6.3 Dropping the AccountDetails view.

Motivation

Apply *Drop View* when a view is no longer required and/or used. This occurs when the view has been replaced by another similar data source, such as another view or a table, or simply when there is no longer the need for that specific query.

Potential Tradeoffs

Dropping a view does not delete any data from your database; however, it does mean that the view is no longer available to the external programs that access it. Views are often used to obtain the data for reports. If the data is still required, the view should have already been replaced by another data source, either a view or a table, or a query to the source data itself. This new data access approach should ideally perform as well or better than the view that is being removed. Views are also used to implement security access control (SAC) to data values within a database. When this is the case, a new SAC strategy for the tables accessed by the view should have been previously implemented and deployed. A view-based security strategy is often a lowest-common denominator approach that can be shared across many applications but is not as flexible as a programmatic SAC strategy (Ambler 2003).

Schema Update Mechanics

To remove the view in Figure 6.3, you must apply the **DROP VIEW** command to *AccountDetails* after the transition period. The following code to drop the *AccountDetails* view is very straightforward—you just mark the view as deprecated and then remove it after the transition date.

```
- drop date = June 14 2007
DROP VIEW AccountDetails;
```

Data-Migration Mechanics

There is no data to migrate for this database refactoring.

Access Program Update Mechanics

You must identify and then update any external programs that reference *AccountDetails*. You may need to refactor SQL code that formerly used *AccountDetails* to now explicitly access the data directly from the source tables. Similarly, any meta data used to generate SQL using *AccountDetails* would need to be updated. The following code shows how you have to change your application code to use data from the base tables:

```
// Before code
stmt.prepare(
  "SELECT * " +
  "FROM AccountDetails "+
  "WHERE CustomerId = ?");
  stmt.setLong(1,customer.getCustomerID);
  stmt.execute();
  ResultSet rs = stmt.executeQuery();

// After code
stmt.prepare(
"SELECT * " +
"FROM Customer, Account " +
"WHERE" +
"  Customer.CustomerId = Account.CustomerId " +
"  AND Customer.CustomerId = ?");
stmt.setLong(1,customer.getCustomerID);
stmt.execute();
ResultSet rs = stmt.executeQuery();
```

Introduce Calculated Column

Introduce a new column based on calculations involving data in one or more tables. (Figure 6.4 depicts two tables, but it could be any number.)

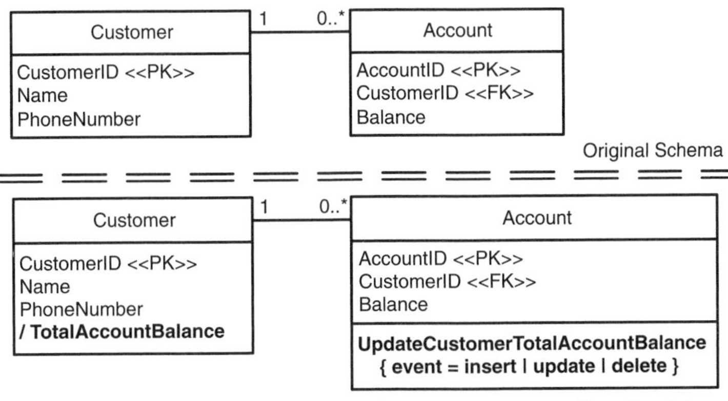

Figure 6.4 Introducing the Customer.TotalAccountBalance calculated column.

Motivation

The primary reason you would apply *Introduce Calculated Column* is to improve application performance by providing prepopulated values for a given property derived from other data. For example, you may want to introduce a calculated column that indicates the credit risk level (for example, exemplary, good risk, bad risk) of a client based on that client's previous payment history with your firm.

Potential Tradeoffs

The calculated column may get out of sync with the actual data values, particularly when external applications are required to update the value. We suggest that you introduce a mechanism, such as a regular batch job or triggers on the source data, which automatically update the calculated column.

Schema Update Mechanics

Applying *Introduce Calculated Column* can be complicated because of data dependencies and the need to keep the calculated column synchronized with the data values it is based on. You will need to do the following:

1. **Determine a synchronization strategy.** Your basic choices are batch jobs, application updates, or database triggers. A batch job can be used when you do not require the value to be updated in real time; otherwise, you need to use one of the other two strategies. When the application(s) are responsible to do the appropriate updates, you run the risk of different applications doing it in different ways. The trigger approach is likely the safer of the two real-time strategies because the logic only needs to be implemented once, in the database. Figure 6.4 assumes the use of triggers.
2. **Determine how to calculate the value.** You have to identify the source data, and how it should be used, to determine the value of *TotalAccount-Balance.*
3. **Determine the table to contain the column.** You have to determine which table should include *TotalAccountBalance.* To do this, ask yourself which business entity does the calculated column best describe. For example, a customer's credit risk indicator is most applicable to the *Customer* entity.
4. **Add the new column.** Add *Customer.TotalAccountBalance* of Figure 6.4 via the *Introduce New Column* transformation (page 301).
5. **Implement the update strategy.** You need to implement and test the strategy chosen in Step 1.

The following code shows you how to add the *Customer.TotalAccountBalance* column and the *UpdateCustomerTotalAccountBalance* trigger, which is run any time the *Account* table is modified:

```
-Create the new column TotalAccountBalance
ALTER TABLE Customer ADD TotalAccountBalance NUMBER;

-Create trigger to keep data in sync.

CREATE OR REPLACE TRIGGER
UpdateCustomerTotalAccountBalance
BEFORE UPDATE OR INSERT OR DELETE
ON Account
REFERENCING OLD AS OLD NEW AS NEW
FOR EACH ROW
DECLARE
```

```
NewBalanceToUpdate NUMBER:=0;
CustomerIdToUpdate NUMBER;
BEGIN
CustomerIdToUpdate := :NEW.CustomerID;
IF UPDATING THEN
  NewBalanceToUpdate := :NEW.Balance-:OLD.Balance;
END IF;
IF INSERTING THEN
  NewBalanceToUpdate := :NEW.Balance;
END IF;
IF DELETING THEN
  NewBalanceToUpdate := -1*:OLD.Balance;
  CustomerIdToUpdate := :OLD.CustomerID;
END IF;
UPDATE Customer SET TotalAccountBalance =
  TotalAccountBalance + NewBalanceToUpdate
  WHERE Customerid = CustomerIdToUpdate;
END;
/
```

Data-Migration Mechanics

There is no data to be migrated per se, although the value of *Customer.TotalAccountBalance* must be populated based on the calculation. This is typically done once using the **UPDATE SQL** command or can be done in batch via one or more scripts. The following code shows you how to set the initial value in *Customer.TotalAccountBalance*:


```
UPDATE Customer SET
  TotalAccountBalance =
    (SELECT SUM(balance) FROM Account
      WHERE Account.CustomerId = Customer.CustomerId)
```

Access Program Update Mechanics

When you introduce the calculated column, you need to identify all the places in external applications where this calculation is used and then rework that code to work with *TotalAccountBalance*. You need to replace existing calculation logic with access to the value of *TotalAccountBalance*. You may discover that the calculation is performed differently in various applications, either because of a bug or because of a different situation, and therefore you will need to negotiate the correct algorithm with your stakeholder(s). The following code shows how an application is used to calculate the total balance by looping through all the accounts of a customer. In the "after version," it simply reads the value into memory when the customer object is retrieved from the database:

```
// Before code
stmt.prepare(
  "SELECT SUM(Account.Balance) Balance FROM Customer, Account " +
    "WHERE Customer.CustomerID = Account.CustomerID "+
    "AND Customer.CustomerID=?");
stmt.setLong(1,customer.getCustomerID);
stmt.execute();
ResultSet rs = stmt.executeQuery();
return rs.getBigDecimal("Balance"));

//After code
return customer.getBalance();
```

Introduce Surrogate Key

Replace an existing natural key with a surrogate key. This refactoring is the opposite of *Replace Surrogate Key With Natural Key* (page 135).

Motivation

There are several reasons why you want to introduce a surrogate key to a table:

- **Reduce coupling.** The primary reason is to reduce coupling between your table schema and the business domain. If part of a natural key is likely to change—for example, if a part number stored within an inventory table is likely to increase in size or change its type (from numeric to alphanumeric)—then having it as a primary key is a dangerous proposition.
- **Increase consistency.** You may want to apply the *Consolidate Key Strategy* (page 168) refactoring, potentially improving performance and reducing code complexity.
- **Improve database performance.** Your database performance may have degraded because of a large composite natural key. (Some databases struggle when a key is made up of several columns.) When you replace the large composite primary key with a single-column surrogate primary key, the database will be able to update the index.

Potential Tradeoffs

Many data professionals prefer natural keys. The debate over surrogate and natural keys is a "religious issue" within the data community, but the reality is that both types of keys have their place. Even though a table has a surrogate primary key, you may still require natural alternate keys to support searching. Because a surrogate key has no business meaning, and because it is typically implemented as a collection of meaningless characters or numbers, your end users cannot use it for searches. As a result, they still need to identify data via natural identifiers. For example, the *InventoryItem* table has a surrogate primary key called *InventoryItemPOID* (POID is short for persistent object identifier) and a natural alternate key called *InventoryID*. Individual items are identified uniquely within the system by the surrogate key but identified by users via the natural key. The value in applying a surrogate key is that it simplifies your key strategy within your database and reduces the coupling between your database schema and your business domain.

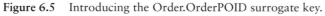

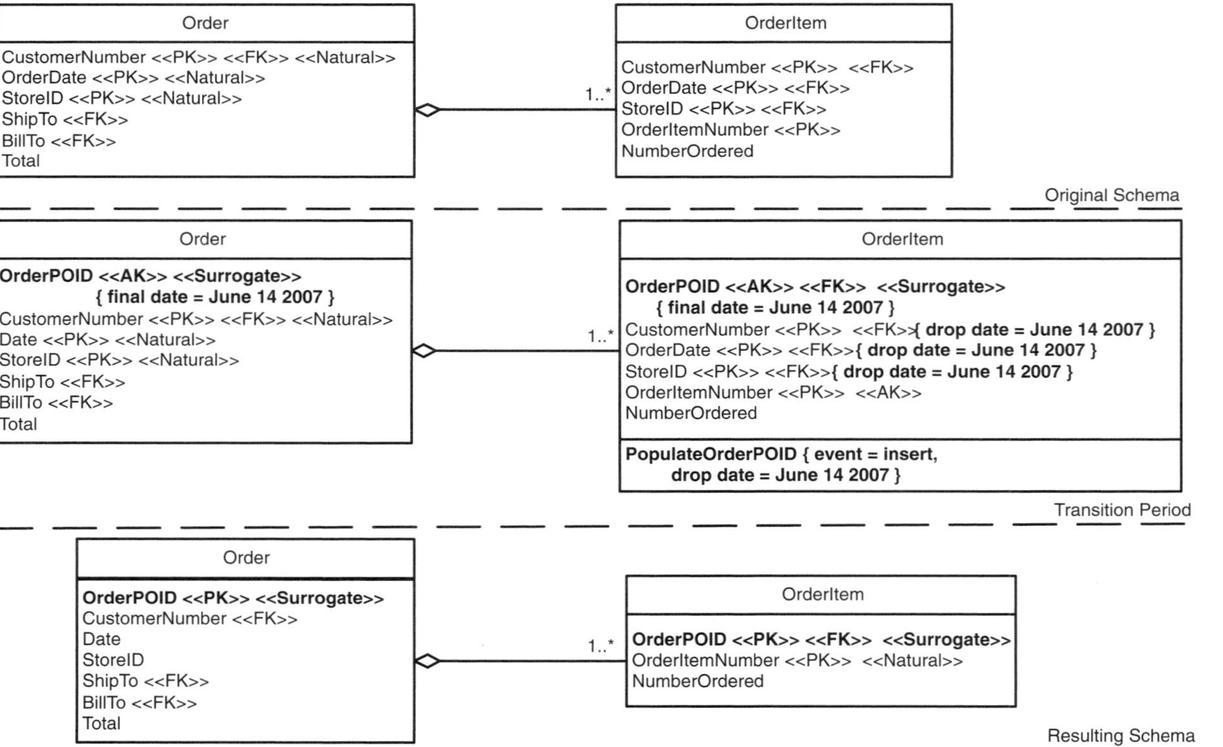

Figure 6.5 Introducing the Order.OrderPOID surrogate key.

Another challenge is that you may implement a surrogate key when it really is not needed. Many people can become overzealous when it comes to implementing keys, and often try to apply the same strategy throughout their schema. For example, in the United States, individual states are identified by a unique two-letter state code (for example, CA for California). This state code is guaranteed to be unique with the United States and Canada; the code for the province of Ontario is ON, and there will never be an American state with that code. The states and provinces are fairly stable entities, there is a large number of codes still available (only 65 of 676 possible combinations have been used to date), and, because of the upheaval it would cause within their own systems, the respective governments are unlikely to change the strategy. Therefore, does it really make sense to introduce a surrogate key to a lookup table listing all the states and provinces? Likely not.

Also, when *OriginalKey* is being used as a foreign key in other tables, you want to apply *Consolidate Key Strategy* (page 168) and make similar updates to those tables. Note that this may be more work than it is worth; you might want to reconsider applying this refactoring.

Schema Update Mechanics

Applying *Introduce Surrogate Key* can be complicated because of the coupling that the original key—in our example, the combination of *CustomerNumber*, *OrderDate*, and *StoreID*—is potentially involved with. Because it is a primary key of a table, it is likely that it also forms (part of) the foreign key back to *Order* from other tables. You will need to do the following:

1. **Introduce the new key column.** Add the column to the target table via the SQL command **ADD COLUMN**. In Figure 6.5, this is *OrderPOID*. This column will need to be populated with unique values.

2. **Add a new index.** A new index based on *OrderPOID* needs to be introduced for *Order*.

3. **Deprecate the original column.** The original key columns must be marked for demotion to alternate key status, or nonkey status as the case may be, at the end of the transition period. In our example, the column will not be deleted at this time from *Order*; they will just no longer be considered the primary key. They will be deleted from *OrderItem*.

4. **Update and possibly add referential integrity (RI) triggers.** Any triggers that exist to maintain referential integrity between tables need to be updated

to work with the corresponding new key values in the other tables. Triggers need to be introduced to populate the value of the foreign key columns during the transition period because the applications may not have been updated to do so.

Figure 6.5 depicts how to introduce *OrderPOID*, a surrogate key, to the *Order* table. You also need to recursively apply *Introduce Surrogate Key* to the *OrderItem* table of Figure 6.5 to make use of the new key column. This is optional. Of course, *OrderItem* could still use the existing composite key made up of the *CustomerNumber*, *OrderDate*, and *StoreID* columns, but for consistency, we have decided to refactor that table, too.

The following SQL code introduces and initially populates the *OrderPOID* column in both the *Order* and *OrderItem* tables. It obtains unique values for *OrderPOID* by invoking the *GenerateUniqueID* stored procedure as needed, which implements the HIGH-LOW algorithm (Ambler 2003). It also introduces the appropriate index required to support *OrderPOID* as a key of *Order*:

```
-Add new surrogate key to Order table
ALTER TABLE Order ADD OrderPOID NUMBER;

-Add new surrogate foreign key to OrderItem table
ALTER TABLE OrderItem ADD OrderPOID NUMBER;

-Assign values to surrogate key column in Order
UPDATE Order SET OrderPOID =
getOrderPOIDFromOrder(CustomerNumber,OrderDate,StoreID);

-Propagate ForeignKey in OrderItem
UPDATE OrderItem SET OrderPOID =
  (SELECT OrderPOID FROM Order
    WHERE CustomerNumber = Order.CustomerNumber
      AND OrderDate = Order.OrderDate
      AND StoreID=Order.StoreID);

CREATE INDEX OrderOrderPOIDIndex ON Order (OrderPOID);
```

Introduce Surrogate Key

To support this new key, we need to add the *PopulateOrderPOID* trigger, which is invoked whenever an insert occurs in *OrderItem*. This trigger obtains the value of *Order.OrderPOID*, as you can see in the following SQL code:

```
CREATE OR REPLACE TRIGGER PopulateOrderPOID
BEFORE INSERT
ON OrderItem
REFERENCING OLD AS OLD NEW AS NEW
FOR EACH ROW
DECLARE
BEGIN
```

```
IF :NEW.OrderPOID IS NULL THEN
  :NEW.OrderPOID :=
getOrderPOIDFromOrder(CustomerNumber,OrderDate,StoreID);
END IF;
IF :NEW.OrderPOID IS NOT NULL THEN
  IF :NEW.CustomerNumber IS NULL
    OR :NEW.OrderDate IS NULL
    OR :NEW.StoreID IS NULL
  THEN
    :NEW.CustomerNumber
      := getCustomerNumberFromOrder(OrderPOID);
      :NEW.OrderDate
:= getOrderDateFromOrder(OrderPOID);
  :NEW.StoreID
:= getStoreIDFromOrder(OrderPOID);
  END IF;
END IF;
END;
/

-June 14 2007
ALTER TABLE OrderItem DROP CONSTRAINT
OrderItemToOrderForeignKey;

ALTER TABLE Order DROP CONSTRAINT
OrderPrimaryKey;


ALTER TABLE Order MODIFY OrderPOID NOT NULL;

ALTER TABLE Order ADD CONSTRAINT OrderPrimaryKey
  PRIMARY KEY (OrderPOID);

ALTER TABLE OrderItem DROP CONSTRAINT
OrderItemPrimaryKey;

ALTER TABLE OrderItem MODIFY OrderPOID NOT NULL;
ALTER TABLE OrderItem ADD CONSTRAINT OrderItemPrimaryKey
  PRIMARY KEY (OrderPOID, OrderItemNumber);


ALTER TABLE OrderItem ADD (CONSTRAINT
OrderItemToOrderForeignKey
  FOREIGN KEY (OrderPOID) REFERENCES Order;


CREATE UNIQUE INDEX OrderNaturalKey ON Order
(CustomerNumber,OrderDate,StoreID);

DROP TRIGGER PopulateOrderPOID;
```

Data-Migration Mechanics

We must generate data in *Order.OrderPOID* and assign these values to the foreign key columns in other tables.

Access Program Update Mechanics

Any external programs referencing the original key columns must be updated to work with *Order.OrderPOID*. You may need to rework the code to do the following:

1. **Assign new types of key values.** If external application code assigns new surrogate key values, instead of the database itself, all external applications need to be reworked to assign values to *Order.OrderPOID*. Minimally, every single program must implement the same algorithm to do so, but a better strategy is to implement a common service that every application invokes.
2. **Join based on the new key.** Many external access programs will define joins involving *Order*, implemented either via hard-coded SQL or via meta data. These joins should be refactored to work with *Order.OrderPOID*.
3. **Retrieve based on the new key.** Some external programs will traverse the database one or more rows at a time, retrieving data based on the key values. These retrievals need to be updated to work with *Order.OrderPOID*.

The following hibernate mapping shows you how the surrogate key is introduced:

```
//Before mapping
<hibernate-mapping>
  <class name="Order" table="ORDER">
    <many-to-one name="customer"
    class="Customer" column="CUSTOMERNUMBER" />
    <property name="orderDate"/>
    <property name="storeID"/>
    <property name="shipTo"/>
    <property name="billTo"/>
    <property name="total"/>
  </class>
</hibernate-mapping>
```

```
//After mapping
<hibernate-mapping>
  <class name="Order" table="ORDER">
    <id name="id" column="ORDERPOID">
      <generator class="OrderPOIDGenerator"/>
    </id>
    <many-to-one name="customer"
     class="Customer" column="CUSTOMERNUMBER" />
    <property name="orderDate"/>
    <property name="storeID"/>
    <property name="shipTo"/>
    <property name="billTo"/>
    <property name="total"/>
  </class>
</hibernate-mapping>
```

Merge Columns

Merge two or more columns within a single table.

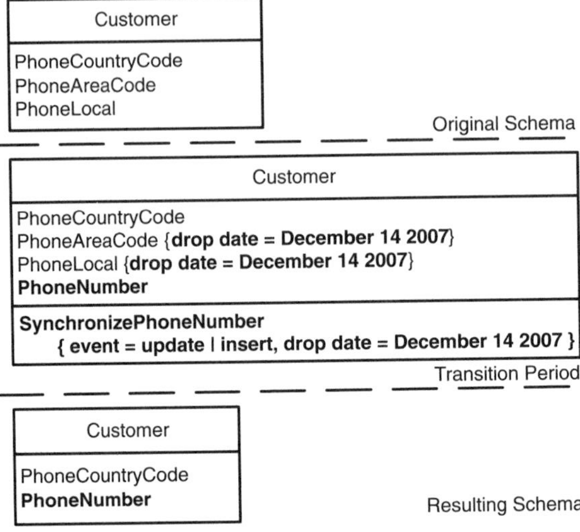

Figure 6.6 Merging columns in the Customer table.

Motivation

There are several reasons why you may want to apply *Merge Columns*:

- **An identical column.** Two or more developers may have added the columns unbeknownst to each other, a common occurrence when the developers are on different teams or when meta data describing the table schema is not available. For example, the *FeeStructure* table has 37 columns, 2 of which are called *CA_INIT* and *CheckingAccountOpeningFee,* and both of which store the initial fee levied by the bank when opening a checking account. The second column was added because nobody was sure what the *CA_INIT* column was really being used for.
- **The columns are the result of overdesign.** The original columns where introduced to ensure that the information was stored in its constituent forms, but actual usage shows that you do not need the fine details that you originally thought. For example, *Customer* table of Figure 6.6 includes

the columns *PhoneCountryCode*, *PhoneAreaCode*, and *PhoneLocal* to represent a single phone number.

- **The actual usage of the columns has become the same.** Several columns were originally added to a table, but over time the way that one or more of them are used has changed to the point where they are all being used for the same purpose. For example, the *Customer* table includes *PreferredCheckStyle* and *SelectedCheckStyle* columns (not shown in Figure 6.6). The first column was used to record which style of checks to send to the customer from next season's selection, and the second column was used to record the style which the customer previously had sent out to them. This was useful 20 years ago when it took several months to order in new checks, but now that they can be printed over night, we have started automatically storing the same value in both columns.

Potential Tradeoffs

This database refactoring can result in a loss of data precision when you merge finely detailed columns. When you merge columns that (you believe) are used for the same purpose, you run the risk that you should in fact be using them for separate things. (If so, you will discover that you need to reintroduce one or more of the original columns.) The usage of the data should determine whether the columns should be merged, something that you will need to explore with your stakeholders.

Schema Update Mechanics

To perform *Merge Columns*, you must do two things. First, you need to introduce the new column. Add the column to the table via the SQL command **ADD COLUMN**. In Figure 6.6, this is *Customer.PhoneNumber*. This step is optional because you may find it possible to use one of the existing columns into which to merge the data. You also need to introduce a synchronization trigger to ensure that the columns remain synchronized with one another. The trigger must be invoked by any change to the columns.

Figure 6.6 shows an example where the *Customer* table initially stores the phone number of a person in three separate columns: *PhoneCountryCode*, *PhoneAreaCode*, and *PhoneLocal*. Over time, we have discovered that few applications are interested in the country code because they are used only within North America. We have also discovered that every application uses both the area code and the local phone number together. Therefore, we have decided to leave the *PhoneCountryCode* alone but to merge the *PhoneAreaCode* and *PhoneLocal* columns into *PhoneNumber,* reflecting the actual usage of the data by the application (because the application does not use *PhoneAreaCode* or *PhoneLocal* individually). We introduced the *SynchronizePhoneNumber* trigger to keep the values in the four columns synchronized.

The following SQL code depicts the DDL to introduce the *PhoneNumber* column and to eventually drop the two original columns:

```
ALTER TABLE Customer ADD PhoneNumber NUMBER(12);
        COMMENT ON Customer.PhoneNumber 'Added as the
        result of merging Customer.PhoneAreaCode and
        Customer.PhoneLocal finaldate = December 14 2007';

-On December 14 2007
ALTER TABLE Customer DROP COLUMN PhoneAreaCode;
ALTER TABLE Customer DROP COLUMN PhoneLocal;
```

Data-Migration Mechanics

You must convert all the data from the original column(s) into the merge column, in this case from *Customer.PhoneAreaCode* and *Customer.PhoneLocal* into *Customer.PhoneNumber*. The following SQL code depicts the DML to initially combine the data from *PhoneAreaCode* and *PhoneLocal* into *PhoneNumber*.

```
/*One-time migration of data from Customer.PhoneAreaCode and Customer.PhoneLocal to
Customer.PhoneNumber. When both the columns are active, there is a need to have a trigger that
keeps both the columns in sync */
UPDATE Customer SET PhoneNumber = PhoneAreaCode*10000000 + PhoneLocal);
```

Access Program Update Mechanics

You need to analyze the access programs thoroughly, and then update them appropriately, during the transition period. In addition to the obvious, you need to work with *Customer.PhoneNumber* rather than the former unmerged columns. Potentially, you must remove merging code. There may be code that combines the existing columns into a data attribute similar to the merged column. This code should be refactored and potentially removed entirely.

Second, you may also need to update data-validation code to work with merged data. Some data-validation code may exist solely because the columns have not yet been merged. For example, if a value is stored in two separate columns, you may have validation code in place that verifies that the values are the same. After the columns are merged, there may no longer be a need for this code.

The before and after code snippet shows how the *getCustomerPhoneNumber()* method changes when we merge the *Customer.PhoneAreaCode* and *Customer.PhoneLocal* columns:

```
//Before code
public String getCustomerPhoneNumber(Customer customer){
  String phoneNumber = customer.getCountryCode();
  phoneNumber.concat(phoneNumberDelimiter());
  phoneNumber.concat(customer.getPhoneAreaCode());
  phoneNumber.concat(customer.getPhoneLocal());
  return phoneNumber;
}

//After code
public String getCustomerPhoneNumber(Customer customer){
  String phoneNumber = customer.getCountryCode();
  phoneNumber.concat(phoneNumberDelimiter());
  phoneNumber.concat(customer.getPhoneNumber());
  return phoneNumber;
}
```

Merge Tables

Merge two or more tables into a single table.

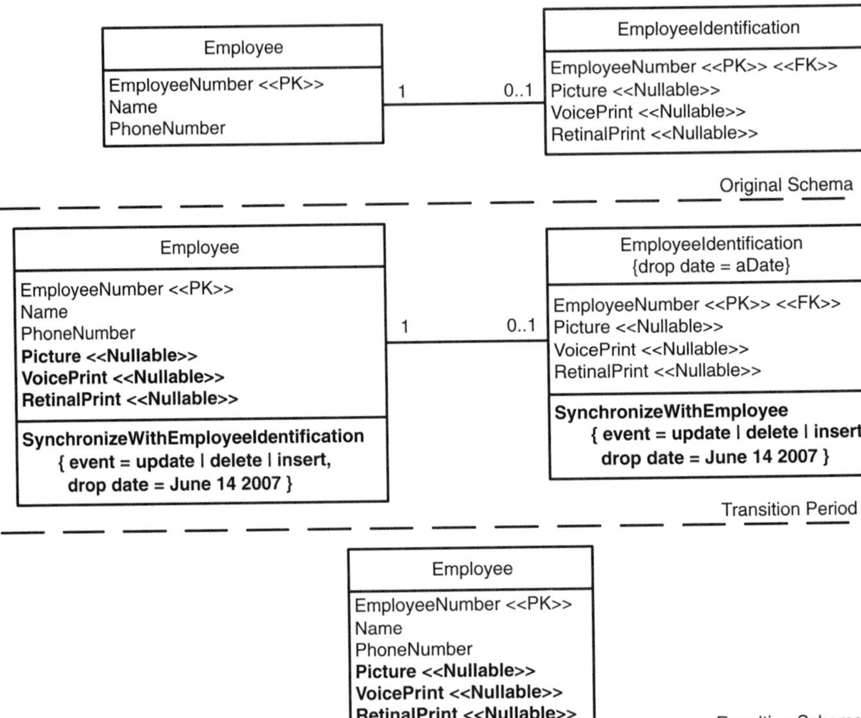

Figure 6.7 Moving all the columns from EmployeeIdentification to Employee.

Motivation

There are several reasons why you may want to apply *Merge Tables*:

- **The tables are the result of over design.** The original tables were introduced to ensure that the information was stored in its constituent forms, but actual usage shows that you do not need the fine details that you originally thought. For example, the *Employee* table includes columns for employee identification, as well as other data, whereas the *EmployeeIdentification* table specifically captures just identification information.

- **The actual usage of the tables has become the same.** Over time, the way that one or more tables are used has changed to the point where several tables are being used for the same purpose. You could also have tables that are related to one another in one-to-one fashion; you may want to merge the tables to avoid making the join to the other table. A good example of this is the *Employee* table mentioned previously. It originally was used to record employee information, but the *EmployeeIdentification* was introduced to store just identification information. Some people did not realize that this table existed, and evolved the *Employee* table to capture similar data.
- **A table is mistakenly repeated.** Two or more developers may have added the tables unbeknownst to each other, a common occurrence when the developers are on different teams or when the meta data describing the table schema is not available. For example, the *FeeStructure* and *FeeSchedule* tables both store the initial fee levied by the bank when opening a checking account. The second table was added because nobody was sure what the *FeeStructure* table was really being used for.

Potential Tradeoffs

Merging two or more tables can result in a loss of data precision when you merge finely detailed tables. When you merge tables that (you believe) are used for the same purpose, you run the risk that you should in fact be using them for separate things. For example, the *EmployeeIdentification* table may have been introduced to separate security-critical information into a single table that had limited access rights. If so, you will discover that you need to reintroduce one or more of the original tables. The usage of the data should determine whether the tables should be merged.

Schema Update Mechanics

As depicted in Figure 6.7, to update the database schema when you perform *Merge Tables,* you must do two things. First, introduce the merged table by adding the columns from *EmployeeIdentification* to *Employee* table via the SQL command **ADD COLUMN**. Note that *Employee* may already include some or all of the required columns, in which case inconsistencies or cluttered domain code may exist; this refactoring should allow for simplification of the application code.

Second, introduce synchronization trigger(s) to ensure that the tables remain synchronized with one another. The trigger(s) must be invoked by any change to the columns. You need to implement the trigger so that cycles do not occur—if the value in one of the original columns changes, *Employee* should be updated, but that update should not trigger the same update to the original tables and so on.

Figure 6.7 depicts an example where the *Employee* table initially stores the employee data. Over time, we have also added *EmployeeIdentification* table that stores employee identification information. Therefore, we have decided to merge the *Employee* and *EmployeeIdentification* tables so that we have all the information regarding the employee at one place. We introduced the *SynchronizeIdentification* trigger to keep the values in the tables synchronized. The following SQL code depicts the DDL to introduce the *Picture*, *VoicePrint*, *RetinalPrint* columns, and then to eventually drop the *EmployeeIdentification* table.

```
ALTER TABLE Employee ADD Picture BINARY;

COMMENT ON Employee.Picture 'Added as the result of merging Employee and EmployeeIdentification
finaldate = December 14 2007';


ALTER TABLE Employee ADD VoicePrint BINARY;

COMMENT ON Employee.VoicePrint 'Added as the result of merging Employee and
EmployeeIdentification finaldate = December 14 2007';


ALTER TABLE Employee ADD RetinalPrint BINARY;

COMMENT ON Employee.RetinalPrint 'Added as the result of merging Employee and
EmployeeIdentification finaldate = December 14 2007';
```

Data-Migration Mechanics

You must copy all the data from the original tables(s) into the merge table—in this case, from *EmployeeIdentification* to *Employee*. This can be done via several means—for example, with an SQL script or with an extract-transform-load (ETL) tool. (With this refactoring, there should not be a transform step.)

The following SQL code depicts the DDL to initially combine the data from the *Employee* and *EmployeeIdentification* tables:

```
/*One-time migration of data from Employee to
EmployeeIdentification. When both the tables are active, there is a need to have a trigger that
keeps both the tables in sync
```

```
*/

UPDATE Employee e SET e.Picture =
  (SELECT ei.Picture FROM
  EmployeeIdentificaion ei
    WHERE
      ei.EmployeeNumber = e.EmployeeNumber);

UPDATE Employee e SET e.VoicePrint =
  (SELECT ei.VoicePrint FROM
  EmployeeIdentificaion ei
    WHERE
      ei.EmployeeNumber = e.EmployeeNumber);


UPDATE Employee e SET e.RetinalPrint =
  (SELECT ei.RetinalPrint FROM
  EmployeeIdentificaion ei
    WHERE
ei.EmployeeNumber = e.EmployeeNumber);


-On December 14 2007
DROP TRIGGER SynchronizeWithEmployee;
DROP TRIGGER SynchronizeWith-
EmployeeIdentification;
DROP TABLE EmployeeIdentification;
```


The following code shows how *SynchronizeWithEmployeeIdentification* and *SynchronizeWithEmployee* triggers are used to keep the values in the tables synchronized:

```
CREATE TRIGGER SynchronizeWithEmployeeIdentification
        BEFORE INSERT OR UPDATE OR DELETE
        ON Employee
        REFERENCING OLD AS OLD NEW AS NEW
        FOR EACH ROW
        DECLARE
        BEGIN
        IF updating THEN
          updateOrCreateEmployeeIdentification;
        END IF;
        IF inserting THEN
          createNewEmployeeIdentification;
        END IF;
        IF deleting THEN
          deleteEmployeeIdentification;
        END IF;
        END;
        /
```

```
CREATE TRIGGER SynchronizeWithEmployee
BEFORE INSERT OR UPDATE OR DELETE
ON EmployeeIdentification
REFERENCING OLD AS OLD NEW AS NEW
FOR EACH ROW
DECLARE
BEGIN
IF updating THEN
  updateOrCreateEmployee;
END IF;
IF inserting THEN
  createNewEmployee;
END IF;
IF deleting THEN
  deleteEmployee;
END IF;
END;
/
```


Access Program Update Mechanics

In addition to the obvious need to work with *Employee* rather than the former unmerged table(s), potential updates you need to make are as follows:

1. **Simplify data access code.** Some access code may exist that accesses two or more of the tables involved with the merge. For example, the *Employee* class may update its information into the two tables in which it is currently stored, tables that have now been merged into one.

2. **Incomplete or contradictory updates.** Now that the data is stored in one place, you may discover that individual access programs worked only with subsets of the data. For example, the *Customer* class currently updates its home phone number information in two tables, yet it is really stored in three tables (which have now been merged into one). Other programs may realize that the data quality in the third table was not very good and may include code that counteracts the problems. For example, a reporting class may convert NULL phone numbers to "Unknown," but now that there are no NULL phone numbers, this code can be removed.

3. **Some merged data is not required by some access programs.** Some of the access programs that currently work with *Employee* need only the data that it contains. However, now that columns from *EmployeeIdentification* have been added, the potential exists that the existing access programs will not update these new columns appropriately. Existing access programs may need to be extended to accept and work with the new columns.

For example, the source table for the *Employee* class may have had a *BirthDate* column merged into it. Minimally, the *Employee* class should not overwrite this column with invalid data, and it should insert an appropriate value when a new customer object is created. You may need to apply *Introduce Default Value* (page 186) to the columns that are merged into *Employee*.

The following example shows example code changes when you apply *Merge Tables* to *Employee* and *EmployeeIdentification*:

```
//Before code
public Employee getEmployeeInformation (Long
employeeNumber) throws SQLException {
  Employee employee = new Employee();

  stmt.prepare(
  "SELECT EmployeeNumber, Name, PhoneNumber " +
  "FROM Employee" +
  "WHERE EmployeeNumber = ?");
  stmt.setLong(1,employeeNumber);
  stmt.execute();
  ResultSet rs = stmt.executeQuery();
  employee.setEmployeeNumber(rs.getLong
  ("EmployeeNumber"));
  employee.setName(rs.getLong("Name"));
  employee.setPhoneNumber(rs.getLong("PhoneNumber"));

  stmt.prepare(
  "SELECT Picture, VoicePrint, RetinalPrint " +
  "FROM EmployeeIdentification" +
  "WHERE EmployeeNumber = ?");
  stmt.setLong(1,employeeNumber);
  stmt.execute();
  rs = stmt.executeQuery();
  employee.setPicture(rs.getBlob("Picture"));
  employee.setVoicePrint(rs.getBlob("VoicePrint"));
  employee.setRetinalPrint(rs.getBlob("RetinalPrint"));

  return employee;
}

//After code
public Employee getEmployeeInformation (Long
employeeNumber) throws SQLException {
  Employee employee = new Employee();

  stmt.prepare(
  "SELECT EmployeeNumber, Name, PhoneNumber " +
  "Picture, VoicePrint, RetinalPrint "+
  "FROM Employee" +
  "WHERE EmployeeNumber = ?");
  stmt.setLong(1,employeeNumber);
```

```
  stmt.execute();
  ResultSet rs = stmt.executeQuery();
  employee.setEmployeeNumber(rs.getLong
  ("EmployeeNumber"));
  employee.setName(rs.getLong("Name"));
  employee.setPhoneNumber(rs.getLong("PhoneNumber"));
  employee.setPicture(rs.getBlob("Picture"));
  employee.setVoicePrint(rs.getBlob("VoicePrint"));
  employee.setRetinalPrint(rs.getBlob("RetinalPrint"));
  return employee;
}
```

Move Column

Migrate a table column, with all of its data, to another existing table.

Motivation

There are several reasons to apply *Move Column*. The first two reasons may appear contradictory, but remember that database refactoring is situational. Common motivations to apply *Move Column* include the following:

- **Normalization.** It is common that an existing column breaks one of the rules of normalization. By moving the column to another table, you can increase the normalization of the source table and thereby reduce data redundancy within your database.
- **Denormalization to reduce common joins.** It is quite common to discover that a table is included in a join simply to gain access to a single column. You can improve performance by removing the need to perform this join by moving the column into the other table.
- **Reorganization of a split table.** You previously performed *Split Table* (page 145), or the table was effectively split in the original design, and you then realize that one more column needs to be moved. Perhaps the column exists in the commonly accessed table but is rarely needed, or perhaps it exists in a rarely accessed table but is needed quite often. In the first case, network performance would be improved by not selecting and then transmitting the column to the applications when it is not required; in the second case, database performance would be improved because few joins would be required.

Potential Tradeoffs

Moving a column to increase normalization reduces data redundancy but may decrease performance if additional joins are required by your applications to obtain the data. Conversely, if you improve performance by denormalizing your schema through moving the column, you will increase data redundancy.

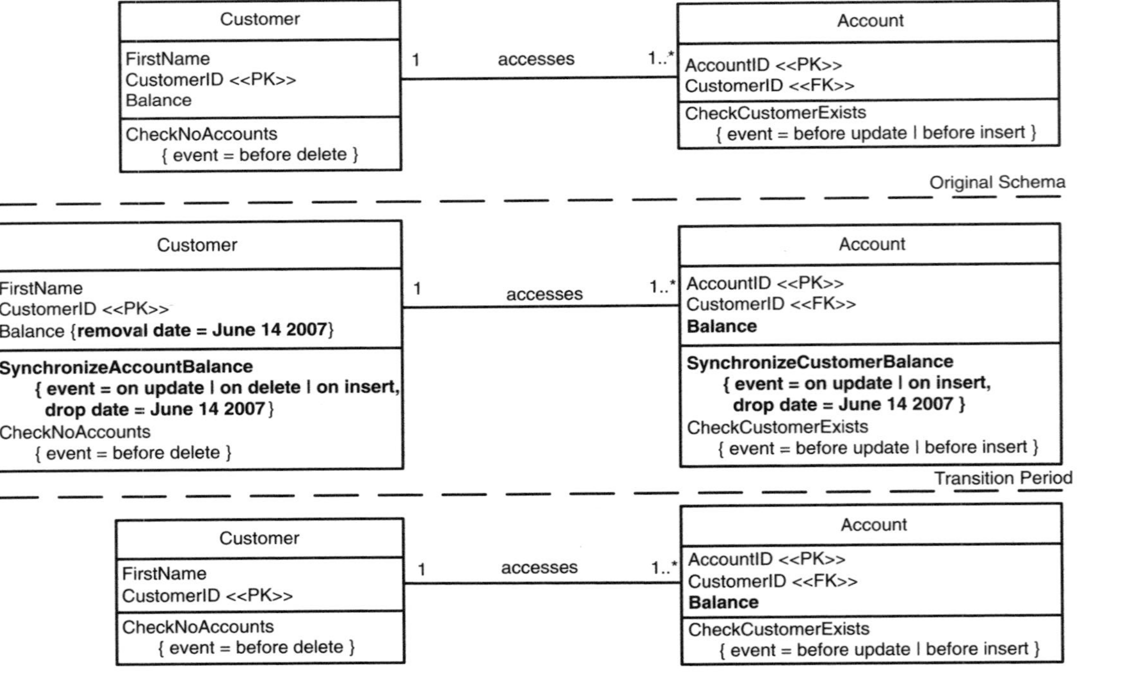

Figure 6.8 Moving the Balance column from Customer to Account.

Schema Update Mechanics

To update the database schema when you perform *Move Column*, you must do the following:

1. **Identify deletion rule(s).** What should happen when a row from one table is deleted? Should the corresponding row in the other table be deleted, should the column value in the corresponding be nulled/zeroed out, should the corresponding value be set to some sort of default value, or should the corresponding value be left alone? This rule will be implemented in trigger code (as discussed later in this section). Note that zero or more deletion triggers may already exist to support referential integrity rules between the tables.

2. **Identify insertion rule(s).** What should happen when a row is inserted into one of the tables? Should a corresponding row in the other table be inserted or should nothing occur? This rule will be implemented in trigger code, and zero or more insertion triggers may already exist.

3. **Introduce the new column.** Add the column to the target table via the SQL command **ADD COLUMN**. In Figure 6.8, this is *Account.Balance*.

4. **Introduce triggers.** You require triggers on both the original and new column to copy data from one column to the other during the transition period. These trigger(s) must be invoked by any change to a row.

Figure 6.8 depicts an example where *Customer.Balance* is moved into the *Account* table. This is a normalization issue—instead of storing a balance each time a customer's account is updated, we can instead store it once for each individual account. During the transition period, the *Balance* column appears in both *Customer* and *Account*, as you would expect.

The existing triggers are interesting. The *Account* table already had a trigger for inserts and updates that checked to see that the corresponding row exists in the *Customer* table, a basic referential integrity (RI) check. This trigger is left alone. The *Customer* table had a delete trigger to ensure that it is not deleted if an *Account* row refers to it, another RI check. The advantage of this is that we do not need to implement a deletion rule for the moved column because we cannot "do the wrong thing" and delete a *Customer* row that has one or more *Account* rows referencing it.

In the following code, we introduce the *Account.Balance* column and the *SynchronizeCustomerBalance* and *SynchronizeAccountBalance* triggers to keep the *Balance* columns synchronized. The code also includes the scripts to drop the scaffolding code after the transition period ends:

```
ALTER TABLE Account ADD Balance NUMBER(32,7);
COMMENT ON Account.Balance 'Moved from Customer table, finaldate = June 14 2007';

COMMENT ON Customer.Balance 'Moved to Account table, dropdate = June 14 2007';

CREATE OR REPLACE TRIGGER SynchronizeCustomerBalance
  BEFORE INSERT OR UPDATE
  ON Account
  REFERENCING OLD AS OLD NEW AS NEW
  FOR EACH ROW
  DECLARE
  BEGIN
    IF :NEW.Balance IS NOT NULL THEN
      UpdateCustomerBalance;
    END IF;
  END;

CREATE OR REPLACE TRIGGER SynchronizeAccountBalance
  BEFORE INSERT OR UPDATE OR DELETE
  ON Customer
  REFERENCING OLD AS OLD NEW AS NEW
  FOR EACH ROW
  DECLARE
  BEGIN
    IF DELETING THEN
      DeleteCustomerIfAccountNotFound;
    END IF;
    IF (UPDATING OR INSERTING) THEN
      IF :NEW.Balance IS NOT NULL THEN
        UpdateAccountBalanceForCustomer;
      END IF;
    END IF;
  END;

-On June 14 2007
ALTER TABLE Customer DROP COLUMN Balance;
DROP TRIGGER SynchronizeCustomerBalance;
DROP TRIGGER SynchronizeAccountBalance;
```

Data-Migration Mechanics

Copy all the data from the original column into the new column—in this case, from *Customer.Balance* to *Account.Balance*. This can be done via several means—for example, with a SQL script or with an ETL tool. (With this refactoring, there should not be a transform step.) The following code depicts the DML to move the *Balance* column values from *Customer* to *Account*:

```
/*One-time migration of data from Customer.Balance to Account.Balance. When both the columns are
active, there is a need to have a trigger that keeps both the balance columns in sync
*/

UPDATE Account SET Balance =
  (SELECT Balance FROM Customer
    WHERE CustomerID = Account.CustomerID);
```

Access Program Update Mechanics

You need to analyze the access programs thoroughly and then update them appropriately during the transition period. Potential updates you need to make are as follows:

1. **Rework joins to use the moved column.** Joins, either hard-coded in SQL or defined via meta data, must be refactored to work with the moved column. For example, when you move *Customer.Balance* to *Account.Balance*, you have to change your queries to get the balance information from *Account* and not from *Customer*.

2. **Add the new table to joins.** The *Account* table must now be included in joins if it is not already included. This may degrade performance.

3. **Remove the original table from joins.** There may be some joins that included the *Customer* table for the sole purpose of joining in the data from *Customer.Balance*. Now that this column has been moved, the *Customer* table can be removed from the join, which could potentially improve performance.

The following code shows you how the *Customer.Balance* column is referenced in the original code and the updated code that works with *Account.Balance*:

```
//Before code
     public BigDecimal getCustomerBalance(Long
     customerId) throws SQLException {
       PreparedStatement stmt = null;
       BigDecimal customerBalance = null;
```

```
        stmt = DB.prepare("SELECT Balance FROM
        Customer " +
                "WHERE CustomerId = ?");
        stmt.setLong(1, customerId.longValue());
        ResultSet rs = stmt.executeQuery();
        if (rs.next()) {
          customerBalance = rs.getBigDecimal("Balance");
        }
        return customerBalance;
}

//After code
      public BigDecimal getCustomerBalance(Long
      customerId) throws SQLException {
        PreparedStatement stmt = null;
        BigDecimal customerBalance = null;
        stmt = DB.prepare(
           "SELECT SUM(Account.Balance) Balance " +
           "FROM Customer, Account " +
           "WHERE Customer.CustomerId=
           Account.CustomerId " +
           "AND CustomerId = ?");
        stmt.setLong(1, customerId.longValue());
        ResultSet rs = stmt.executeQuery();
        if (rs.next()) {
          customerBalance = rs.getBigDecimal("Balance");
        }
        return customerBalance;
}
```

Rename Column

Rename an existing table column.

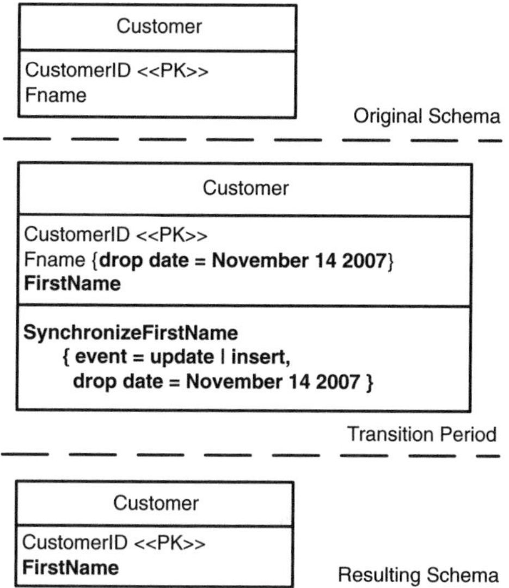

Figure 6.9 Renaming the Customer.FName column.

Motivation

The primary reasons to apply *Rename Column* are to increase the readability of your database schema, to conform to accepted database naming conventions in your enterprise, or to enable database porting. For example, when you are porting from one database product to another, you may discover that the original column name cannot be used because it is a reserved keyword in the new database.

Potential Tradeoffs

The primary trade-off is the cost of refactoring the external applications that access the column versus the improved readability and/or consistency provided by the new name.

Schema Update Mechanics

To rename a column, you must do the following:

1. **Introduce the new column.** In Figure 6.9, we first add *FirstName* to the target table via the SQL command **ADD COLUMN.**
2. **Introduce a synchronization trigger.** As you can see in Figure 6.9, you require a trigger to copy data from one column to the other during the transition period. This trigger must be invoked by any change to the data row.
3. **Rename other columns.** If *FName* is used in other tables as (part of) a foreign key, you may want to apply *Rename Column* recursively to ensure naming consistency. For example, if *Customer.CustomerNumber* is renamed *as Customer.CustomerID*, you may want to go ahead and rename all instances of *CustomerNumber* in other tables. Therefore, *Account.CustomerNumber* will now be renamed to *Account.CustomerID* to keep the column names consistent.

Rename Column

The following code depicts the DDL to rename *Customer.FName* to *Customer.FirstName*, creates the *SynchronizeFirstName* trigger that synchronizes the data during the transition period, and removes the original column and trigger after the transition period ends:

```
ALTER TABLE Customer ADD FirstName VARCHAR(40);

COMMENT ON Customer.FirstName 'Renaming of FName column, finaldate = November 14 2007';

COMMENT ON Customer.FName 'Renamed to FirstName,
dropdate = November 14 2007';

UPDATE Customer SET FirstName = FName;

CREATE OR REPLACE TRIGGER SynchronizeFirstName
BEFORE INSERT OR UPDATE
ON Customer
REFERENCING OLD AS OLD NEW AS NEW
FOR EACH ROW
DECLARE
BEGIN
  IF INSERTING THEN
    IF :NEW.FirstName IS NULL THEN
      :NEW.FirstName := :NEW.FName;
    END IF;
    IF :NEW.Fname IS NULL THEN
      :NEW.FName := :NEW.FirstName;
```

```
    END IF;
  END IF;

  IF UPDATING THEN
    IF NOT(:NEW.FirstName=:OLD.FirstName) THEN
      :NEW.FName:=:NEW.FirstName;
    END IF;
    IF NOT(:NEW.FName=:OLD.FName) THEN
      :NEW.FirstName:=:NEW.FName;
    END IF;
  END IF;
  END;
/

-On Nov 30 2007
DROP TRIGGER SynchronizeFirstName;
ALTER TABLE Customer DROP COLUMN FName;
```

Data-Migration Mechanics

You need to copy all the data from the original column into the new column, in this case from *FName* to *FirstName*. See the refactoring *Move Data* (page 192) for details.

Rename Column

Access Program Update Mechanics

External programs that reference *Customer.FName* must be updated to reference columns by its new name. You should simply have to update any embedded SQL and/or mapping meta data. The following hibernate mapping files show how your mapping files would change when the *fName* column is renamed:

```
//Before mapping
<hibernate-mapping>
<class name="Customer" table="Customer">
  <id name="id" column="CUSTOMERID">
      <generator class="CustomerIdGenerator"/>
  </id>
  <property name="fName"/>
</class>
</hibernate-mapping>
```

```
//Transition mapping
<hibernate-mapping>
<class name="Customer" table="Customer">
  <id name="id" column="CUSTOMERID">
      <generator class="CustomerIdGenerator"/>
  </id>
  <property name="fName"/>
  <property name="firstName"/>
</class>
</hibernate-mapping>

//After mapping
<hibernate-mapping>

<class name="Customer" table="Customer">
  <id name="id" column="CUSTOMERID">
      <generator class="CustomerIdGenerator"/>
  </id>
  <property name="firstName"/>
</class>
</hibernate-mapping>
```

Rename Table

Rename an existing table.

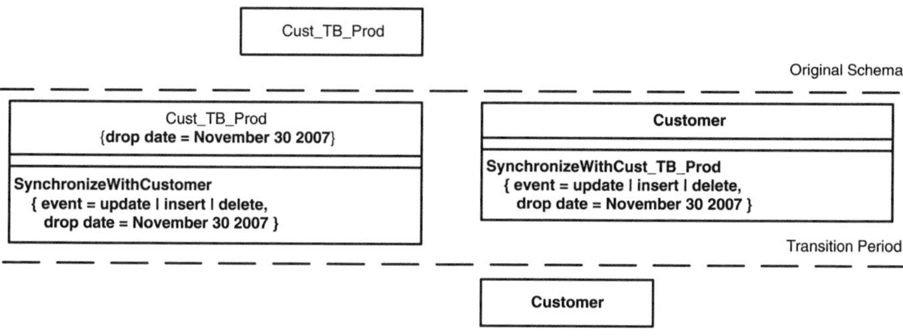

Figure 6.10 Renaming the Cust_TB_Prod table to Customer.

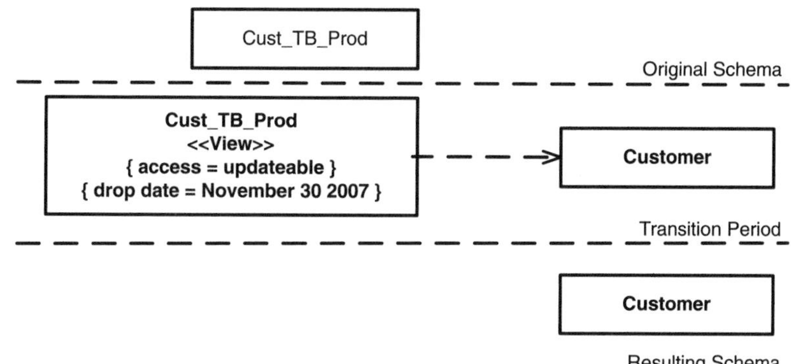

Figure 6.11 Renaming the Cust_TB_Prod table to Customer via a view.

Motivation

The primary reason to apply *Rename Table* is to clarify the table's meaning and intent in the overall database schema or to conform to accepted database naming conventions. Ideally, these reasons are one in the same.

Potential Tradeoffs

The primary tradeoff is the cost to refactoring the external applications that access the table versus the improved readability and/or consistency provided by the new name.

Schema Update Mechanics via a New Table

To perform *Rename Table*, you create a new table using the SQL command **CREATE TABLE**, in this case *Customer*. If any columns of *Cust_TB_Prod* are used in other tables as (part of) a foreign key, you must refactor those constraints and/or indices implementing the foreign key to refer to *Customer*.

We want to rename *Cust_TB_Prod* to *Customer* as depicted in Figure 6.10. The *SynchronizeCust_TB_Prod* and *SynchronizeCustomer* triggers keep the two tables synchronized with each other. Each trigger is invoked by any change to a row in the *Cust_TB_Prod or Customer* table, respectively. The following code depicts the DDL to rename the table and introduce the triggers:


```
CREATE TABLE Customer
  (FirstName VARCHAR(40),
  LastName VARCHAR(40),
);

COMMENT ON Customer 'Renaming of Cust_TB_Prod,
finaldate = September 14 2006';

COMMENT ON Cust_TB_Prod 'Renamed to Customer,
dropdate = September 14 2006';

CREATE OR REPLACE TRIGGER SynchronizeCustomer
BEFORE INSERT OR UPDATE
ON Cust_TB_Prod
REFERENCING OLD AS OLD NEW AS NEW
FOR EACH ROW
DECLARE
BEGIN
IF updating THEN
  findAndUpdateIfNotFoundCreateCustomer;
END IF;
IF inserting THEN
  createNewIntoCustomer;
END IF;
IF deleting THEN
  deleteFromCustomer;
```

```
END IF;
END;
/

CREATE OR REPLACE TRIGGER SynchronizeCust_TB_Prod
BEFORE INSERT OR UPDATE
ON Customer
REFERENCING OLD AS OLD NEW AS NEW
FOR EACH ROW
DECLARE
BEGIN
IF updating THEN
       findAndUpdateIfNotFoundCreateCust_TB_Prod;
END IF;
IF inserting THEN
  createNewIntoCust_TB_Prod;
END IF;
IF deleting THEN
  deleteFromCust_TB_Prod;
END IF;
END;
/
```

Schema Update Mechanics via an Updateable View

The second approach is to rename the table and then introduce an updateable view with the original name of the table. Note that some database products supports the **RENAME** option of the **ALTER TABLE** command. If yours does not, you must re-create the table with the new name, and then load the data into the table. You should schedule the drop of the old table so that it is not accidentally used by someone. As you see in Figure 6.11, the updateable view is needed during the transition period to support external access programs that have yet to be refactored to use the renamed table. This strategy is viable only if your database supports updateable views.

Figure 6.11 shows how to rename the table using a view. You simply use the **RENAME TO** clause of **ALTER TABLE** SQL command to rename the table and create the view, as shown here:

```
ALTER TABLE Cust_tb_Prod RENAME TO Customer;

CREATE VIEW Cust_tb_Prod AS
  SELECT * FROM Customer;
```

As with the new table approach, if any columns of *Cust_TB_Prod* are used in other tables as (part of) a foreign key, you must re-create those constraints and/or indices implementing the foreign key to refer to *Customer*.

Data-Migration Mechanics

With the updateable view approach, you do not need to migrate data. However, with the new table approach, you must first copy the data. Copy all the data from the original table into the new table—in this case, from *Cust_TB_Prod* to *Customer*. Second, you must introduce triggers on both the original and new table to copy data from one table to the other during the transition period. These triggers must be invoked by any change to the tables. You need to implement the triggers so that cycles do not occur—if *Cust_TB_Prod* changes, *Customer* must also be updated, but that update should not trigger the same update to *Cust_TB_Prod* and so on. The following code shows how to copy the data from *Cust_TB_Prod* into *Customer*:

```
INSERT INTO Customer
  SELECT * FROM CUST_TB_PROD;
```

Access Program Update Mechanics

External access programs must be refactored to work with *Customer* rather than *Cust_TB_Prod*. The following hibernate mapping shows the change you have to make when you rename the *Cust_TB_Prod* table:

```
//Before mapping
<hibernate-mapping>
<class name="Customer" table="Cust_TB_Prod">
.....
</class>
</hibernate-mapping>

//After mapping
<hibernate-mapping>
<class name="Customer" table="Customer">
.....
</class>
</hibernate-mapping>
```

Rename View

Rename an existing view.

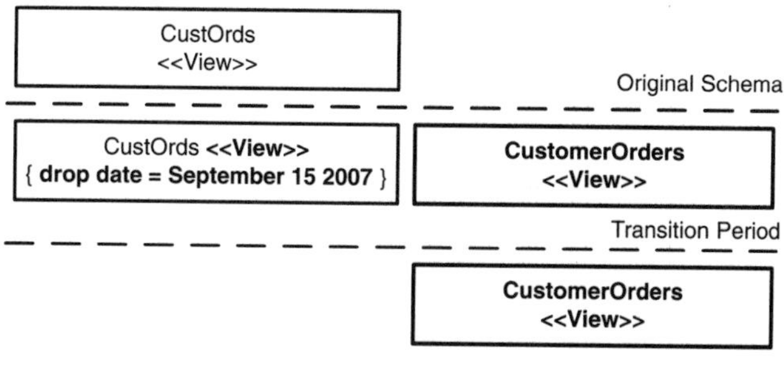

Figure 6.12 Renaming the CustOrds view to CustomerOrders.

Motivation

The primary reason to apply *Rename View* is to increase the readability of your database schema or to conform to accepted database naming conventions. Ideally, these reasons are one in the same.

Potential Tradeoffs

The primary tradeoff is the cost of refactoring the external applications that access the view versus the improved readability and/or consistency provided by the new name.

Schema Update Mechanics

To perform *Rename View*, you must do the following:

1. **Introduce the new view.** Create a new view using the SQL command **CREATE VIEW**. In Figure 6.12, this is *CustomerOrders*, the definition of which has to match with *CustOrds*.

2. **Deprecate the original view.** After you create *CustomerOrders*, you want to indicate that *CustOrds* should no longer be updated with new features or bug fixes.

3. **Redefine the old view.** You should redefine *CustOrds* to be based on *CustomerOrders* to avoid duplicate code streams. The benefit is that any changes to *CustomerOrders*, such as a new data source for a column, will propagate to *CustOrds* without any additional work.

The following code depicts the DDL to create *CustomerOrders*, which is identical to the code that was used to create *CustOrds*:

```
CREATE VIEW CustomerOrders AS
SELECT
  Customer.CustomerCode,
  Order.OrderID,
  Order.OrderDate,
  Order.ProductCode
FROM Customer,Order
WHERE
  Customer.CustomerCode = Order.CustomerCode
  AND Order.ShipDate = TOMORROW
;

COMMENT ON CustomerOrders 'Renamed from CustOrds,
CustOrds dropdate = September 15 2007';
```


The following code drops and then re-creates the *CustOrds* so that it derives its results from the *CustomerOrders*:

```
DROP VIEW CustOrds;

CREATE VIEW CustOrds AS
SELECT CustomerCode, OrderID, OrderDate, ProductCode
FROM CustomerOrders
;
```

Data-Migration Mechanics

There is no data to migrate for this database refactoring.

Access Program Update Mechanics

You must refactor all the external programs currently accessing *CustOrds* to access *CustomerOrders*. In the case of hard-coded SQL, this will simply be the update of the **FROM/INTO** clauses, and in the case of meta data-driven approaches, the update of the name within the representation for this view.

The following code shows how a reference to *CustOrds* should be changed to *CustomerOrders*:

```
// Before code
stmt.prepare(
  "SELECT * " +
  "FROM CustOrds "+
  "WHERE CustomerId = ?");
  stmt.setLong(1,customer.getCustomerID);
  stmt.execute();
  ResultSet rs = stmt.executeQuery();

// After code
stmt.prepare(
  "SELECT * " +
  "FROM CustomerOrders " +
  "WHERE " +
  "  CustomerId = ?");
  stmt.setLong(1,customer.getCustomerID);
  stmt.execute();
  ResultSet rs = stmt.executeQuery();
```

Replace LOB With Table

Replace a large object (LOB) column that contains structured data with a new table or with new columns in the same table. LOBs are typically stored as either a binary large object (BLOB), a variable character (VARCHAR), or in some cases as XML data.

Motivation

The primary reason to replace a LOB with a table is because you need to treat parts of the LOB as distinct data elements. This is quite common with XML data structures that have been stored in a single column, often to avoid "shredding" the structure into individual columns.

Potential Tradeoffs

The advantage of storing a complex data structure in a single column is that you can quickly get that specific data structure easily. This proves particularly valuable when existing code already works with the data structure in question and merely needs to use the database as a handy file-storage mechanism. By replacing the LOB with a table, or perhaps several tables if the structure of the data contained within the LOB is very complex, you can easily work with the individual data elements within your database. You also make the data more accessible to other applications that may not need the exact structure contained within the LOB. Furthermore, if the LOB contains some data that is already present within your database, you can potentially use those existing data sources to represent the appropriate portions of the LOB, reducing data redundancy (and thus integrity errors). The disadvantage of this approach is the increased time and complexity required to shred the data to store it within the database and similarly to retrieve and convert it back into the required structure.

Schema Update Mechanics

As you see in Figure 6.13, applying *Replace LOB With Table* is straightforward. You need to do the following:

1. **Determine a table schema.** You need to analyze *Customer.MailingAddress* to determine the data that it contains, and then develop a table schema to store that data. If the structure contained within *MailingAddress* is

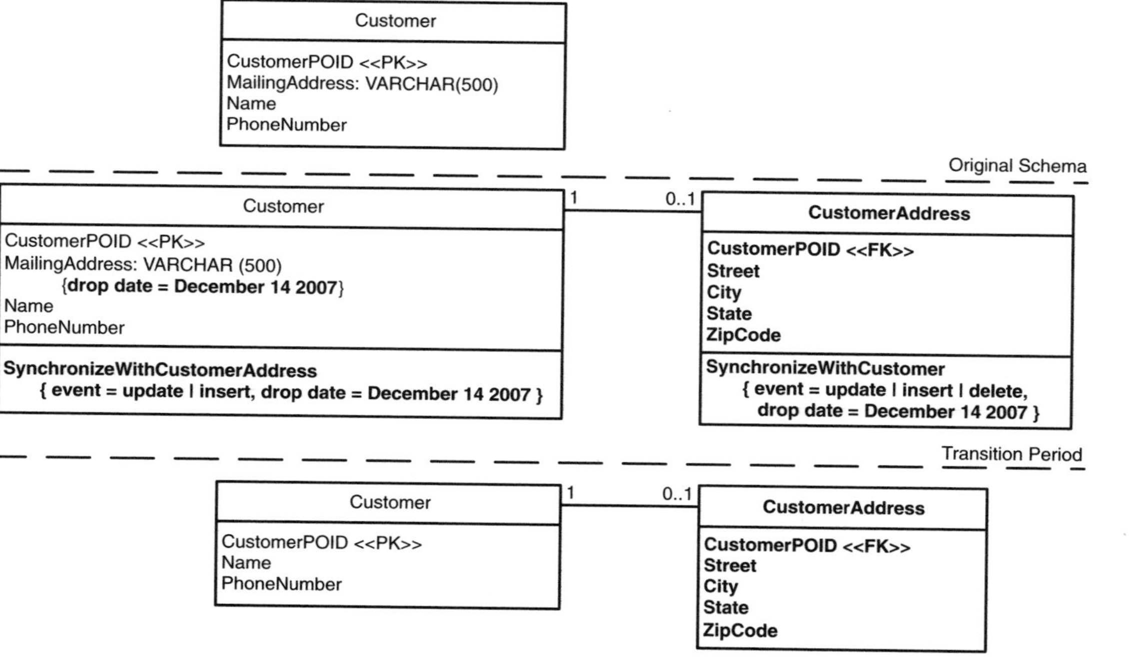

Figure 6.13 Replacing a LOB with a table.

complex, you either need to have smaller LOB columns within the new table or recursively apply *Replace LOB With Table* to deal with these smaller structures.

2. **Add the table.** In Figure 6.13, this is *CustomerAddress*. The columns of this table are the primary key of *Customer*, the *CustomerPOID* column, and the new columns containing the data from *MailingAddress*.
3. **Deprecate the original column.** *MailingAddress* must be marked for deletion at the end of the deprecation period.
4. **Add a new index.** For performance reasons, you may need to introduce an new index for *CustomerAddress* via the **CREATE INDEX** command.
5. **Introduce synchronization triggers.** *Customer* will require a trigger to populate the values in *CustomerAddress* appropriately. This trigger will need to shred the *MailingAddress* structure and store it appropriately. Similarly, a trigger on *CustomerAddress* is needed to update *Customer* during the transition period.

The code to create the *CustomerAddress* table, add an index, define the synchronization triggers, and eventually drop the column and triggers is shown here:


```
CREATE TABLE CustomerAddress (
  CustomerPOID NUMBER NOT NULL,
  Street VARCHAR(40),
  City VARCHAR(40),
  State VARCHAR(40),
  ZipCode VARCHAR(10)
);

CREATE INDEX IndexCustomerAddress ON
  CustomerAddress(CustomerPOID);

-Triggers to keep the tables synchronized
CREATE OR REPLACE TRIGGER SynchronizeWithCustomerAddress
BEFORE INSERT OR UPDATE OR DELETE
ON Customer
REFERENCING OLD AS OLD NEW AS NEW
FOR EACH ROW
DECLARE
BEGIN
  IF updating THEN
    FindOrCreateCustomerAddress;
  END IF;
  IF inserting THEN
    CreateCustomerAddress;
  END IF;
```

```
  IF deleting THEN
    DeleteCustomerAddress;
  END IF;
END;
/

CREATE OR REPLACE TRIGGER SynchronizeWithCustomer
BEFORE INSERT OR UPDATE OR DELETE
ON Customer
REFERENCING OLD AS OLD NEW AS NEW
FOR EACH ROW
DECLARE
BEGIN
  IF updating OR inserting THEN
    FindAndUpdateCustomer;
  END IF;
  IF deleting THEN
    UpdateCustomerNullAddress;
  END IF;
END;
/

-On Dec 14 2007
DROP TRIGGER SynchronizeWithCustomerAddress;
DROP TRIGGER SynchronizeWithCustomer;

ALTER TABLE Customer DROP COLUMN MailingAddress;
```


Data-Migration Mechanics

CustomerAddress must be populated by shredding and then copying the data contained in *Customer.MailingAddress*. The value of *Customer.CustomerPOID* must also be copied to maintain the relationship. If *MailingAddress* has a NULL or empty value, a row in *CustomerAddress* does not need to be created. This can be accomplished via one or more SQL scripts, as you see in the following code:

```
INSERT INTO CustomerAddress
  SELECT
    CustomerPOID,
    ExtractStreet(MailingAddress),
    ExtractCity(MailingAddress),
    ExtractState(MailingAddress),
    ExtractZipCode(MailingAddress)
  FROM Customer
    WHERE MailingAddress IS NOT NULL;
```

Access Program Update Mechanics

You must identify any external programs referencing *Customer.MailingAddress* so that they can be updated to work with *CustomerAddress* as appropriate. You will need to do the following:

1. **Remove translation code.** External programs could have code that shreds the data within *MailingAddress* to work with its subdata elements, or they could contain code that takes the source data elements and builds the format to be stored into *MailingAddress*. This code will no longer be needed with the new data structure.
2. **Add translation code.** Conversely, some external programs may require the exact data structure contained within *MailingAddress*. If several applications require this, you should consider introducing stored procedures or introduce a library within the database to do this translation, enabling reuse.
3. **Write code to access the new table.** After you add *CustomerAddress*, you have to write application code that uses this new table rather than *MailingAddress*.

The following code shows how the code to retrieve data attributes from *Customer.MailingAddress* is replaced with a **SELECT** against the *CustomerAddress* table:

```
// Before code
public Customer findByCustomerID(Long customerPOID) {
  Customer customer = new Customer();
  stmt = DB.prepare("SELECT CustomerPOID, " +
    "MailingAddress, Name, PhoneNumber " +
    "FROM Customer " +
    "WHERE CustomerPOID = ?");
  stmt.setLong(1, customerPOID);
  stmt.execute();
  ResultSet rs = stmt.executeQuery();
  if (rs.next()) {
    customer.setCustomerId(rs.getLong("CustomerPOID"));
    customer.setName(rs.getString("Name"));
    customer.setPhoneNumber(rs.getString
    ("PhoneNumber"));
    String mailingAddress = rs.getString
    ("MailingAddress");
    customer.setStreet(extractStreet(mailingAddress));
    customer.setCity(extractCity(mailingAddress));
    customer.setState(extractState(mailingAddress));
    customer.setZipCode(extractZipCode(mailingAddress));
  }
 return customer;
 }
```

```
// After code
public Customer findByCustomerID(Long customerPOID) {
  Customer customer = new Customer();
  stmt = DB.prepare("SELECT CustomerPOID, "+
    "Name, PhoneNumber, "+
    "Street, City, State, ZipCode " +
  "FROM Customer, CustomerAddress " +
  "WHERE Customer.CustomerPOID = ? " +
  "AND Customer.CustomerPOID =
  CustomerAddress.CustomerPOID");
  stmt.setLong(1, customerPOID);
  stmt.execute();
  ResultSet rs = stmt.executeQuery();
  if (rs.next()) {
    customer.setCustomerId(rs.getLong("CustomerPOID"));
    customer.setName(rs.getString("Name"));
    customer.setPhoneNumber(rs.getString
    ("PhoneNumber"));
    customer.setStreet(rs.getString("Street"));
    customer.setCity(rs.getString("City"));
    customer.setState(rs.getSring("State"));
    customer.setZipCode(rs.getString("ZipCode"));
  }
return customer;
}
```

Replace Column

Replace an existing nonkey column with a new one.

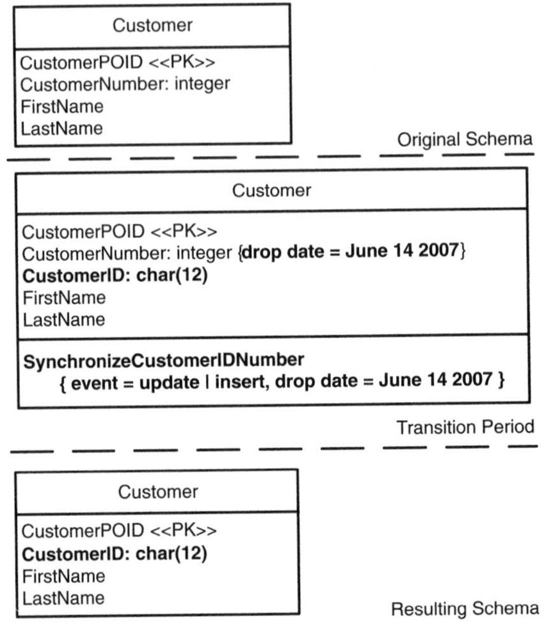

Figure 6.14 Replacing the Customer.CustomerNumber column.

For replacing a column that is part of a key, either the primary key or an alternate key, see the *Introduce Surrogate Key* (page 85) and *Replace Surrogate Key With Natural Key* (page 135) refactorings.

Motivation

There are two reasons why you want to apply *Replace Column*. First, the most common reason is that usage of the column has changed over time, requiring you to change its type. For example, you previously had a numeric customer identifier, but now your business stakeholders have made it alphanumeric. Second, this may be an intermediate step to implement other refactorings. Another common reason to replace an existing column is that it is often an important step in merging two similar data sources, or applying

Consolidate Key Strategy (page 168) because you need to ensure type and format consistency with another column.

Potential Tradeoffs

A significant risk when replacing a column is information loss when transferring the data to the replacement column. This is particularly true when the types of the two columns are significantly different—converting from a **CHAR** to a **VARCHAR** is straightforward as is **NUMERIC** to **CHAR**, but converting **CHAR** to **NUMERIC** can be problematic when the original column contains non-numeric characters.

Schema Update Mechanics

To apply *Replace Column*, you must do the following:

1. **Introduce the new column.** Add the column to the target table via the SQL command **ADD COLUMN**. In Figure 6.14, this is *CustomerID*.
2. **Deprecate the original column.** *CustomerNumber* must be marked for deletion at the end of your chosen transition period.
3. **Introduce a synchronization trigger.** As you can see in Figure 6.14, you require a trigger to copy data from one column to the other during the transition period. This trigger must be invoked by any change to a data row.
4. **Update other tables.** If *CustomerNumber* is used in other tables as part of a foreign key, you will want to replace those columns similarly, as well as update any corresponding index definitions.

The following SQL code depicts the DDL to replace the column, create the synchronization trigger, and eventually drop the column and trigger after the transition period:

```
ALTER TABLE Customer ADD CustomerID CHAR(12);

COMMENT ON Customer.CustomerID 'Replaces CustomerNumber column, finaldate = 2007-06-14';

COMMENT ON Customer.CustomerNumber 'Replaced with CustomerID, dropdate = 2007-06-14';


CREATE OR REPLACE TRIGGER SynchronizeCustomerIDNumber
BEFORE INSERT OR UPDATE
ON Customer
```

```
REFERENCING OLD AS OLD NEW AS NEW
FOR EACH ROW
DECLARE
  BEGIN
  IF :NEW.CustomerID IS NULL THEN
    :NEW.CustomerID:=
      formatCustomerNumber(:New.CustomerNumber);
  END IF;
  IF :NEW.CustomerNumber IS NULL THEN
    :New.CustomerNumber := :New.CustomerID;
  END IF;
END;
/

-On June 14 2007
DROP TRIGGER SynchronizeCustomerIDNumber;
ALTER TABLE Customer DROP COLUMN CustomerNumber;
```

Data-Migration Mechanics

The data must be initially copied from *CustomerNumber* to *CustomerID* and then kept synchronized during the transition period (for example, via stored procedures). As described earlier, this can be problematic with the data formats are significantly different from one another. Before applying *Replace Column*, you may discover that you need to apply one or more data quality refactorings to clean up the source data first. The code to copy the values into the new column is shown here:

```
UPDATE Customer SET CustomerID = CustomerNumber;
```

Access Program Update Mechanics

The primary issue is that external programs need to be refactored to work with the new data type and format of *CustomerID*. This could imply that conversion code be written that converts back and forth between the old data format and the new. A longer-term strategy, although potentially a more expensive one, would be to completely rework all the external program code to use the new data format. The following code snippet shows you how the column name and the data type needs to change in the application code:

```
// Before code
public Customer findByCustomerID(Long customerID) {
  Customer customer = new Customer();
  stmt = DB.prepare("SELECT CustomerPOID, " +
    "CustomerNumber, FirstName, LastName " +
    "FROM Customer " +
```

```
      "WHERE CustomerPOID = ?");
    stmt.setLong(1, customerID);
    stmt.execute();
    ResultSet rs = stmt.executeQuery();
    if (rs.next()) {
      customer.setCustomerPOID(rs.getLong
("CustomerPOID"));
      customer.setCustomerNumber(rs.getInt
("CustomerNumber"));
      customer.setFirstName(rs.getString("FirstName"));
      customer.setLastName(rs.getString("LastName"));
    }
return customer;
}

// After code
public Customer findByCustomerID(Long customerID) {
  Customer customer = new Customer();
  stmt = DB.prepare("SELECT CustomerPOID, " +
    "CustomerID, FirstName, LastName " +
    "FROM Customer " +
    "WHERE CustomerPOID = ?");
  stmt.setLong(1, customerID);
  stmt.execute();
  ResultSet rs = stmt.executeQuery();
  if (rs.next()) {
    customer.setCustomerPOID(rs.getLong
("CustomerPOID"));
    customer.setCustomerID(rs.getString("CustomerID"));
    customer.setFirstName(rs.getString("FirstName"));
    customer.setLastName(rs.getString("LastName"));
  }
return customer;
}
```

Replace One-To-Many With Associative Table

Replace a one-to-many association between two tables with an associative table.

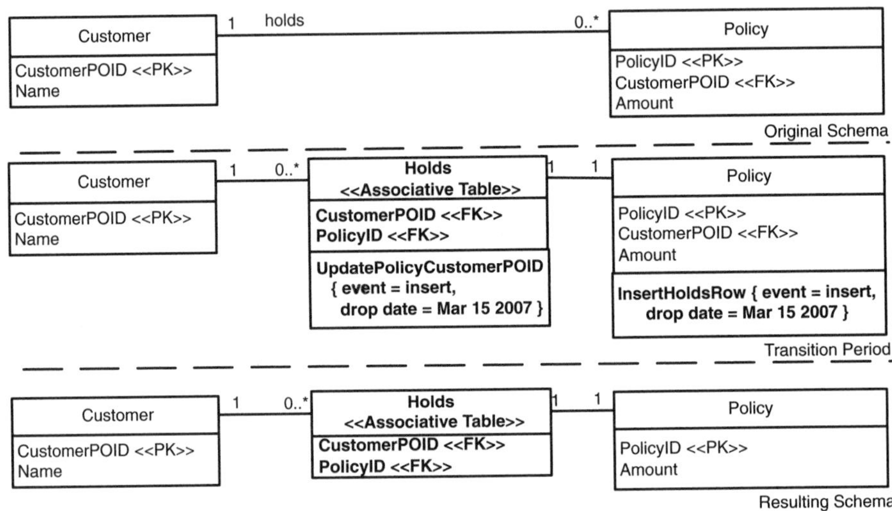

Figure 6.15 Replacing a one-to-many with an associative table.

Motivation

The primary reason to introduce an associative table between two tables is to implement a many-to-many association between them later on. It is quite common for a one-to-many association to evolve into a many-to-many association. For example, any given employee currently has at most one manager. (The president of the company is the only person without a manager.) However, the company wants to move to a matrix organization structure where people can potentially report to several managers. Because a one-to-many association is a subset of a many-to-many association, the new associative table would implement the existing hierarchical organization structure yet be ready for the coming matrix structure. You may also want to add information to the relationship itself that does not belong to either of the existing tables.

Potential Tradeoffs

You are overbuilding your database schema when you use an associative table to implement a one-to-many association. If the association is not likely to evolve into a many-to-many relationship, it is not advisable to take this approach. When you add associative tables, you are increasing the number of joins you have to make to get to the relevant data, thus degrading performance and making it harder to understand the database schema.

Schema Update Mechanics

To apply *Replace One-To-Many With Associative Table*, you must do the following:

1. **Add the associative table.** In Figure 6.15, this is *Holds*. The columns of this table are the combination of the primary keys of *Customer* and *Policy*. Note that some tables may not necessarily have a primary key, although this is rare—when this is the case, you may decide to apply the *Introduce Surrogate Key* refactoring.

2. **Deprecate the original column.** Because we no longer maintain the relationship directly from *Policy* to *Customer*, *Policy.CustomerPOID* must be marked for deletion at the end of the transition period, because it is currently used to maintain the one-to-many relationship with *Customer* but will no longer be needed.

3. **Add a new index.** A new index for *Holds* should be introduced via the *Introduce Index* (page 248) refactoring.

4. **Introduce synchronization triggers.** *Policy* will require a trigger that will populate the key values in the *Holds* table, if the appropriate values do not already exist, during the transition period. Similarly, there will need to be a trigger on *Holds* that verifies that *Policy.CustomerPOID* is populated appropriately.

The code to add the *Holds* table, to add an index on *Holds*, to add the synchronization triggers, and finally to drop the old schema and triggers is shown here:

```
CREATE TABLE Holds (
  CustomerPOID BIGINT,
  PolicyID INT,
);
```

```
CREATE INDEX HoldsIndex ON Holds
    (CustomerPOID, PolicyID);

CREATE OR REPLACE TRIGGER InsertHoldsRow
BEFORE INSERT OR UPDATE OR DELETE
ON Policy
REFERENCING OLD AS OLD NEW AS NEW
FOR EACH ROW
DECLARE
BEGIN
  IF updating THEN
    UpdateInsertHolds;
  END IF;
  IF inserting THEN
    CreateHolds;
  END IF;
  IF deleting THEN
    RemoveHolds;
  END IF;
END;
/

CREATE OR REPLACE TRIGGER UpdatePolicyCustomerPOID
BEFORE INSERT OR UPDATE OR DELETE
ON Holds
REFERENCING OLD AS OLD NEW AS NEW
FOR EACH ROW
BEGIN
IF updating THEN
  UpdateInsertPolicy;
END IF;
IF inserting THEN
  CreatePolicy;
END IF;
IF deleting THEN
  RemovePolicy;
END IF;
END;
/

-On Mar 15 2007
DROP TRIGGER InsertHoldsRow;
DROP TRIGGER UpdatePolicyCustomerPOID;
ALTER TABLE customer
DROP COLUMN balance;
```

Set a Naming Convention

There are two common naming conventions for associative tables—either assign the table the same name as the original association, as we have done, or concatenate the two table names, which would have resulted in *CustomerPolicy* for the name.

Data-Migration Mechanics

The associative table must be populated by copying the values of *Policy.CustomerPOID* and *Policy.PolicyID* into *Holds.CustomerPOID* and *Holds.PolicyID*, respectively. This can be accomplished via a simple SQL script, as follows:

```
INSERT INTO Holds (CustomerPOID,PolicyID)
  SELECT CustomerPOID,PolicyID FROM Policy
```

Access Program Update Mechanics

To update external programs, you must do the following:

1. **Remove updates to the foreign key.** Any code to assign values to *Policy.CustomerPOID* should be refactored to write to *Holds* to maintain the association properly.
2. **Rework joins.** Many external access programs will define joins involving *Customer* and *Policy*, implemented either via hard-coded SQL or via meta data. These joins should be refactored to work with *Holds*.
3. **Rework retrievals.** Some external programs will traverse the database one or more rows at a time, retrieving data based on the key values, traversing from *Policy* to *Customer*. These retrievals will need to be updated similarly.

The following code shows how to change your application code so that retrieval of data is now done via a join using the associative table:

```
//Before code
stmt.prepare(
  "SELECT Customer.CustomerPOID, Customer.Name, " +
  "Policy.PolicyID,Policy.Amount " +
  "FROM Customer, Policy" +
```

```
  "WHERE Customer.CustomerPOID = Policy.CustomerPOID " +
  "AND Customer.CustomerPOID = ? ");
stmt.setLong(1,customerPOID);
ResultSet rs = stmt.executeQuery();

//After code
stmt.prepare(
  "SELECT Customer.CustomerPOID, Customer.Name, " +
  "Policy.PolicyID,Policy.Amount " +
  "FROM Customer, Holds, Policy" +
  "WHERE Customer.CustomerPOID = Holds.CustomerPOID " +
  "AND Holds.PolicyId = Policy.PolicyId " +
  "AND Customer.CustomerPOID = ? ");
stmt.setLong(1,customerPOID);
ResultSet rs = stmt.executeQuery();
```

Replace Surrogate Key With Natural Key

Replace a surrogate key with an existing natural key. This refactoring is the opposite of *Introduce Surrogate Key* (page 85).

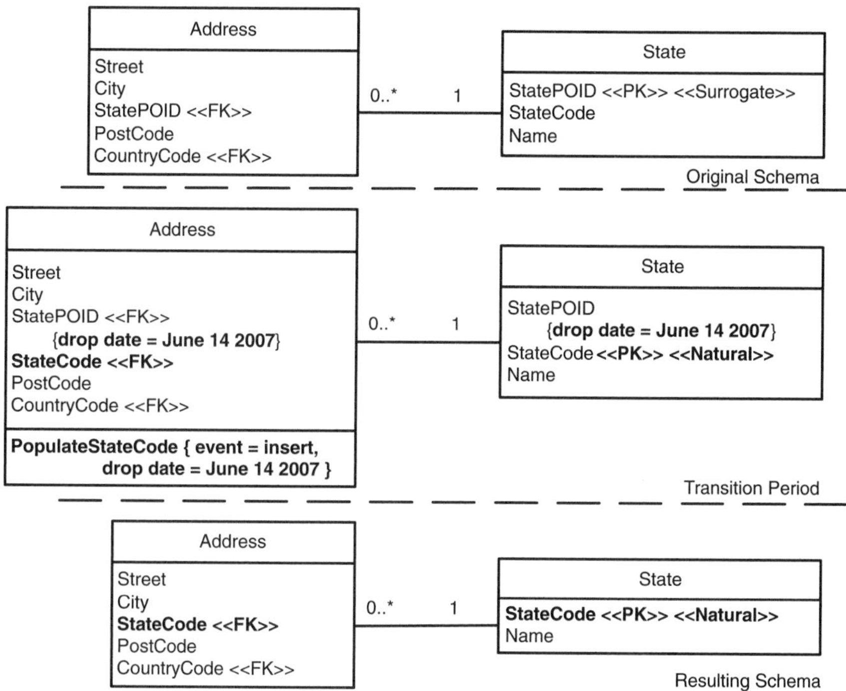

Figure 6.16 Replacing a surrogate key with a natural key.

Motivation

There are several reasons to apply *Replace Surrogate Key with Natural Key*:

- **Reduce overhead.** When you replace a surrogate key with an existing natural key, you reduce the overhead within your table structure of maintaining the additional surrogate key column(s).
- **To consolidate your key strategy.** To support *Consolidate Key Strategy* (page 168), you may decide to first replace an existing surrogate primary key with the "official" natural key.

- **Remove nonrequired keys.** You may have discovered that a surrogate key was introduced to a table when it really was not needed. It is always better to remove unused indexes to improve performance.

Potential Tradeoffs

Although many data professionals debate the use of surrogate versus natural keys, the reality is that both types of keys have their place. When you have tables with natural keys, each external application, as well as the database itself, must access data from each table in its own unique way. Sometimes, the key will be a single numeric column, sometimes a single character column, or sometimes a combination of several columns. With a consistent surrogate key strategy, tables are accessed in the exact same manner, enabling you to simplify your code. Thus, by replacing a surrogate key with a natural key, you potentially increase the complexity of the code that accesses your database. The primary advantage is that you simplify your table schema.

Schema Update Mechanics

Applying *Replace Surrogate Key With Natural Key* can be complicated because of the coupling that the surrogate key is potentially involved with. Because it is a primary key of a table, it is likely that it also forms (part of) foreign keys within other tables. You will need to do the following:

1. **Identify the column(s) to form the new primary key.** In Figure 6.16, this is *StateCode*. (This could be several columns.) *StateCode* must have a unique value within each row for it to qualify to be a primary key.

2. **Add a new index.** If one does not already exist, a new index based on *StateCode* needs to be introduced for *State*.

3. **Deprecate the original column.** *StatePOID* must be marked for deletion at the end of the transition period.

4. **Update coupled tables.** If *StatePOID* is used in other tables as part of a foreign key, you will want to update those tables to use the new key. You must remove the column(s) using *Drop Column* (page 172), which currently corresponds to *StatePOID*. You also need to add new column(s) that correspond to *StateCode* if those columns do not already exist. The corresponding index definition(s) need to be updated to reflect this change. When *StatePOID* is used in many tables, you may want to consider updating the tables one at a time to simplify the effort.

5. **Update and possibly add RI triggers.** Any triggers that exist to maintain referential integrity between tables must be updated to work with the corresponding *StateCode* values in the other tables.

Figure 6.16 depicts how to remove *State.StatePOID*, a surrogate key, replacing it with the existing *State.StateCode* as key. To support this new key, we must add the *PopulateStateCode* trigger, which is invoked whenever an insert occurs in *Address*, obtaining the value of *State.StateCode*.

```
CREATE OR REPLACE TRIGGER PopulateStateCode
  BEFORE INSERT
  ON Address
  REFERENCING OLD AS OLD NEW AS NEW
  FOR EACH ROW
  DECLARE
  BEGIN
    IF :NEW.StateCode IS NULL THEN
      :NEW.StateCode := getStatePOIDFromState(StatePOID);
    END IF;
  END;
/

ALTER TABLE Address ADD (CONSTRAINT
AddressToStateForeignKey FOREIGN KEY (StateCode)
REFERENCES State;

-June 14 2007
ALTER TABLE Address DROP CONSTRAINT
AddressToStateForeignKey;
ALTER TABLE State DROP CONSTRAINT StatePrimaryKey;
ALTER TABLE State MODIFY StateCode NOT NULL;
ALTER TABLE State ADD CONSTRAINT StatePrimaryKey
      PRIMARY KEY (StateCode);
DROP TRIGGER PopulateStateCode;
```

Data-Migration Mechanics

There is no data to migrate for this database refactoring.

Access Program Update Mechanics

To update external access programs, you need to do the following:

1. **Remove surrogate key code.** The code to assign values to the surrogate key column (which may be implemented either within external applications or the database) should no longer be invoked. It may not even be needed any longer at all.

2. **Joining based on the new key.** Many external access programs will define joins involving *State*, implemented either via hard-coded SQL or via meta data. These joins should be refactored to work with *StateCode*, not *StatePOID*.

3. **Retrievals based on the new key.** Some external programs will traverse the database one or more rows at a time, retrieving data based on the key values. These retrievals must be updated similarly.

The following hibernate mappings show how the referenced tables must refer to the new keys, and how the POID columns are no longer generated:

```
//Before mapping
<hibernate-mapping>
<class name="State" table="STATE">
  <id name="id" column="STATEPOID">
    <generator class="IdGenerator"/>
  </id>
  <property name="stateCode" />
  <property name="name" />
</class>
</hibernate-mapping>

<hibernate-mapping>
<class name="Address" table="ADDRESS">
  <id name="id" column="ADDRESSID" >
    <generator class="IdGenerator"/>
  </id>
  <property name="streetLine" />
  <property name="city"  />
  <property name="postalCode"  />
  <many-to-one name="state" class="State"
    column="STATEPOID" not-null="true"/>
  <many-to-one name="country" class="Country"
    column="COUNTRYID" not-null="true"/>
</class>
</hibernate-mapping>

//After mapping
<hibernate-mapping>
<class name="State" table="STATE">
  <property name="stateCode" />
  <property name="name" />
</class>
</hibernate-mapping>

<hibernate-mapping>
<class name="Address" table="ADDRESS">
```

```
  <id name="id" column="ADDRESSID" >
    <generator class="IdGenerator"/>
  </id>
  <property name="streetLine" />
  <property name="city"  />
  <property name="postalCode"  />
  <many-to-one name="state" class="State"
    column="STATECODE" not-null="true"/>
  <many-to-one name="country" class="Country"
    column="COUNTRYID" not-null="true"/>
</class>
</hibernate-mapping>
```

Split Column

Split a column into one or more columns within a single table.

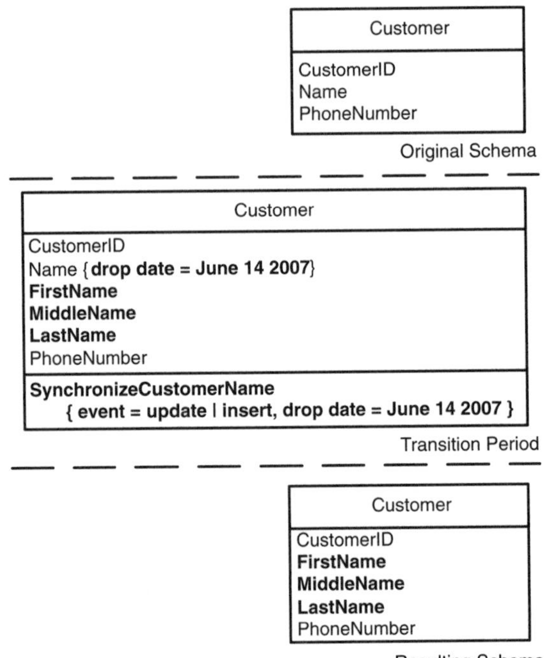

Figure 6.17 Splitting the Customer.Name column.

Note: If one or more of the new columns needs to appear in another table, first apply *Split Column* and then apply *Move Column* (page 103).

Motivation

There are two reasons why you may want to apply *Split Column*. First, you have a need for fine-grained data. For example, the *Customer* table has a *Name* column, which contains the full name of the person, but you want to split this column so that you can store *FirstName, MiddleName*, and *LastName* as independent columns.

Second, the column has several uses. The original column was introduced to track the *Account* status, and now you are also using it to track the type of *Account*. For example, the *Account.Status* column contains the status of the account (such as *Open, Closed, OverDrawn*, and so on). Unknowingly, someone else has also started using it for account type information such as *Checking, Savings*, and so on. We need to split these usages into their own fields to avoid introduction of bugs because of dual usage.

Potential Tradeoffs

This database refactoring can result in duplication of data when you split columns. When you split a column that (you believe) is used for different purposes, you run the risk that you should in fact be using the new columns for same things. (If so, you will discover that you need to apply *Merge Columns*.) The usage of a column should determine whether it should be split.

Schema Update Mechanics

To perform *Split Column*, you must first introduce the new columns. Add the column to the table via the SQL command **ADD COLUMN**. In Figure 6.17, this is *FirstName, MiddleName*, and *LastName*. This step is optional because you may find it possible to use one of the existing columns into which to split the data. Then you must introduce a synchronization trigger to ensure that the columns remain in sync with one another. The trigger must be invoked by any change to the columns.

Figure 6.17 depicts an example where the *Customer* table initially stores the name of a person in the column *Name*. Over time, we have discovered that few applications are interested in the full name, but instead need components of the full name, in particular the last name of the customer. We have also discovered that many applications include duplicate code to split the *Name* column, a source of potential bugs. Therefore, we have decided to split the *Name* column into *FirstName, MiddleName*, and *LastName* columns, reflecting the actual usage of the data. We introduced the *SynchronizeCustomerName* trigger to keep the values in the columns synchronized. The following code implements the changes to the schema:

```
ALTER TABLE Customer ADD FirstName VARCHAR(40);

COMMENT ON Customer.FirstName 'Added as the result of splitting Customer.Name finaldate =
December 14 2007';

ALTER TABLE Customer ADD MiddleName VARCHAR(40);

COMMENT ON Customer.MiddleName 'Added as the result of splitting Customer.Name finaldate =
December 14 2007';
```

```
ALTER TABLE Customer ADD LastName VARCHAR(40);

COMMENT ON Customer.LastName 'Added as the result of splitting Customer.Name finaldate = December
14 2007';

COMMENT ON Customer.Name 'Replaced with FirstName,
LastName and MiddleName, will be dropped December 14 2007';

-Trigger to keep all the split columns in sync
CREATE OR REPLACE TRIGGER SynchronizeCustomerName
  BEFORE INSERT OR UPDATE
  ON Customer
  REFERENCING OLD AS OLD NEW AS NEW
  FOR EACH ROW
  DECLARE
  BEGIN
    IF :NEW.FirstName IS NULL THEN
      :NEW.FirstName := getFirstName(Name);
    END IF;
    IF :NEW.MiddleName IS NULL THEN
      :NEW.MiddleName := getMiddleName(Name);
    END IF;
    IF :NEW.LastName IS NULL THEN
      :NEW.LastName := getLastName(Name);
    END IF;
END;
/


-On December 14 2007
ALTER TABLE Customer DROP COLUMN Name;
DROP TRIGGER SynchronizeCustomerName;
```


Data-Migration Mechanics

You must copy all the data from the original column(s) into the split columns—in this case, from *Customer.Name* into *FirstName, MiddleName*, and, *LastName*. The following code depicts the DML to initially split the data from *Name* into the three new columns. (The source code for the three stored functions that are invoked are not shown for the sake of brevity.)

```
/*One-time migration of data from Customer.Name to Customer.FirstName,  Customer.MiddleName, and
Customer.LastName. When both set of columns are active, there is a need to have a trigger that
keeps both set of columns in sync
*/

UPDATE Customer SET FirstName = getFirstName(Name);
UPDATE Customer SET MiddleName = getMiddleName(Name);
UPDATE Customer SET LastName = getLastName(Name);
```

Access Program Update Mechanics

You need to analyze the access programs thoroughly, and then update them appropriately, during the transition period. In addition to the obvious need to work with *FirstName, MiddleName,* and *LastName* rather than the former columns, potential updates you need to make are as follows:

1. **Remove splitting code.** There may be code that splits the existing columns into a data attribute similar to the split columns. This code should be refactored and potentially removed entirely.
2. **Update data-validation code to work with split data.** Some data-validation code may exist that exists solely because the columns have not been split. For example, if a value is stored in the *Customer.Name* column, you may have validation code in place that verifies that the values contain the *FirstName* and *LastName*. After the column is split, there may no longer be a need for this code.
3. **Refactor the user interface.** After the original column is split, the presentation layer should make use of the finer-grained data, if it was not doing so already, as appropriate.

The following code shows how the application makes use of the finer-grained data available to it:

```
//Before code
public Customer findByCustomerID(Long customerID)  {
Customer customer = new Customer();
stmt = DB.prepare("SELECT CustomerID, "+
"Name, PhoneNumber " +
"FROM Customer " +
"WHERE CustomerID = ?");
stmt.setLong(1, customerID);
stmt.execute();
ResultSet rs = stmt.executeQuery();
if (rs.next()) {
 customer.setCustomerId(rs.getLong("CustomerID"));
 String name = rs.getString("Name");
 customer.setFirstName(getFirstName(name));
 customer.setMiddleName(getMiddleName(name));
 customer.setLastName(getMiddleName(name));
 customer.setPhoneNumber(rs.getString("PhoneNumber"));
}
return customer;
}

//After code
public Customer findByCustomerID(Long customerID)  {
Customer customer = new Customer();
```

```
stmt = DB.prepare("SELECT CustomerID, "+
"FirstName, MiddleName, LastName, PhoneNumber " +
"FROM Customer " +
"WHERE CustomerID = ?");
stmt.setLong(1, customerID);
stmt.execute();
ResultSet rs = stmt.executeQuery();
if (rs.next()) {
  customer.setCustomerId(rs.getLong("CustomerID"));
  customer.setFirstName(rs.getString("FirstName"));
  customer.setMiddleName(rs.getString("MiddleName"));
  customer.setLastName(rs.getString("LastName"));
  customer.setPhoneNumber(rs.getString("PhoneNumber"));
}
return customer;
}
```

Split Table

Vertically split (for example, by columns) an existing table into one or more tables.

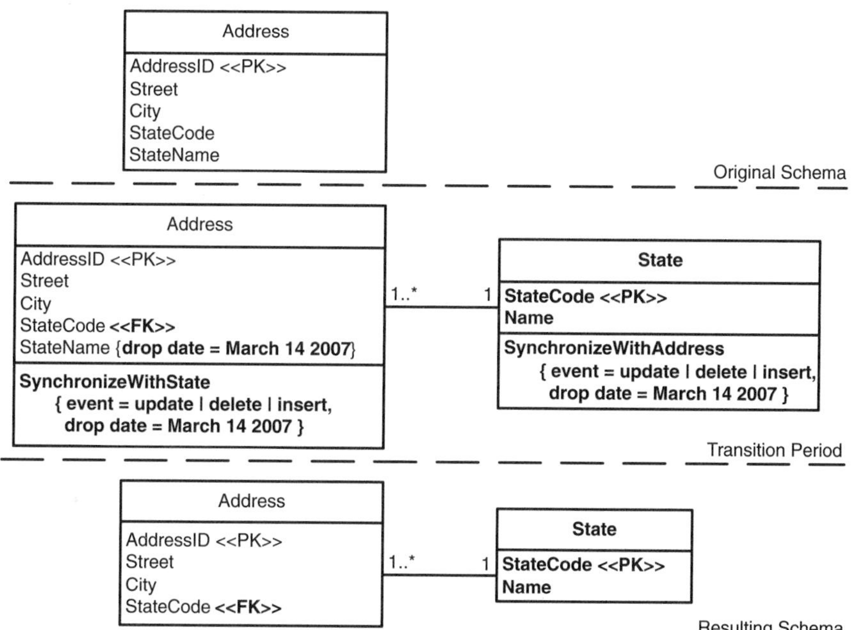

Figure 6.18 Splitting the Address table.

Note: If the destination of the split columns happens to be an existing table, then in reality you would be applying *Move Column(s)* (page 103). To split a table horizontally (for example, by rows), apply *Move Data* (page 192).

Motivation

There are several reasons why you may want to apply *Split Table*:

- **Performance improvement.** It is very common for most applications to require a core collection of data attributes of any given entity, and then a specific subset of the noncore data attributes. For example, the core columns of the *Employee* table would include the columns required to store their name, address, and phone numbers; whereas noncore columns would include the *Picture* column as well as salary information. Because *Employee.Picture* is large, and required only by a few applications, you would want to consider splitting it off into its own table. This would help to improve retrieval access times for applications that select all columns from the *Employee* table yet do not require the picture.

- **Restrict data access.** You may want to restrict access to some columns, perhaps the salary information within the *Employee* table, by splitting it off into its own table and assigning specific security access control (SAC) rules to it.
- **Reduce repeating data groups (apply 1NF).** The original table may have been designed when requirements were not yet finalized, or by people who did not appreciate why you need to normalize data structures (Date 2001; Ambler 2003). For example, the *Employee* table may store descriptions of the five previous evaluation reviews for the person. This information is a repeating group that you would want to split off into an *EmployeeEvaluation* table.

Potential Tradeoffs

When you split a table that (you believe) is used for different purposes, you run the risk that you would in fact be using the new tables for same things; if so, you will discover that you need to apply *Merge Tables* (page 96). The usage of a table should determine whether it should be split.

Schema Update Mechanics

To perform *Split Table*, you must first add the table(s) via the SQL command **CREATE TABLE**. This step is optional because you may find it possible to use an existing table(s) into which to move the columns. In this situation, you should repeatedly apply the *Move Column* refactoring (page 103). Second, you must introduce a trigger to ensure that the columns remain synchronized with one another. The trigger must be invoked by any change to the tables. You need to implement the trigger so that cycles do not occur.

Figure 6.18 depicts an example where the *Address* table initially stores the address information along with the state code and state name. To reduce data duplication, we have decided to split *Address* table into *Address* and *State* tables, reflecting the current refactor of the table design. We introduced the *SynchronizeWithAddress* and *SynchronizeWithState* triggers to keep the values in the tables synchronized:

```
CREATE TABLE State (
  StateCode VARCHAR(2) NOT NULL,
  Name VARCHAR(40) NOT NULL,
  CONSTRAINT PKState
    PRIMARY KEY (StateCode)
);

COMMENT ON State.Name 'Added as the result of splitting Address into Address and State  drop date
= December 14 2007';

-Trigger to keep all the split tables in sync
CREATE OR REPLACE TRIGGER SynchronizeWithAddress
BEFORE INSERT OR UPDATE
ON Address
REFERENCING OLD AS OLD NEW AS NEW
FOR EACH ROW
DECLARE
BEGIN
  IF updating THEN
    FindOrCreateState;
  END IF;
  IF inserting THEN
    CreateState;
  END IF;
END;
/


CREATE OR REPLACE TRIGGER SynchronizeWithState
BEFORE UPDATE OF Statename
ON State
REFERENCING OLD AS OLD NEW AS NEW
FOR EACH ROW
DECLARE
BEGIN
  IF updating THEN
    FindAndUpdateAllAddressesForStateName;
  END IF;
END;
/

-On December 14 2007
ALTER TABLE Address DROP COLUMN StateName;
DROP TRIGGER SynchronizeWithAddress;
DROP TRIGGER SynchronizeWithState;
```


Data-Migration Mechanics

You must copy all the data from the original column(s) into the new table's columns. In the case of Figure 6.18, this would be from *Address.StateCode* and

Address.StateName into *State.StateCode* and *State.Name*, respectively. The following code shows how to initially migrate this data:

```
/*One-time migration of data from Address.StateCode and Address.StateName to State. When both set
of columns are active, there is a need to have a trigger that keeps both set of columns in sync
*/

INSERT INTO State (StateCode, Name)
  SELECT StateCode,StateName FROM Address
  WHERE StateCode IS NOT NULL AND StateName IS NOT NULL
  GROUP BY StateCode, StateName;
```

Access Program Update Mechanics

You must analyze the access programs thoroughly, and then update them appropriately, during the transition period. In addition to the obvious need to work with the new columns rather than the former columns, potential updates you will need to make are as follows:

1. **Introduce new table meta data.** If you are using a meta data-based persistence framework, you must introduce new meta data for *State* and change the meta data for *Address*.
2. **Update SQL code.** Similarly, any embedded SQL code that accesses *Address* must be updated to join in *State* where appropriate. This may slightly reduce performance of this code.
3. **Refactor the user interface.** After the original table is split, the presentation layer should make use of the finer-grained data, if it was not doing so already, as appropriate.

The following hibernate mappings show how we split the *Address* table and create a new *State* table:

```
//Before mapping
<hibernate-mapping>
<class name="Address" table="ADDRESS">
  <id name="id" column="ADDRESSID">
    <generator class="IdGenerator"/>
  </id>
  <property name="street" />
  <property name="city" />
  <property name="stateCode" />
  <property name="stateName" />
</class>
</hibernate-mapping>
```

```
//After mapping

//Address table
<hibernate-mapping>
<class name="Address" table="ADDRESS">
  <id name="id" column="ADDRESSID">
    <generator class="IdGenerator"/>
  </id>
  <property name="street" />
  <property name="city" />
  <many-to-one name="state" class="State"
    column="STATECODE" not-null="true"/>
</class>
</hibernate-mapping>

//State table
<hibernate-mapping>
<class name="State" table="STATE">
  <id name="stateCode" column="stateCode">
    <generator class="assigned"/>
  </id>
  <property name="stateName" />
</class>
</hibernate-mapping>
```

Chapter 7

Data Quality Refactorings

Data quality refactorings are changes that improve the quality of the information contained within a database. Data quality refactorings improve and/or ensure the consistency and usage of the values stored within the database. The data quality refactorings are as follows:

- Add Lookup Table
- Apply Standard Codes
- Apply Standard Type
- Consolidate Key Strategy
- Drop Column Constraint
- Drop Default Value
- Drop Non-Nullable Constraint
- Introduce Column Constraint
- Introduce Common Format
- Introduce Default Value
- Make Column Non-Nullable
- Move Data
- Replace Type Code With Property Flags

Common Issues When Implementing Data Quality Refactorings

Because data quality refactorings change the values of the data stored within your database, several issues are common to all of them. As a result, you need to do the following:

1. **Fix broken constraints.** You may have constraints defined on the affected data. If so, you can apply *Drop Column Constraint* (page 172) to first remove the constraint and then apply *Introduce Column Constraint* (page 180) to add the constraint back, reflecting the values of the improved data.

2. **Fix broken views.** Views will often reference hard-coded data values in their **WHERE** clauses, usually to select a subset of the data. As a result, these views may become broken when the values of the data change. You will need to find these broken views by running your test suite and by searching for view definitions that reference the columns in which the changed data is stored.

3. **Fix broken stored procedures.** The variables defined within a stored procedure, any parameters passed to it, the return value(s) calculated by it, and any SQL defined within it are potentially coupled to the values of the improved data. Hopefully, your existing tests will reveal business logic problems arising from the application of any data quality refactorings; otherwise, you will need to search for any stored procedure code accessing the column(s) in which the changed data is stored.

4. **Update the data.** You will likely want to lock the source data rows during the update, affecting performance and availability of the data for the application(s). You can take two strategies to do this. First, you can lock all the data and then do the updates at that time. Second, you can lock subsets of the data, perhaps even just a single row at a time, and do the update just on the subset. The first approach ensures consistency but risks performance degradation with large amounts of data—updating millions of rows can take time, preventing applications from making updates during this period. The second approach enables applications to work with the source data during the update process but risks inconsistency between rows because some will have the older, "low-quality" values, whereas other rows will have been updated.

Add Lookup Table

Create a lookup table for an existing column.

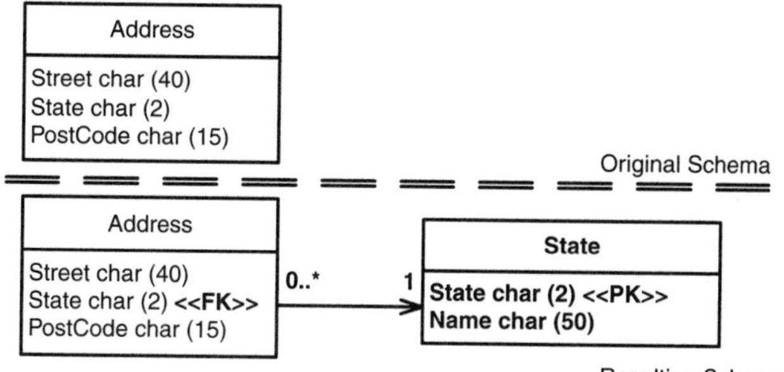

Figure 7.1 Adding a State lookup table.

Motivation

There are several reasons why you may want to apply *Add Lookup Table*:

- **Introduce referential integrity.** You may want to introduce a referential integrity constraint on an existing *Address.State* to ensure the quality of the data.

- **Provide code lookup.** Many times you want to provide a defined list of codes in your database instead of having an *enumeration* in every application. The lookup table is often cached in memory.

- **Replace a column constraint.** When you introduced the column, you added a column constraint to ensure that a small number of correct code values persisted. But, as your application(s) evolved, you needed to introduce more code values, until you got to the point where it was easier to maintain the values in a lookup table instead of updating the column constraint.

- **Provide detailed descriptions.** In addition to defining the allowable codes, you may also want to store descriptive information about the codes. For example, in the *State* table, you may want to relate the code CA to California.

Potential Tradeoffs

There are two issues to consider when adding a lookup table. The first is data population—you need to be able to provide valid data to populate the lookup table. Although this sounds simple in practice, the implication is that you must have an agreement as to the semantics of the existing data values in *Address.State* of Figure 7.1. This is easier said than done. For example, in the case of introducing a *State* lookup table, some applications may work with all 50 U.S. states, whereas others may also include the four territories (Puerto Rico, Guam, the District of Columbia, and the U.S. Virgin Islands). In this situation, you may either need to add two lookup tables, one for the 50 states and the other for the territories, or implement a single table and then the appropriate validation logic within applications that only need a subset of the lookup data.

The second issue is that there will be a performance impact resulting from the addition of a foreign key constraint. (See the refactoring *Add Foreign Key Constraint* on page 204 for details.)

Schema Update Mechanics

As depicted in Figure 7.1, to update the database schema, you must do the following:

1. **Determine the table structure.** You must identify the column(s) of the lookup table (*State*).
2. **Introduce the table.** Create *State* in the database via the **CREATE TABLE** command.
3. **Determine lookup data.** You have to determine what rows are going to be inserted in the *State*. Consider applying the *Insert Data* refactoring (page 296).
4. **Introduce referential constraint.** To enforce referential integrity constraints from the code column in the source table(s) to *State*, you must apply the *Add Foreign Key* refactoring.

The following code depicts the DDL to introduce the *State* table and add a foreign key constraint between it and *Address*:

```
--Create the lookup table.
CREATE TABLE State (
  State CHAR(2) NOT NULL,
```

```
  Name CHAR(50),
  CONSTRAINT PKState
    PRIMARY KEY (State)
);

--Introduce Foreign Key to the lookup table
ALTER TABLE Address ADD CONSTRAINT FK_Address_State
  FOREIGN KEY (State) REFERENCES State;
```

Data-Migration Mechanics

You must ensure that the data values in *Address.State* have corresponding values in *State*. The easiest way to populate *State.State* is to copy the unique values from *Address.State*. With this automated approach, you need to remember to inspect the resulting rows to ensure that invalid data values are not introduced—if so, you need to update both *Address* and *State* appropriately. When there are descriptive information columns, such as *State.Name*, you must provide the appropriate values; this is often done manually via a script or a data-administration utility. An alternative strategy is to simply load the values into the State table from an external file.

The following code depicts the DDL to populate the *State* table with distinct values from the *Address.State* column. We then cleanse the data, in this case ensuring that all addresses use the code TX instead of Tx or tx or Texas. The final step is to provide state names corresponding to each state code. (In the example, we populate values for just three states.)


```
--Populate data in the lookup table
INSERT INTO State (State)
  SELECT DISTINCT UPPER(State) FROM Address;

--Update the Address.StateCode to valid values and
clean data

UPDATE Address SET State = 'TX' WHERE
UPPER(State) ='TX';
...
--Now provide state names
UPDATE State SET Name = 'Florida' WHERE State='FL';
UPDATE State SET Name = 'Illinois' WHERE State='IL';
UPDATE State SET Name = 'California' WHERE State='CA';
```

Access Program Update Mechanics

When you add *State*, you have to ensure that external programs now use the data values from the lookup table. The following code shows how external programs can now get the name of the state from the *State* table; in the past, they would have to get this information from an internally hard-coded collection:

```
// After code
ResultSet rs = statement.executeQuery(
  "SELECT State, Name FROM State");
```

Some programs may choose to cache the data values, whereas others will access *State* as needed—caching works well because the values in *State* rarely change. Furthermore, if you are also introducing a foreign key constraint along with *Lookup Table*, external programs will need to handle any exceptions thrown by the database. See the *Add Foreign Key* refactoring (page 204) for details.

Apply Standard Codes

Apply a standard set of code values to a single column to ensure that it conforms to the values of similar columns stored elsewhere in the database.

Motivation

You may need to apply *Apply Standard Codes* to do the following:

- **Cleanse data.** When you have the same semantic meaning for different code values in your database, it is generally better to standardize them so that you can apply standard logic across all data attributes. For example, in Figure 7.2, when the values in *Country.Code* is USA and *Address.CountryCode* is US, you have a potential problem because you can no longer accurately join the two tables. Apply a consistent value, one or the other, throughout your database.
- **Support referential integrity.** When you want to apply *Add Foreign Key Constraint* (page 204) to tables based on the code column, you need to standardize the code values first.
- **Add a lookup table.** When you are applying *Add Lookup Table* (page 153), you often need to first standardize the code values on which the lookup is based.
- **Conform to corporate standards.** Many organizations have detailed data and data modeling standards that development teams are expected to conform to. Often when applying *Use Official Data Source* (page 271), you discover that your current data schema does not follow your organization's standards and therefore needs to be refactored to reflect the official data source code values.
- **Reduce code complexity.** When you have a variety of values for the semantically same data, you will be writing extra program code to deal with the different values. For example, your existing program code of *countryCode = 'US' || countryCode = 'USA'*. . . would be simplified to something like *country Code = 'USA'*.

Before

Address			
Street	City	State	CountryCode
123 Main St.	Borington	ON	CAN
456 Elm St.	Hickton	CA	USA
4321 Oak Lane	New York	NY	US

Country	
CountryCode	Name
CAN	Canada
USA	United States

After

Address			
Street	City	State	CountryCode
123 Main St.	Borington	ON	**CA**
456 Elm St.	Hickton	CA	**US**
4321 Oak Lane	New York	NY	US

Country	
CountryCode	Name
CA	Canada
US	United States

Figure 7.2 Applying standard state codes.

Potential Tradeoffs

Standardizing code values can be tricky because they are often used in many places. For example, several tables may use the code value as a foreign key to another table; therefore, not only does the source need to be standardized but so do the foreign key columns. Second, the code values may be hard-coded in one or more applications, requiring extensive updates. For example, applications that access the *Country* table may have the value USA hard-coded in SQL statements, whereas applications that use the *Address* table have US hard-coded.

Schema Update Mechanics

To *Apply Standard Codes* to the database schema, you must do the following:

1. **Identify the standard values. You need to settle on the "official" values for the code.** Are the values being provided from existing application tables or are they being provided by your business users? Either way, the values must be accepted by your project stakeholder(s).
2. **Identify the tables where the code is stored.** You must identify the tables that include the code column. This may require extensive analysis and many iterations before you discover all the tables where the code is used. Note that this refactoring is applied a single column at a time; you will potentially need to apply it several times to ensure consistency across your database.
3. **Update stored procedures.** When you standardize code values, the stored procedures that access the affected columns may need to be updated. For example, if *getUSCustomerAddress* has the **WHERE** clause as *Address.CountryCode*="USA", this needs to change to *Address.Country Code*="US".

Data-Migration Mechanics

When you standardize on a particular code, you must update all the rows where there are nonstandard codes to use the standard ones. If you are updating small numbers of rows, a simple SQL script that updates the target table(s) is sufficient. When you have to update large amounts of data, or in cases where the code in transactional tables is being changed, apply *Update Data* (page 310) instead.

The following code depicts the DML to update data in the *Address* and *Country* tables to use the standard code values:

```
UPDATE Address SET CountryCode = 'CA' WHERE CountryCode = 'CAN';
UPDATE Address SET CountryCode = 'US' WHERE CountryCode = 'USA';

UPDATE Country SET CountryCode = 'CA' WHERE CountryCode = 'CAN';
UPDATE Country SET CountryCode = 'US' WHERE CountryCode = 'USA';
```

Access Program Update Mechanics

When *Apply Standard Codes* is applied, the following aspects of external programs must be examined:

1. **Hard-coded WHERE clauses.** You may need to update SQL statements to have the correct values in the **WHERE** clause. For example, if the *Country.Code* row values changes from 'US' to 'USA', you will have to change your **WHERE** clause to use the new value.
2. **Validation code.** Similarly, you may need to update source code that validates the values of data attributes. For example, code that looks like *countryCode = 'US'* must be updated to use the new code value.
3. **Lookup constructs.** The values of codes may be defined in various programming "lookup constructs" such as constants, enumerations, and collections for use throughout an application. The definition of these lookup constructs must be updated to use the new code values.
4. **Test code.** Code values are often hard-coded into testing logic and/or test data generation logic; you will have to change these to now use the new values.

The following code shows you the before and after state of the method to read U.S. addresses:

```
// Before code
stmt = DB.prepare("SELECT addressId, line1, line2,
city, state, zipcode, country FROM address WHERE
countrycode = ?");
stmt.setString(1,"USA");
stmt.execute();
ResultSet rs = stmt.executeQuery();
```

```
//After code
stmt = DB.prepare("SELECT addressId, line1, line2,
city, state, zipcode, country FROM address WHERE
countrycode = ?");
stmt.setString(1,"US");
stmt.execute();
ResultSet rs = stmt.executeQuery();
```

Apply Standard Type

Ensure that the data type of a column is consistent with the data type of other similar columns within the database.

Motivation

The refactoring *Apply Standard Types* can be used to do the following:

- **Ensure referential integrity.** When you want to apply *Add Foreign Key* (page 204) to all tables storing the same semantic information, you need to standardize the data types of the individual columns. For example, Figure 7.3 shows how all the phone number columns are refactored to be stored as integers. Another common example occurs when you have *Address.ZipCode* stored as a **VARCHAR** data type and *Customer.Zip* stored as **NUMERIC** data type; you should standardize on one data type so that you can apply referential integrity constraints.
- **Add a lookup table.** When you are applying *Add Lookup Table* (page 153), you will want a consistent type used for the two code columns.
- **Conform to corporate standards.** Many organizations have detailed data and data modeling standards that development teams are expected to conform to. Often, when applying *Use Official Data Source* (page 271), you discover that your current data schema does not follow your standards and therefore needs to be refactored to reflect the official data source type.
- **Reduce code complexity.** When you have a variety of data types for semantically the same data, you require extra program code to handle the different column types. For example, phone number-validation code for the *Customer*, *Branch*, and *Employee*, classes could be refactored to use a shared method.

Potential Tradeoffs

Standardizing data types can be tricky because the individual columns are often referred to in many places. For example, several application classes may reference the column, code that will need to change when you change the column's data type. Second, when you are attempting to change the data type of a column, you may have situations when the source data cannot be converted to the

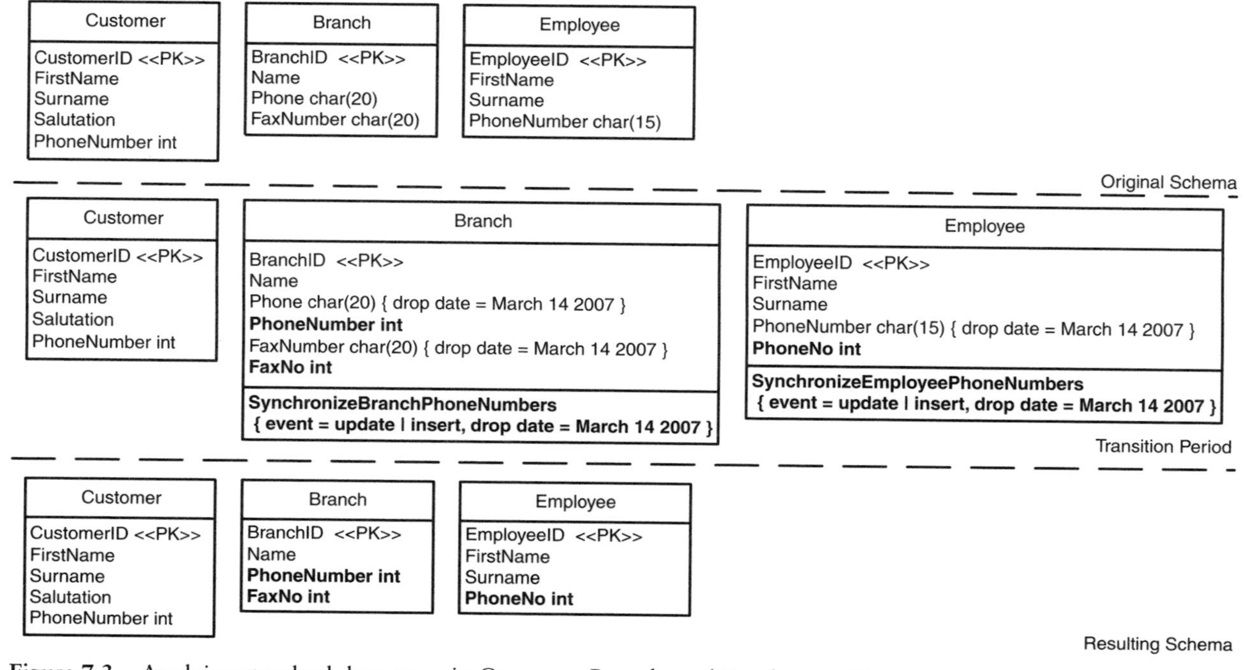

Figure 7.3 Applying standard data types in Customer, Branch, and Employee tables.

destination data type. For example, when you change *Customer.Zip* to **NUMERIC** data type, you may not be able to convert international postal codes such as R2D 2C3 that contain character data.

Schema Update Mechanics

To apply this refactoring, you must first identify the standard data type. You need to settle on the "official" data type for the columns. This data type must handle all existing data and external access programs must be able to handle it. (Older languages sometimes cannot process new data types.) Then you must identify the tables that include column(s) where the data type needs to change. This may require extensive analysis and many iterations before you find out all the tables where the column needs to change. Note that this refactoring is applied to a single column at a time; therefore, you will potentially need to apply it several times to ensure consistency across your database.

Figure 7.3 depicts how we change the *Branch.Phone, Branch.FaxNumber*, and *Employee.PhoneNumber* columns to use the same data type of integer—the column *Customer.PhoneNumber* is already an integer and therefore does not need to be refactored. Although this would really be three individual refactorings, because the three columns appear in the same table it behooves us to bundle these three refactorings together.

The following code depicts the three refactorings required to change the *Branch.Phone, Branch.FaxNumber*, and *Employee.Phone* columns. We are going to add a new column to the tables using *Introduce New Column* (page 301). Because we want to provide some time for all the applications to migrate to the new columns, during this transition phase we are going to maintain both the columns and also synchronize the data in them:

```
ALTER TABLE Branch ADD COLUMN PhoneNumber INT;
COMMENT ON Branch.PhoneNumber "Replaces Phone,
dropdate=2007-03-27"

ALTER TABLE Branch ADD COLUMN FaxNo INT;
COMMENT ON Branch.FaxNo "Replaces FaxNumber,
dropdate=2007-03-27"

ALTER TABLE Employee ADD PhoneNo INT;
COMMENT ON Employee.PhoneNo "Replaces PhoneNumber,
dropdate=2007-03-27"
```

The following code depicts how to synchronize changes in the *Branch.Phone*, *Branch.FaxNumber*, and *Employee.Phone* columns with the existing columns:

```
CREATE OR REPLACE TRIGGER SynchronizeBranchPhoneNumbers
  BEFORE INSERT OR UPDATE
  ON Branch
  REFERENCING OLD AS OLD NEW AS NEW
  FOR EACH ROW
  DECLARE
  BEGIN
    IF :NEW.PhoneNumber IS NULL THEN
      :NEW.PhoneNumber := :NEW.Phone;
    END IF;
    IF :NEW.Phone IS NULL THEN
      :NEW.Phone := :NEW.PhoneNumber;
    END IF;
    IF :NEW.FaxNumber IS NULL THEN
      :NEW.FaxNumber := :NEW.FaxNo;
    END IF;
    IF :NEW.FaxNo IS NULL THEN
      :NEW.FaxNo := :NEW.FaxNumber;
    END IF;
  END;
/

CREATE OR REPLACE TRIGGER SynchronizeEmployeePhoneNumbers
  BEFORE INSERT OR UPDATE
  ON Employee
  REFERENCING OLD AS OLD NEW AS NEW
  FOR EACH ROW
  DECLARE
  BEGIN
    IF :NEW.PhoneNumber IS NULL THEN
      :NEW.PhoneNumber := :NEW.PhoneNo;
    END IF;
    IF :NEW.PhoneNo IS NULL THEN
      :NEW.PhoneNo := :NEW.PhoneNumber;
    END IF;
  END;
/

--Update Existing data for the first time
UPDATE Branch SET
PhoneNumber = formatPhone(Phone),
FaxNo = formatPhone(FaxNumber);
UPDATE Employee SET
  PhoneNo = formatPhone(PhoneNumber);

--Drop the old columns on Mar 23 2007
ALTER TABLE Branch DROP COLUMN Phone;
ALTER TABLE Branch DROP COLUMN FaxNumber;
```

```
ALTER TABLE Employee DROP COLUMN PhoneNumber;
DROP TRIGGER SynchronizeBranchPhoneNumbers;
DROP TRIGGER SynchronizeEmployeePhoneNumbers;
```

Data-Migration Mechanics

When small numbers of rows need to be converted, you will likely find that a simple SQL script that converts the target column(s) is sufficient. When you want to convert large amounts of data, or you have complicated data conversions, consider applying *Update Data* (page 310).

Access Program Update Mechanics

When *Apply Standard Type* is applied, the external programs should be updated in the following manner:

1. **Change application variables data type.** You need to change the program code so that its data types match the data type of the column.
2. **Database interaction code.** The code that saves, deletes, and retrieves data from this column must be updated to work with the new data type. For example, if the *Customer.Zip* has changed from a character to numeric data type, you must change your application code from *customerGateway.getString("ZIP")* to *customerGateway.getLong ("ZIP")*.
3. **Business logic code.** Similarly, you may need to update application code that works with the column. For example, comparison code such as *Branch.Phone* = 'XXX-XXXX' must be updated to look like *Branch .Phone* = XXXXXXX.

The following code snippet shows the before and after state of the class that finds the *Branch* row for a given *BranchID* when we change data type of *PhoneNumber* to a **Long** from a **String:**

```
// Before code
stmt = DB.prepare("SELECT BranchId, Name, PhoneNumber, "
          "FaxNumber FROM branch WHERE BranchId = ?");
stmt.setLong(1,findBranchId);
stmt.execute();
ResultSet rs = stmt.executeQuery();
if (rs.next()) {
  rs.getLong("BranchId");
  rs.getString("Name");
  rs.getString("PhoneNumber");
  rs.getString("FaxNumber");
}
```

```
//After code
stmt = DB.prepare("SELECT BranchId, Name, PhoneNumber, "+
           "FaxNumber FROM branch WHERE branchId = ?");
stmt.setLong(1,findBranchId);
stmt.execute();
ResultSet rs = stmt.executeQuery();
if (rs.next()) {
  rs.getLong("BranchId");
  rs.getString("Name");
  rs.getLong("PhoneNumber");
  rs.getString("FaxNumber");
}
```

Consolidate Key Strategy

Choose a single key strategy for an entity and apply it consistently throughout your database.

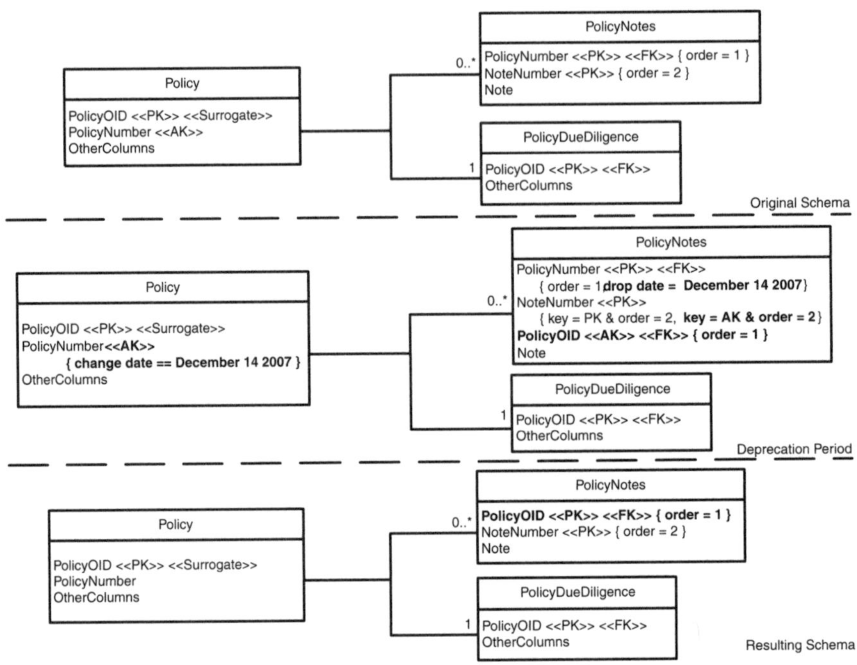

Figure 7.4 Consolidating the key strategy for the Policy table.

Motivation

Many business entities have several potential keys. There is usually one or more keys with business meaning, and fundamentally you can always assign a surrogate key column to a table. For example, your *Customer* table may have *CustomerPOID* as the primary key and both *CustomerNumber* and *SocialSecurityNumber* as alternate/secondary keys. There are several reasons why you would want to apply *Consolidate Key Strategy*:

- **Improve performance.** You likely have an index for each key that the database needs to insert, update, and delete in a manner that performs well.

- **Conform to corporate standards.** Many organizations have detailed data and data modeling guidelines that development teams are expected to conform to, guidelines that indicate the preferred keys for entities. Often when applying *Use Official Data Source* (page 271), you discover that your current data schema does not follow your standards and therefore needs to be refactored to reflect the official data source code values.

- **Improve code consistency.** When you have a variety of keys for a single entity, you have code that implements access to the table in various ways. This increases the maintenance burden for those working with that code because they must understand each approach being used.

Potential Tradeoffs

Consolidating key strategies can be difficult. Not only do you need to update the schema of *Policy* in Figure 7.4, you also need to update the schema of any tables that include foreign keys to *Policy* that do not use your chosen key strategy. To do this, you need to apply *Replace Column* (page 126). You may also find that your existing set of keys does not contain a palatable option for the "one, true key," and therefore you need to apply either *Introduce Surrogate Key* (page 85) or *Introduce Index* (page 248).

Schema Update Mechanics

To implement this refactoring within your database schema, you must do the following:

1. **Identify the proper key.** You need to settle on the "official" key column(s) for the entity. Ideally, this should reflect your corporate data standards, if any.

2. **Update the source table schema.** The simplest approach is to use the current primary key and to stop using the alternate keys. With this strategy, you simply drop the indices, if any, supporting the key. This approach still works if you choose to use one of the alternate keys rather than the current primary key. However, if none of the existing keys work, you may need to apply *Introduce Surrogate Key*.

3. **Deprecate the unwanted keys.** Any existing keys that are not to be the primary key, in this case *PolicyNumber*, should be marked that they will no longer be used as keys after the transition period. Note that you may want to retain the uniqueness constraint on these columns, even though you are not going to use them as keys anymore.

4. **Add a new index.** If one does not already exist, a new index based on the official key needs to be introduced for *Policy* via *Introduce Index* (page 248).

Figure 7.4 shows how we consolidate the key strategy for *Policy* to use only *PolicyOID* for the key. To do this, the *Policy.PolicyNumber* is deprecated to indicate that it will no longer be used as a key as of December 14, 2007, and *PolicyNotes.PolicyOID* is introduced as a new key column to replace *PolicyNotes.PolicyNumber*. The following code adds the *PolicyNotes.PolicyNumber* column:

```
ALTER TABLE PolicyNotes ADD PolicyOID CHAR(16);
```

The following code is run after the transition period ends to drop *PolicyNotes.PolicyNumber* and the index for the alternate key based on *Policy.PolicyNumber*:

```
COMMENT ON Policy 'Consolidation of keys to use only PolicyPOID, dropdate = <<2007-12-14>>'
DROP INDEX PolicyIndex2;

COMMENT ON PolicyNotes 'Consolidation of keys to use only PolicyPOID, therefore drop the
PolicyNumber column, dropdate = <<2007-12-14>>'

ALTER TABLE PolicyNotes ADD CONSTRAINT
  PolicyNotesPolciyOID_PK
  PRIMARY KEY (PolicyOID, NoteNumber);

ALTER TABLE PolicyNotes DROP COLUMN PolicyNumber;
```


Data-Migration Mechanics

Tables with foreign keys maintaining relationships to *Policy* must now implement foreign keys that reflect the chosen key strategy. For example, the *PolicyNotes* table originally implemented a foreign key based on *Policy.PolicyNumber*. It must now implement a foreign key based on *Policy.PolicyOID*. The implication is that you will need to potentially apply *Replace Column* (page 126) to do so, and this refactoring requires you to copy the data from the source column (the value in *Policy.PolicyOID*) to the *PolicyNotes.PolicyOID* column. The following code sets the value of the *PolicyNotes.PolicyNumber* column:

```
UPDATE PolicyNotes
          SET PolicyNotes.PolicyOID = Policy.PolicyOID
  WHERE PolicyNotes.PolicyNumber = Policy.PolicyNumber;
```

Access Program Update Mechanics

When this refactoring is applied, the primary task is to ensure that existing SQL statements use the official primary key column in **WHERE** clauses to ensure continued good performance of joins. For example, the before code joined the *Policy*, *PolicyNotes*, and *PolicyDueDiligence* tables by a combination of the *PolicyOID* and *PolicyNumber* columns. The "after code" code joins them based solely on the *PolicyOID* column:

```
// Before code
stmt.prepare(
 "SELECT Policy.Note FROM Policy, PolicyNotes " +
 "WHERE Policy.PolicyNumber = PolicyNotes.PolicyNumber "+
 "AND Policy.PolicyOID=?");
stmt.setLong(1,policyOIDToFind);
stmt.execute();
ResultSet rs = stmt.executeQuery();

//After code
stmt.prepare(
 "SELECT Policy.Note FROM Policy, PolicyNotes " +
 "WHERE Policy.PolicyOID = PolicyNotes.PolicyOID "+
 "AND Policy.PolicyOID=?");
stmt.setLong(1,policyOIDToFind);
stmt.execute();
ResultSet rs = stmt.executeQuery();
```

Drop Column Constraint

Remove a column constraint from an existing table.

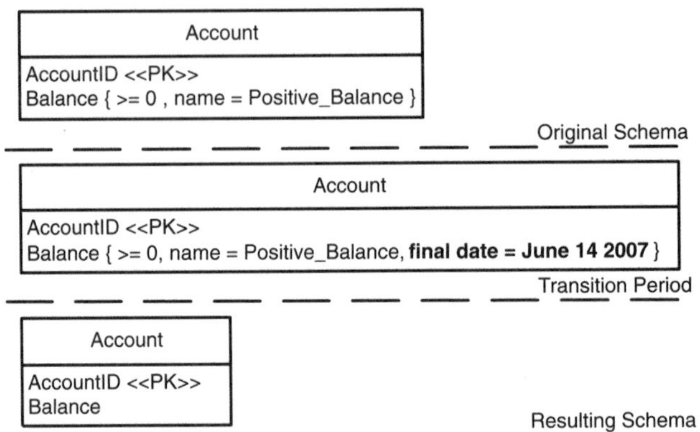

Figure 7.5 Dropping the column constraint from the Account table.

When you need to remove a referential integrity constraint on a column, you should consider the use of *Drop Foreign Key Constraint* (page 213).

Motivation

The most common reason why you want to apply *Drop Column Constraint* is that the constraint is no longer applicable because of changes in business rules. For example, perhaps the *Address.Country* column is currently constrained to the values of "US" and "Canada", but now you are also doing business internationally and therefore have addresses all over the world. A second reason is that the constraint is applicable to only a subset of the applications that access the column, perhaps because of changes in some applications but not others. For example, some applications may be used in international settings, whereas others are still only North American—because the constraint is no longer applicable to all applications, it must be removed from the common database and implemented in the applications that actually need it. As a side effect, you may see some minor performance improvements because the database no longer needs to do the work of enforcing the constraint. A third reason is that the column has been refactored, perhaps *Apply Standard Codes* (page 157) or *Apply*

Standard Type (page 162) have been applied to it and now the column constraint needs to be dropped, refactored, and then reapplied via *Introduce Column Constraint* (page 180).

Potential Tradeoffs

The primary challenge with this refactoring is that you potentially need to implement the constraint logic in the subset of applications that require it. Because you are implementing the same logic in several places, you are at risk of implementing it in different ways.

Schema Update Mechanics

To update the database schema, you must simply drop the constraint from *Balance* via the **DROP CONSTRAINT** clause of the **ALTER TABLE** SQL command. Figure 7.5 depicts an example where the constraint is that the *Account.Balance* column be positive; this constraint is being removed to support the ability to allow accounts to be overdrawn. The following code depicts the DDL to drop the constraint on *Account.Balance* column:

```
ALTER TABLE Account DROP CONSTRAINT Positive_Balance;
```


Data-Migration Mechanics

There is no data to migrate for this database refactoring.

Access Program Update Mechanics

The access programs working with this column will include logic to handle any errors being thrown by the database when the data being written to the column does not conform to the constraint. You need to remove this code from the programs.

Drop Default Value

Remove the default value that is provided by a database from an existing table column.

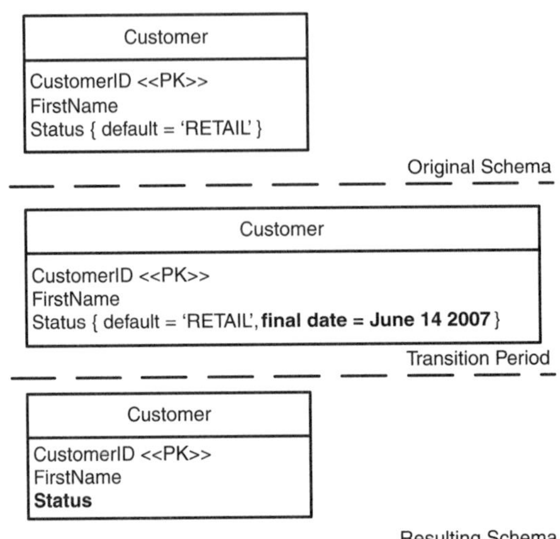

Figure 7.6 Dropping the default value for the Customer.Status column.

Motivation

We often use *Introduce Default Value* (page 186) when we want the database to persist some of the columns with data, when those columns are not being assigned any data from the application. When we no longer have a need for the database to insert data for some of the columns, because the application is providing the data that is needed, in many cases we may no longer want the database to persist the default value, because we want the application to provide the value for the column in question. In this situation, we make use of *Drop Default Value* refactoring.

Potential Tradeoffs

There are two potential challenges to consider regarding to this refactoring. First, there may be unintended side effects. Some applications may assume that a default value is persisted by the database and therefore exhibit different behavior now that columns in new rows that formerly would have some value are null now. Second, you need to improve the exception handling of external programs, which may be more effort than it is worth. If a column is non-nullable and data is not provided by the application, the database will throw an exception, which the application will not be expecting.

Schema Update Mechanics

To update the schema to remove a default value, you must remove the default value from the column of the table in the database using the **MODIFY** clause of the **ALTER TABLE** command. The following code depicts the steps to remove the default value on the *Customer.Status* column of Figure 7.6. From a database point of view, a default value of null is the same as having no default value:

```
ALTER TABLE Customer MODIFY Status DEFAULT NULL;
```

Data-Migration Mechanics

There is no data to migrate for this database refactoring.

Access Program Update Mechanics

If some access programs depend on the default value to be used by the table, you either need to add data validation code to counteract the change to the table or consider backing out of this refactoring.

The following code shows how your application code has to provide the value for the column now instead of depending on the database to provide the default value:

```
//Before code
public void createRetailCustomer
  (long customerId,String firstName) {
  stmt = DB.prepare("INSERT into customer" +
    "(Customerid, FirstName) " +
    "values (?, ?)");
  stmt.setLong(1, customerId);
  stmt.setString(2, firstName);
  stmt.execute();
}
```

```
//After code
public void createRetailCustomer
  (long customerId,String firstName) {
  stmt = DB.prepare("INSERT into customer" +
    "(Customerid, FirstName, Status) " +
    "values (?, ?, ?)");
  stmt.setLong(1, customerId);
  stmt.setString(2, firstName);
  stmt.setString(3, RETAIL);
  stmt.execute();
}
```

Drop Non-Nullable

Change an existing non-nullable column such that it accepts null values.

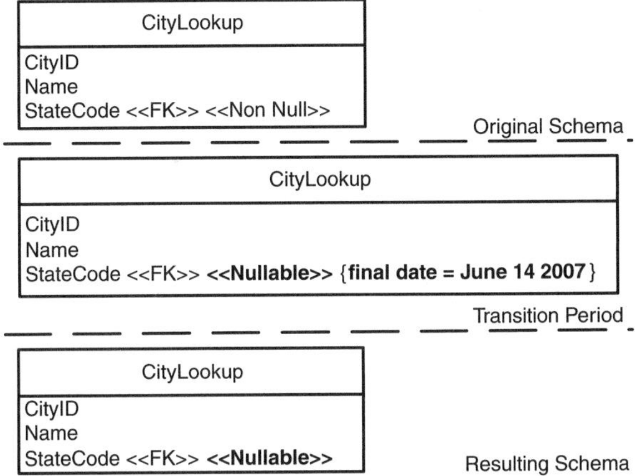

Figure 7.7 Making the CityLookup.StateID column nullable.

Motivation

There are two primary reasons to apply this refactoring. First, your business process has changed so that now parts of the entity are persisted at different times. For example, one application may create the entity, not assign a value to this column right away, and another application update the row at a later time. Second, during transition periods, you may want a particular column to be nullable. For example, when one of the applications cannot provide a value for the column because of some refactoring that the application is going through, you want to change the non-nullable constraint for a limited amount of time during the transition phase so that the application can continue working. Later on, you will apply *Make Column Non-Nullable* (page 189) to revert the constraint back to the way it was.

Potential Tradeoffs

Every application that accesses this column must be able to accept a null value, even if it merely ignores it or more likely assumes an intelligent default when it discovers the column is null. If there is an intelligent default value, you should consider the refactoring *Introduce Default Value* (page 186), too.

Schema Update Mechanics

To perform this refactoring you must simply remove the **NOT NULL** constraint from the column. This is done via the SQL command **ALTER TABLE MODIFY COLUMN**. The following code shows how to make *CityLookup.StateCode* nullable:

```
-- On 2007-06-14
ALTER TABLE CityLookup MODIFY StateCode NULL;
```

Data-Migration Mechanics

There is no data to migrate for this database refactoring.

Access Program Update Mechanics

You must refactor all the external programs currently accessing *CityLookup.StateCode* so that the code can appropriately handle null values. Because null values can be persisted, they can therefore be retrieved, implying that we need to add null value checking code. Furthermore, you want to rework any code that checks for null value exceptions that are no longer being thrown by the database.

The following code sample shows how to add null checking logic to application code:

```
//Before code
public StringBuffer getAddressString(Address address) {
  StringBuffer stringAddress = new StringBuffer();
  stringAddress = address.getStreetLine1();
  stringAddress.append(address.getStreetLine2());
  stringAddress.append(address.getCity());
  stringAddress.append(address.getPostalCode());

  stringAddress.append(states.getNameFor
  (address.getStateCode()));
  return stringAddress;
}
```

```
//After code
public StringBuffer getAddressString(Address address) {
  StringBuffer stringAddress = new StringBuffer();
  stringAddress = address.getStreetLine1();
  stringAddress.append(address.getStreetLine2());
  stringAddress.append(address.getCity());
  stringAddress.append(address.getPostalCode());
  String statecode = address.getStateCode;
  if (statecode != null) {
    stringAddress.append(states.getNameFor
    (stateCode()));
  }
  return stringAddress;
}
```

Introduce Column Constraint

Introduce a column constraint in an existing table.

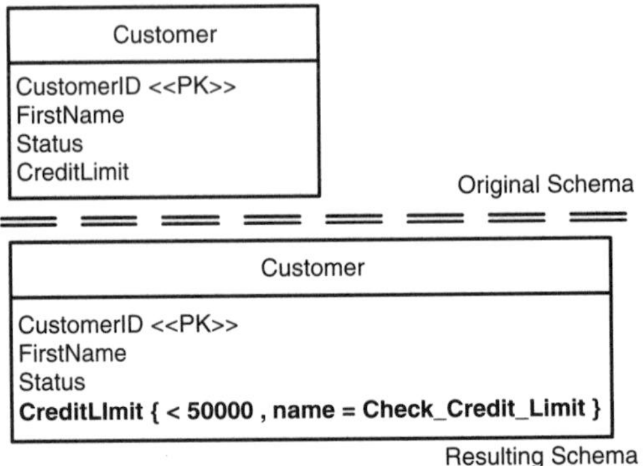

Figure 7.8 Introducing a constraint to the Customer.CreditLimit column.

When you have a need to add a non-nullable constraint on a column, you should consider the use of *Make Column Non-Nullable* refactoring (page 189). When you need to add a referential integrity constraint on a column, you should consider the use of *Add Foreign Key* (page 204).

Motivation

The most common reason why you want to apply *Introduce Column Constraint* is to ensure that all applications interacting with your database persist valid data in the column. In other words, column constraints are typically used to implement common, and relatively simple, data-validation rules.

Potential Tradeoffs

The primary issue is whether there is truly a common constraint for this data element across all programs that access it. Individual applications may have their own unique version of a constraint for this column. For example, the *Customer* table could have a *FavoriteColor* column. Your corporate standard might be the values "Red", "Green", and "Blue", yet for competitive reasons one application may allow the color "Yellow" as a fourth value, whereas two other applications will only allow "Red" and "Blue". You could argue that there should be one consistent standard across all applications, but the reality is that individual applications have good reasons for doing things a certain way. The implication is that because individual applications will implement their own versions of business rules, that even in the best of circumstances you will discover that you will have existing data within your database that does not meet the constraint conditions. One strategy is to write a script that crawls through your database tables and then reports on any constraint violations, identifying data to be fixed. These processes will be run in batch mode during nonbusy hours for the database and the application.

You may also apply this refactoring because you need to refactor an existing column constraint. Refactorings such as *Apply Standard Codes* (page 157) and *Apply Standard Type* (page 162) could force you to change the underlying code value or data type respectively of the column, requiring you to reintroduce the constraint.

Schema Update Mechanics

As depicted in Figure 7.8, to update the database schema you must simply introduce a constraint on the column, in this case *Customer.CreditLimit*. As you can see in the following code, you do this via the **ADD CONSTRAINT** clause of the **ALTER TABLE** SQL command. In this case, the credit limit must be less than $50,000 as a fraud-prevention tactic:


```
ALTER TABLE Customer ADD CONSTRAINT
  Check_Credit_Limit CHECK (CreditLimit < 50000.00);
```

Data-Migration Mechanics

Although not a data migration per se, a significant primary challenge with this refactoring is to make sure that existing data conforms to the constraint that is being applied on the column. You first need to define the constraint by working with your project stakeholders to identify what needs to be done to the data values that do not conform to the constraint being applied. Then you need to fix the source data. You may need to apply *Update Data* (page 310), as appropriate, to ensure that the values stored in this column conform to the constraint.

Access Program Update Mechanics

You need to ensure that the access programs can handle any errors being thrown by the database when the data being written to the column does not conform to the constraint. You need to look for every point in the programs where an insert or update is being done to the table, and then add the proper exception handling code, as shown in the following code:

```
//Before code
stmt = conn.prepare(
  "INSERT INTO Customer "+
  "(CustomerID,FirstName,Status,CreditLimit) "+
  "VALUES (?,?,?,?)");
stmt.setLong(1,customerId);
stmt.setString(2,firstName);
stmt.setString(3,status);
stmt.setBigDecimal(4,creditLimit);
stmt.executeUpdate();
}

//After code
stmt = conn.prepare(
  "INSERT INTO Customer "+
  "(CustomerID,FirstName,Status,CreditLimit) "+
  "VALUES (?,?,?,?)");
stmt.setLong(1,customerId);
stmt.setString(2,firstName);
stmt.setString(3,status);
stmt.setBigDecimal(4,creditLimit);
try {
  stmt.executeUpdate();
} catch (SQLException exception){
    while (exception != null) {
      int errorCode = e.getErrorCode();
      if (errorCode = 2290) {
            handleCreditLimitExceeded();
      }
    }
}
```

Introduce Common Format

Apply a consistent format to all the data values in an existing table column.

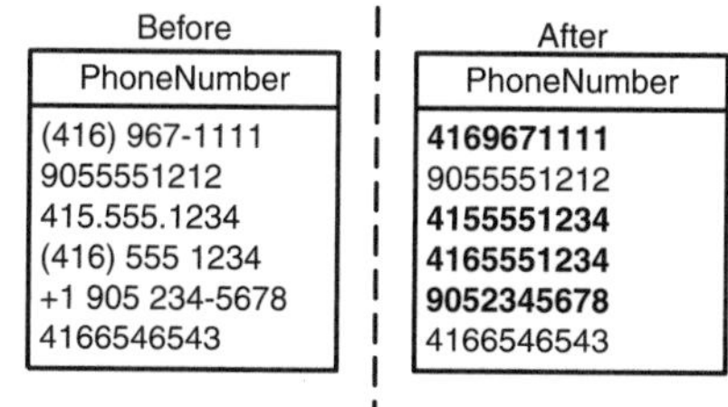

Figure 7.9 Applying a common format to the Address.PhoneNumber column.

Motivation

You typically apply *Introduce Common Format* to simplify external program code. When the same data is stored in different formats, external programs require unnecessarily complex logic to work with your data. It is generally better to have the data in uniform format so that applications interfacing with your database do not have to handle multiple formats. For example, when the values in *Customer.Phonenumber* are '4163458899', '905-777-8889', and '(990) 345-6666', every application accessing that column must be able to parse all three formats. This problem is even worse when an external program parses the data in several places, often because the program is poorly designed. A common format enables you to reduce the validation code dealing with *Customer.Phonenumber* and to reduce the complexity of your display logic—although the data is stored as 1234567890, it might be output in a report as (123) 456-7890.

Another common reason is to conform to your existing corporate standards. Often when applying *Use Official Data Source* (page 271), you discover that your current data format differs from that of the "official" data source, and therefore your data needs to be reformatted for consistency.

Potential Tradeoffs

Standardizing the format for the data values can be tricky when multiple formats exist within the same column. For example, the *Customer.Phonenumber* column could be stored using 15 different formats—you would need code that can detect and then convert the data in each row to the standard format.

Luckily, the code to do this conversion should already exist within one or more external programs.

Schema Update Mechanics

To *Introduce Common Format* to a column, you must first identify the standard format. You need to settle on the "official" format for the data values. The data format may be an existing standard or it may be a new one defined by your business stakeholders, but either way the format must be accepted by your project stakeholder(s). Then, you must identify the column(s) where the format needs to be applied. You apply *Introduce Common Format* one column at a time; smaller refactorings are always easier to implement and then deploy into production. You will potentially need to apply it several times to ensure consistency across your database.

Data-Migration Mechanics

The first step is to identify the various formats currently being used within the column, often a simple **SELECT** statement will get you this information, to help you understand what your data migration code needs to do. The second step is to write the code to convert the existing data into the standard format. You may want to write this code using either standard SQL data manipulation language (DML), an application programming language such as Java or C#, or with an extract-transform-load (ETL) tool. When small numbers of rows need to be updated, a simple SQL script that updates the target table(s) is sufficient. When you want to update a large amount of data, or in cases where the code in transactional tables is being changed, apply *Update Data* (page 310) instead.

The following code depicts the DML to update data in the *Customer* table:

```
UPDATE Customer SET PhoneNumber =
      REPLACE(PhoneNumber,'-','');

UPDATE Customer SET PhoneNumber =
      REPLACE(PhoneNumber,' ','');

UPDATE Customer SET PhoneNumber =
      REPLACE(PhoneNumber,'(','');

UPDATE Customer SET PhoneNumber =
      REPLACE(PhoneNumber,')','');
```

```
UPDATE Customer SET PhoneNumber =
      REPLACE(PhoneNumber,'+1','');

UPDATE Customer SET PhoneNumber =
      REPLACE(PhoneNumber,'.','');
```

As you can see, we are updating one type of format at a time. You can also encapsulate the individual changes using a stored procedure, as shown here:

```
UPDATE Address SET PhoneNumber =
FormatPhoneNumber(PhoneNumber);
```

Access Program Update Mechanics

When *Introduce Common Format* is applied, the following aspects of the external programs must be examined:

1. **Cleansing code.** Your external programs will contain logic that accepts the various formats and converts them to the format that they want to work with. You may even be able to use some of this existing code as the basis for your data migration code above.
2. **Validation code.** You may need to update source code that validates the values of data attributes. For example, code that looks for formats such as Phonenumber = 'NNN-NNN-NNNN' must be updated to use the new data format.
3. **Display code.** Your user interface code will often include logic to display data elements in a specific format, often one that is not being used for storage (for example, NNNNNNNNNN for storage, (NNN) NNN-NNNN for display). This includes display logic for both your screens and reports.
4. **Test data.** Your test data, or test data generation code, must now be changed to conform to the new standard data format. You may also want to add new test cases to test for data rows in inappropriate formats.

Introduce Default Value

Let the database provide a default value for an existing table column.

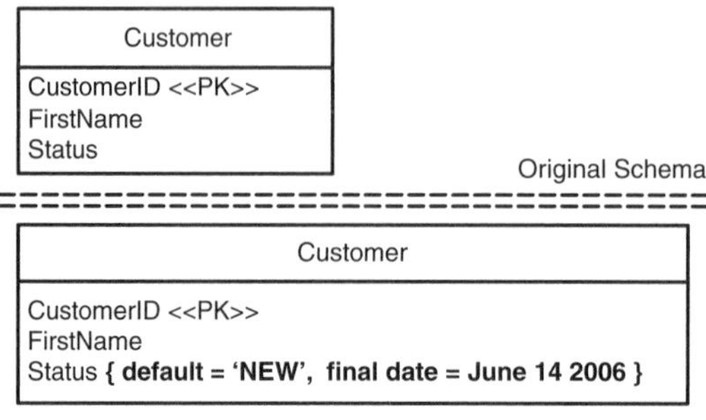

Figure 7.10 Introducing a default value on the Customer.Status column.

Motivation

We often want the value of a column to have a default value populated when a new row is added to a table. However, the insert statements may not always populate that column, often because the column has been added after the original insert was written or simply because the application code that is submitting the insert does not require that column. Generally, we have found that *Introduce Default Value* is useful when we want to make the column non-nullable later on (see the database refactoring *Make Column Non-Nullable* on page 189).

Potential Tradeoffs

There are several potential challenges to consider regarding this refactoring:

- **Identifying a true default can be difficult.** When many applications share the same database, they may have different default values for the same column, often for good reasons. Or it may simply be that your business stakeholders cannot agree on a single value—you need to work closely with them to negotiate the correct value.
- **Unintended side effects.** Some applications may assume that a null value within a column actually means something and will therefore exhibit

different behavior now that columns in new rows that formerly would have been null now are not.

- **Confused context.** When a column is not used by an application, the default value may introduce confusion over the column's usage with the application team.

Schema Update Mechanics

This is a single-step refactoring. You merely use the SQL **ALTER TABLE** command to define the default value for the column. An effective date for this refactoring is optionally indicated to tell people when this default value was first introduced into the schema. The following code shows how you would introduce a default value on the *Customer.Status* column, as depicted in Figure 7.10:

```
ALTER TABLE Customer MODIFY Status DEFAULT 'NEW';

COMMENT ON Customer.Status 'Default value of NEW will be inserted when there is no data present
on the insert as of June 14 2006';
```

Data-Migration Mechanics

The existing rows may already have null values in this column, rows that will not be automatically updated as a result of adding a default value. Furthermore, there may be invalid values in some rows, too. You need to examine the values contained in the column—simply looking at a unique list of values may suffice—to determine whether you need to do any updates. If appropriate, you need to write a script that runs through the table to introduce the default value to these rows.

Access Program Update Mechanics

On the surface, it seems unlikely that access programs would be affected by the introduction of a default value; however, appearances can be deceiving. Potential issues you may run across include the following:

1. **Invariants are broken by the new value.** For example, a class may assume that the value of a color column is red, green, or blue, but the default value has now been defined as yellow.

2. **Code exists to apply default values.** There may now be extraneous source code that checks for a null value and introduces the default value programmatically. This code should be removed.

3. **Existing source code assumes a different default value.** For example, existing code may look for the default value of none, which was set programmatically in the past, and if found it gives users the option to change the color. Now the default value is yellow, so this code will never be invoked.

You need to analyze the access programs thoroughly, and then update them appropriately, before introducing a default value to a column.

Make Column Non-Nullable

Change an existing column such that it does not accept any null values.

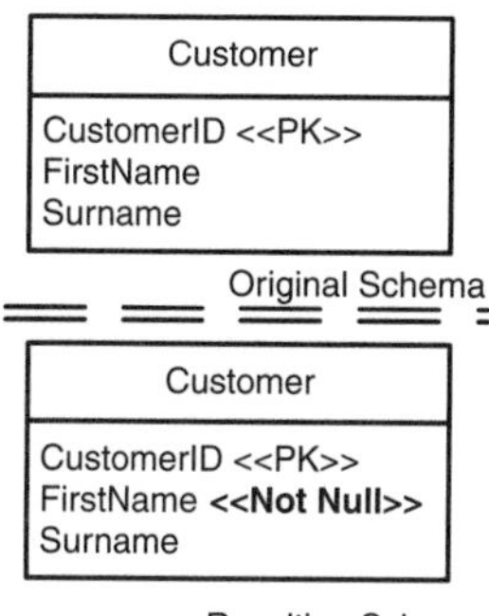

Figure 7.11 Making the Customer.FirstName column non-nullable.

Motivation

There are two reasons to apply *Make Column Non-Nullable*. First, you want to enforce business rules at the database level such that every application updating this column is forced to provide a value for it. Second, you want to remove repetitious logic within applications that implement a not-null check—if you are not allowed to insert a null value, you will never receive one.

Potential Tradeoffs

Any external program that updates rows within the given table must provide a value for the column—some programs may currently assume that the column is nullable and therefore not provide such a value. Whenever an update or insertion occurs, you must ensure that a value is provided, implying that the external programs need to be updated and/or the database itself must provide a valid value. One technique we have found useful is to assign a default value using *Introduce Default Value* (page 186) for this column.

Schema Update Mechanics

As depicted in Figure 7.11, to perform *Make Column Non-Nullable*, you must simply add a **NOT NULL** constraint to the column. This is done via the SQL command **ALTER TABLE**, as shown in the following code:

```
ALTER TABLE Customer
  MODIFY FirstName NOT NULL;
```

Depict Models Simply

Figure 7.11 shows an interesting style issue—it does not indicate in the original schema that *FirstName* is nullable. Because it is common to assume that columns that are not part of the primary key are nullable, it would merely clutter the diagram to include the stereotype of <<nullable>> on most columns. Your diagrams are more readable when you depict them simply.

Data-Migration Mechanics

You may need to clean the existing data because you cannot make a column non-nullable if there are existing rows with a null value in the column. To address this problem, write a script that replaces the rows containing a null with an appropriate value.

The following code shows how to clean the existing data to support the change depicted in Figure 7.11. The initial step is to make sure that the *FirstName* column does not contain any null values; if it does, we have to update the data in the table:

```
SELECT count(FirstName) FROM Customer
  WHERE
    FirstName IS NULL;
```

If we do find rows where *Customer.FirstName* is null, we have to go ahead and apply some algorithm and make sure that *Customer.FirstName* does not contain any null values. In this example, we set *Customer.FirstName* to '???' to indicate that we need to update this record. This strategy was chosen carefully by our project stakeholders because the data being changed is critical to the business:

```
UPDATE Customer SET FirstName='???'
  WHERE
    FirstName IS NULL;
```

Access Program Update Mechanics

You must refactor all the external programs currently accessing *Customer.FirstName* to provide an appropriate value whenever they modify a row within the table. Furthermore, they must also detect and then handle any new exceptions that are thrown by the database.

If you are unsure about where all this column is used and do not have a way to change all those instances, you can apply the database refactoring *Introduce Default Value* (page 186) so that the database provides a default value when no value is provided by the application. This may be an interim strategy for you—after sufficient time has passed and you believe that the access programs have been updated, or at least until you are willing to quickly deal with the handful of access programs that were not updated, you can apply *Drop Default Value* (page 174) and thereby improve performance.

The following code shows the before and after state when the *Make Column Non-Nullable* refactoring is applied. In the example, we have decided to throw an exception when null values are found:

```
//Before code
stmt = conn.prepare(
  "INSERT INTO Customer "+
  "(CustomerID,FirstName,Surname) "+
  "VALUES (?,?,?,)");
stmt.setLong(1,customerId);
stmt.setString(2,firstName);
stmt.setString(3,surname);
stmt.executeUpdate();
}

//After code
if (firstName == null) {
  throw new CustomerFirstNameCannotBeNullException();
};
stmt = conn.prepare(
  "INSERT INTO Customer "+
  "(CustomerID,FirstName,Surname) "+
  "VALUES (?,?,?,)");
stmt.setLong(1,customerId);
stmt.setString(2,firstName);
stmt.setString(3,surname);
stmt.executeUpdate();
}
```

Move Data

Move the data contained within a table, either all or a subset of its columns, to another existing table.

Schema:

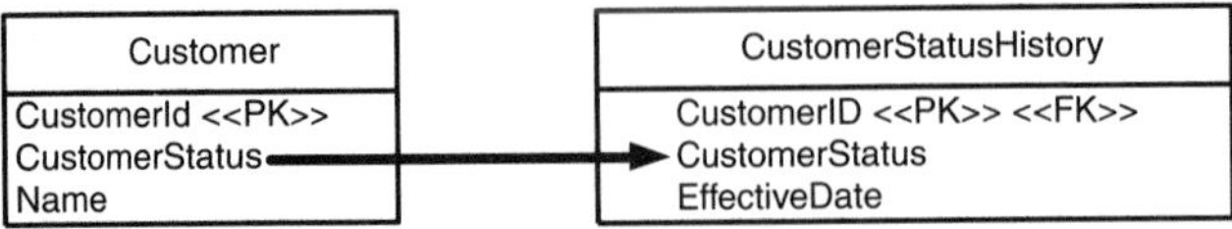

Data Values Before:

Customer		
CustomerID	CustomerStatus	Name
1	Active	Allen, B.
2	Pending	Jordan, H.
3	Active	Wayne, B.
4	Active	Parker, P.
5	In Arrears	Banner, B.

Data Values After:

Customer		
CustomerID	CustomerStatus	Name
1	**NULL**	Allen, B.
2	**NULL**	Jordan, H.
3	**NULL**	Wayne, B.
4	**NULL**	Parker, P.
5	**NULL**	Banner, B.

CustomerStatusHistory		
CustomerID	CustomerStatus	EffectiveDate
1	**Active**	**2006-04-09**
2	**Pending**	**2006-04-09**
3	**Active**	**2006-04-09**
4	**Active**	**2006-04-09**
5	**In Arrears**	**2006-04-09**

Figure 7.12 Moving status data from Customer to CustomerStatusHistory.

Motivation

You typically want to apply *Move Data* as the result of structural changes with your table design; but as always, application of this refactoring depends on the situation. You may want to apply *Move Data* as the result of the following:

- **Column renaming.** When you rename a column, the process is first to introduce a new column with the new name, move the original data to the new column, and then remove the original column using *Drop Column* (page 72).

- **Vertically splitting a table.** When you apply *Split Table* (page 145) to vertically reorganize an existing table, you need to move data from the source table into the new tables that have been split off from it.
- **Horizontally splitting a table.** Sometimes a horizontal slice of data is moved from a table into another table with the same structure because the original table has grown so large that performance has degraded. For example, you might move all the rows in your *Customer* table that represent European customers into a *EuropeanCustomer* table. This horizontal split might be the first step toward building an inheritance hierarchy (for example, *EuropeanCustomer* inherits from *Customer*) within your database and/or because you intend to add specific columns for Europeans.
- **Splitting a column.** With *Split Column* (page 140), you need to move data to the new column(s) from the source.
- **Merging a table or column.** Applying *Merge Tables* (page 96) or *Merge Columns* (page 92) requires you to move data from the source(s) into the target(s).
- **Consolidation of data without involving structural changes.** Data is often stored in several locations. For example, you may have several customer-oriented tables, one to store Canadian customer information and several for customers who live in various parts of the United States, all of which have the same basic structure. As the result of a corporate reorganization, the data for the provinces of British Columbia and Alberta are moved from the *CanadianCustomer* table to the *WestCoastCustomer* table to reflect the data ownership within your organization.
- **Move data before removing a table or column.** Applying *Drop Table* (page 77) or *Drop Column* (page 72) may require you to apply *Move Data* first if some or all of the data stored in the table or column is still required.

Potential Tradeoffs

Moving data between columns can be tricky at any time, but it is particularly challenging when millions of rows are involved. While the move occurs, the applications accessing the data may be impacted—you will likely want to lock the data during the move—affecting performance and availability of the data for the application, because the applications now cannot access data during this move.

Schema Update Mechanics

To perform *Move Data*, you must first identify data to move and any dependencies on it. Should the corresponding row in the other table be deleted or should the column value in the corresponding be nulled/zeroed out, or should the corresponding value be left alone? Is the row being moved or are we just moving some column(s).

Second, you must identify the data destination. Where is the data being moved to? To another table or tables? Is the data being transformed while its being moved? When you move rows, you must make sure that all the dependent tables that have foreign key references to the table where the data is being moved to now reference the table where the destination of the move is.

Data-Migration Mechanics

When small amounts of data need to be moved, you will likely find that a simple SQL script that inserts the source data into the target location, and then deletes the source, is sufficient. For large amounts of data, you must take a more sophisticated approach because of the time it will take to move the data. You may need to export the source data and then import it into the target location. You can also use database utilities such as Oracle's SQLLDR or a bulk loader.

Figure 7.12 depicts how we moved the data within the *Customer.Status* column to *CustomerStatusHistory* table to enable us to track the status of a customer over a period of time. The following code depicts the DML to move the data from the *Customer.Status* column to the *CustomerStatusHistory*. First, we insert the data into the *CustomerStatusHistory* from the *Customer* table, and later we update the *Customer.Status* column to **NULL**:

```
INSERT INTO CustomerStatusHistory (CustomerId,Status,EffectiveDate)
SELECT CustomerId,Status,Sysdate FROM Customer;
UPDATE Customer SET Status = NULL;
```

Access Program Update Mechanics

When *Move Data* is applied as the result of another database refactoring, the applications should have been updated to reflect that refactoring. However, when *Move Data* is applied to support a reorganization of data within an existing schema, it is possible that external application code will need to be updated. For example, **SELECT** clauses may need to be reworked to access the moved data from the new source(s) for it. The following code snippet shows how the *getCustomerStatus()* method changes:

```
//Before code
public String getCustomerStatus(Customer customer) {
  return customer.getStatus();
}

//After code
public String getCustomerStatus(Customer customer) throws SQLException {
  stmt.prepare(
    "SELECT Status "+
    "FROM CustomerStatusHistory " +
    "WHERE " +
    "CustomerId = ? "+
    "AND EffectiveDate < TRUNC(SYSDATE) "+
    "ORDER BY EffectiveDate DESC");
    stmt.setLong(1,customer.getCustomerId);
  ResultSet rs = stmt.execute();
  if (rs.next()) {
    return rs.getString("Status");
  }
  throw new CustomerStatusNotFoundInHistoryException();
}
```

Replace Type Code With Property Flags

Replace a code column with individual property flags, usually implemented as Boolean columns, within the same table column.

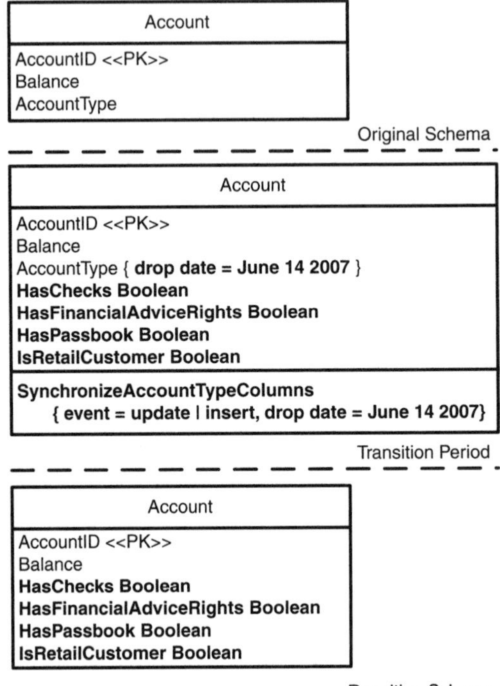

Figure 7.13 Replacing the AccountType code column with property flags.

Note that some database products support native Boolean columns. In other database products, you can use alternative data types for Boolean values (for example, NUMBER(1) in Oracle, where a value 1 means TRUE and 0 means FALSE).

Motivation

The refactoring *Replace Type Code With Property Flags* is used to do the following:

- **Denormalize for performance.** When you want to improve performance, by having a column for each instance of the type code. For example, the

Address.Type column has values of *Home* and *Business*; it would be replaced by *isHome* and *isBusiness* property flag columns. This enables a more efficient search because it is faster to compare two Boolean values than it is to compare two string values.

- **Simplify selections.** Type code columns work well when the types are mutually exclusive; when they are not, however, they become problematic to search on. For example, assume that it is possible for an address to be either a home or a business. With the type code approach, you would need the *Address.Type* column values of *Home*, *Business*, and *HomeAnd Business*, for example. To obtain a list of all business addresses, you would need to run a query along the lines of **SELECT * FROM Address WHERE Type = "Business" OR Type = "HomeAndBusiness"**. As you can imagine, this query would need to be updated if a new kind of address type, such as a vacation home address, was added that could also be a potential business. With the property flag column approach, the query would look like **SELECT * FROM Address WHERE isBusiness = TRUE**. This query is simple and would not need to be changed if a new address type was added.
- **Decouple applications from type code values.** When you have multiple applications using *Account.AccountType* of Figure 7.13, making changes to the values becomes difficult because most applications will have hard coded the values. When these type codes are replaced with property flag columns, the applications will only have to check for the standard TRUE or FALSE values. With a type code column, the applications are coupled to the name of the column and the values within the column; with property flag columns, the applications are merely coupled to the names of the columns.

Potential Tradeoffs

Every time you want to add a new type of value, you must change the table structure. For example, when you want to add a money market account type, you must add the *isMoneyMarket* column to the *Account* table. This will not be desirable after awhile because tables with large numbers of columns are more difficult to understand than tables with smaller numbers of columns. The result of joins with this table increase in size each time you add a new type column. However, it is very easy to add a column independent of the rest of the columns. With the type code column approach, the column is coupled to all the applications accessing it.

Schema Update Mechanics

To *Replace Type Code With Property Flags* to your database table, you must do the following:

1. **Identify the type code to replace.** Find the type code column that you need to replace, which is *Account.AccountType* in our example. You should also find out the instances of the type code to replace—for example, when you want to replace the *AddressType* code, you need to find all the different types of addresses, and replace all of the instances of *AddressType*.

2. **Introduce property flag columns.** After you have identified the instances of the type codes that you want to replace, you have to add those many columns to the table using *Introduce New Column* (page 301). In Figure 7.13, we are going to add the *HasChecks*, *HasFinancialAdviceRights*, *HasPassbook*, and *IsRetailCustomer* columns to *Account*.

3. **Remove the type code column.** After all the type codes have been converted to property flags, you have to remove the type code column using *Drop Column* (page 72).

Figure 7.13 shows how we change the *Account.AccountType* column to use type flag columns for every instance of the *AccountType* data. In the example, we have four different types of accounts that will be converted to type flag columns, named *HasChecks, HasFinancialAdviceRights, HasPassbook*, and *isRetailCustomer*. The following SQL depicts how to add the four type flag columns to the *Account* table, the synchronization trigger during the transition period, the code to drop the original column, and the trigger after the transition period ends:

```
ALTER TABLE Account ADD COLUMN HasChecks Boolean;
COMMENT ON Account.HasChecks "Replaces AccountType of Checks"

ALTER TABLE Account ADD COLUMN HasFinancialAdviceRights Boolean;
COMMENT ON Account.HasFinancialAdviceRights "Replaces AccountType of FinancialAdviceRights"

ALTER TABLE Account ADD COLUMN HasPassbook Boolean;
COMMENT ON Account.HasPassbook "Replaces AccountType of Passbook"

ALTER TABLE Account ADD COLUMN isRetailCustomer Boolean;
COMMENT ON Account. isRetailCustomer "Replaces
AccountType of RetailCustomer"

CREATE OR REPLACE TRIGGER SynchronizeAccountTypeColumns
BEFORE INSERT OR UPDATE
ON ACCOUNT
REFERENCING OLD AS OLD NEW AS NEW
FOR EACH ROW
```

```
DECLARE
BEGIN
  IF (:NEW.HasChecks IS NULL AND :NEW.AccountType = 'CHECKS') THEN
    :NEW.HasChecks := TRUE;
  END IF;
  IF (:NEW.HasFinancialAdviceRights IS NULL AND :NEW.AccountType = 'FINANCIALADVICERIGHTS') THEN
    :NEW.HasFinancialAdviceRights := TRUE;
  END IF;
  IF (:NEW.HasPassbook IS NULL AND :NEW.AccountType = 'PASSBOOK') THEN
    NEW.HasPassbook := TRUE;
  END IF;
  IF (:NEW.isRetailCustomer IS NULL AND
:NEW.AccountType = 'RETAILCUSTOMER') THEN
    :NEW.isRetailCustomer := TRUE;
  END IF;
END;
/

--On June 14 2007
ALTER TABLE Account DROP COLUMN AccountType;
DROP TRIGGER SynchronizeAccountTypeColumns;
```

Data-Migration Mechanics

You have to write data-migration scripts to update the property flags based on the value of the type code you can use *Update Data* (page 310). During the transition phase, when the type code column and the type flag columns also exist, we have to keep the columns synchronized, so that the applications using the data get consistent information. This can be achieved by using database triggers. The following SQL syntax shows how to update the existing data in the *Account* table (see *Update Data* for details):


```
UPDATE Account SET HasChecks = TRUE
  WHERE AccountType = 'CHECKS';
UPDATE Account SET HasChecks = FALSE
  WHERE HasChecks != TRUE;

UPDATE Account SET HasFinancialAdviceRights = TRUE
  WHERE AccountType = 'FINANCIALADVICERIGHTS';
UPDATE Account SET HasFinancialAdviceRights = FALSE
  WHERE HasFinancialAdviceRights != TRUE;

UPDATE Account SET HasPassbook = TRUE
  WHERE Accounttype = 'PASSBOOK';
UPDATE Account SET HasPassbook = FALSE
  WHERE HasPassbook != TRUE;
```

```
UPDATE Account SET isRetailCustomer = TRUE
  WHERE Accounttype ='RETAILCUSTOMER';
UPDATE Account SET isRetailCustomer = FALSE
  WHERE isRetailCustomer!= TRUE;
```

Access Program Update Mechanics

When *Replace Type Code With Property Flags* is applied, you need to update external programs in two ways. First, the SQL code (or meta data) that saves, deletes, and retrieves data from this column must be updated to work with the individual type flag columns and not *AccountType*. For example, when we have **SELECT * FROM Account WHERE AccountType = 'XXXX'**, this SQL will change to **SELECT * FROM Account WHERE isXXXX = TRUE**. Similarly, you will have to change the program code to update the type flag columns rather than *AccountType* during an insert or update operation.

Second, you may need to update application code that works with the column. For example, comparison code such as **Customer.AddressType = 'Home'** must be updated to work with *isHome*.

The following code depicts how the *Account* class changes when you replace the account type code with property flags:


```
//Before code
public class Account {

private Long accountID;
private BigDecimal balance;
private String accountType;
private Boolean FALSE = Boolean.FALSE;
private Boolean TRUE = Boolean.TRUE;

public Long getAccountID() {
  return accountID;
}

public BigDecimal getBalance() {
  return balance;
}

public Boolean HasChecks() {
  return accountType.equals("CHECKS");
}

public Boolean HasFinancialAdviceRights() {
  return accountType.equals("FINANCIALADVICERIGHTS");
}

public Boolean HasPassBook() {
  return accountType.equals("PASSBOOK");
}
```

```
public Boolean IsRetailCustomer() {
  return accountType.equals("RETAILCUSTOMER");
}
}

//After code
public class Account {

private Long accountID;
private BigDecimal balance;
private Boolean HasChecks;
private Boolean HasFinancialAdviceRights;
private Boolean HasPassBook;
private Boolean IsRetailCustomer;

public Long getAccountID() {
  return accountID;
}

public BigDecimal getBalance() {
  return balance;
}

public Boolean HasChecks() {
  return HasChecks;
}

public Boolean HasFinancialAdviceRights() {
  return HasFinancialAdviceRights;
}

public Boolean HasPassBook() {
  return HasPassBook;
}

public Boolean IsRetailCustomer() {
  return IsRetailCustomer;
}
}
```

Chapter 8

Referential Integrity Refactorings

Referential integrity refactorings are changes that ensure that a referenced row exists within another table and/or that ensures that a row that is no longer needed is removed appropriately. The referential integrity refactorings are as follows:

- Add Foreign Key Constraint
- Add Trigger For Calculated Column
- Drop Foreign Key Constraint
- Introduce Cascading Delete
- Introduce Hard Delete
- Introduce Soft Delete
- Introduce Trigger For History

Add Foreign Key Constraint

Add a foreign key constraint to an existing table to enforce a relationship to another table.

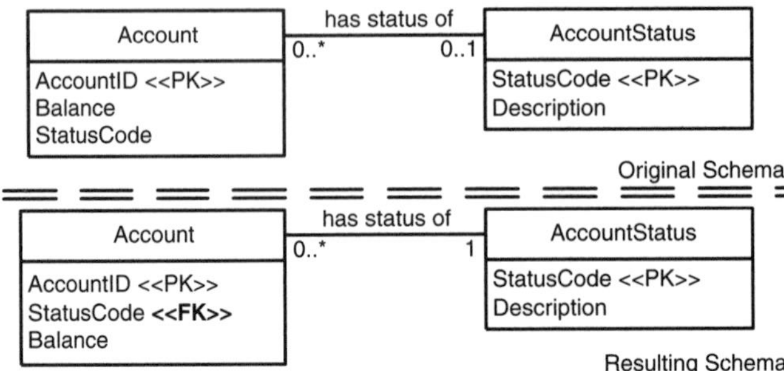

Figure 8.1 Adding a foreign key constraint to the Account.AccountStatus column.

Motivation

The primary reason to apply *Add Foreign Key Constraint* is to enforce data dependencies at the database level, ensuring that the database enforces some referential integrity (RI) business rules preventing invalid data from being persisted. This is particularly important when several applications access the same database because you cannot count on them enforcing data-integrity rules consistently.

Potential Tradeoffs

Foreign key constraints reduce performance within your database because the existence of the row in the foreign table will be verified whenever the source row is updated. Furthermore, when adding a foreign key constraint to the database, you must be careful about the order of inserts, updates, and deletions. For example, in Figure 8.1, you cannot add a row in *Account* without the corresponding row in *AccountStatus*. The implication is that your application, or your persistence layer as the case may be, must be aware of the table dependencies in the database. Luckily, many databases allow commit-time enforcing of the database constraints, enabling you to insert/update or delete rows in any order as long as data integrity is maintained at commit time. This type of feature makes development easy and provides higher incentive to use foreign key constraints.

Schema Update Mechanics

As depicted in Figure 8.1, to update the schema to add a foreign key constraint, you must do the following:

1. **Choose a constraint checking strategy.** Depending on your database product, it will support one or two ways to enforce foreign keys. First, with the immediate checking method, the foreign key constraint is checked when the data is inserted/updated or deleted from the table. The immediate checking method is better at failing faster and will force you to consider the order of database changes (inserts, updates, and deletes). Second, with the deferred checking method, the foreign key constraint is checked when the transaction is committed from the application. This method allows you the flexibility to not worry about the order of database changes because the constraints are checked at commit time. This approach also enables you to cache all the dirty objects and write them in a batch; you just have to make sure that at commit time the database is in a clean state. In either case, the database returns an exception when the first foreign key constraint fails. (There could be several.)

2. **Create the foreign key constraint.** Create the foreign key constraint in the database via the **ADD CONSTRAINT** clause of the **ALTER TABLE** statement. The database constraint should be named according to your database naming conventions for clarity and effective error reporting by the database. If you are using the commit-time checking of constraints, there may be performance degradation because the database will be checking the integrity of the data at commit time, a significant problem with tables with millions of rows.

3. **Introduce an index for the primary key of the foreign table (optional).** Databases use select statements on the referenced tables to verify whether the data being entered in the child table is valid. If the *AccountStatus.StatusCode* column does not have an index, you may experience significant performance degradation and need to consider applying the *Introduce Index* (page 248) database refactoring. When you create an index, you will increase the performance of constraint checking, but you will be decreasing the performance of update, insert, and delete on *AccountStatus* because the database now has to maintain the added index.

The following code depicts the steps to add a foreign key constraint to the table. In this example, we are creating the constraint such that the foreign key constraint is checked immediately upon data modification:

```
ALTER TABLE Account
  ADD CONSTRAINT FK_Account_AccountStatus
  FOREIGN KEY (StatusCode)
  REFERENCES AccountStatus;
```

In this example, we are creating the foreign key constraint such that the foreign key is checked at commit time:

```
ALTER TABLE Account
  ADD CONSTRAINT FK_Account_AccountStatus
  FOREIGN KEY (StatusCode)
  REFERENCES AccountStatus
  INITIALLY DEFERRED;
```

Data-Migration Mechanics

To support the addition of a foreign key constraint to a table, you may discover that you need to update the existing data within the database first. This is a multi-step process:

1. **Ensure the referenced data exists.** First, we need to ensure that the rows being referred to exist in *AccountStatus*. You need to analyze the existing data in both *Account* and *AccountStatus* to determine whether there are missing rows in *AccountStatus*. The easiest way to do this is to compare the count of the number of rows in *Account* to the count of the number of rows resulting in the join of *Account* and *AccountStatus*.

2. **Ensure that the foreign table contains all required rows.** If the counts are different, either you are missing rows in *AccountStatus* and/or there are incorrect values in *Account.StatusCode*. First, create a list of unique values of *Account.StatusCode* and compare it with the list of values from *AccountStatus.StatusCode*. If the first list contains values that are valid but do not appear in the second list, *AccountStatus* needs to be updated. Second, there may still be valid values that appear in neither list but are still valid within your business domain. To identify these values, you need to work closely with your project stakeholders; better yet, just wait until they actually need the data rows and then add them at that time.

3. **Ensure that source table's foreign key column contains valid values.** Update the lists from the previous step. Any differences in the list must

now be the result of invalid or missing values in the *Account.StatusCode* column. You need to update these rows appropriately, either with an automated script that sets a default value or by manually updating them.

4. **Introduce a default value for the foreign key column.** You may optionally need to make the database insert default values when the external programs do not provide a value for *Account.StatusCode*. See the database refactoring *Introduce Default Value* (page 186).

For the example of Figure 8.1, you must ensure that the data before the foreign key constraint is added is clean; if it is not, you must update the data. Let's assume that we have some *Account* rows where the status is not set or is not part of the *AccountStatus* table. In this situation, you must update the *Account.Status* column to some known value that exists in the *AccountStatus* table:

```
UPDATE Account SET Status = 'DORMANT'
  WHERE
    Status NOT IN (SELECT StatusCode FROM AccountStatus)
    AND Status IS NOT NULL;
```

In other cases, you may have the *Account.Status* containing a null value. If so, update the *Account.Status* column with a known value, as shown here:

```
UPDATE Account SET Status = 'NEW'
  WHERE Status IS NULL;
```

Access Program Update Mechanics

You must identify and then update any external programs that modify data in the table where the foreign key constraint was added. Issues to look for include the following:

1. **Similar RI code.** Some external programs will implement the RI business rule that will now be handled via the foreign key constraint within the database. This code should be removed.

2. **Different RI code.** Some external programs will include code that enforces different RI business rules than what you are about to implement. This implication is that you either need to reconsider adding this foreign key constraint because there is no consensus within your organization regarding the business rule that it implements or you need to rework the code to work based on this new version (from its point of view) of the business rule.

3. **Nonexistent RI code.** Some external programs will not even be aware of the RI business rule pertaining to these data tables.

All external programs must be updated to handle any exception(s) thrown by the database as the result of the new foreign key constraint. The following code shows how the application code needs to change to handle exceptions throws by the database:

```
// Before code
stmt = conn.prepare(
  "INSERT INTO Account(AccountID,StatusCode,Balance) "+
  "VALUES (?,?,?)";
stmt.setLong(1,accountId);
stmt.setString(2,statusCode);
stmt.setBigDecimal(3,balance);
stmt.executeUpdate();

//After code
stmt = conn.prepare(
  "INSERT INTO Account(AccountID,StatusCode,Balance) "+
  "VALUES (?,?,?)";
stmt.setLong(1,accountId);
stmt.setString(2,statusCode);
stmt.setBigDecimal(3,balance);
try {
  stmt.executeUpdate();
} catch (SQLException exception){
      int errorCode = exception.getErrorCode();
      if (errorCode = 2291) {
          handleParentRecordNotFoundError();
      }
      if (errorCode = 2292) {
          handleParentDeletedWhenChildFoundError();
      }
}
```

Add Trigger For Calculated Column

Introduce a new trigger to update the value contained in a calculated column. The calculated column may have been previously introduced by the *Introduce Calculated Column* refactoring (page 81).

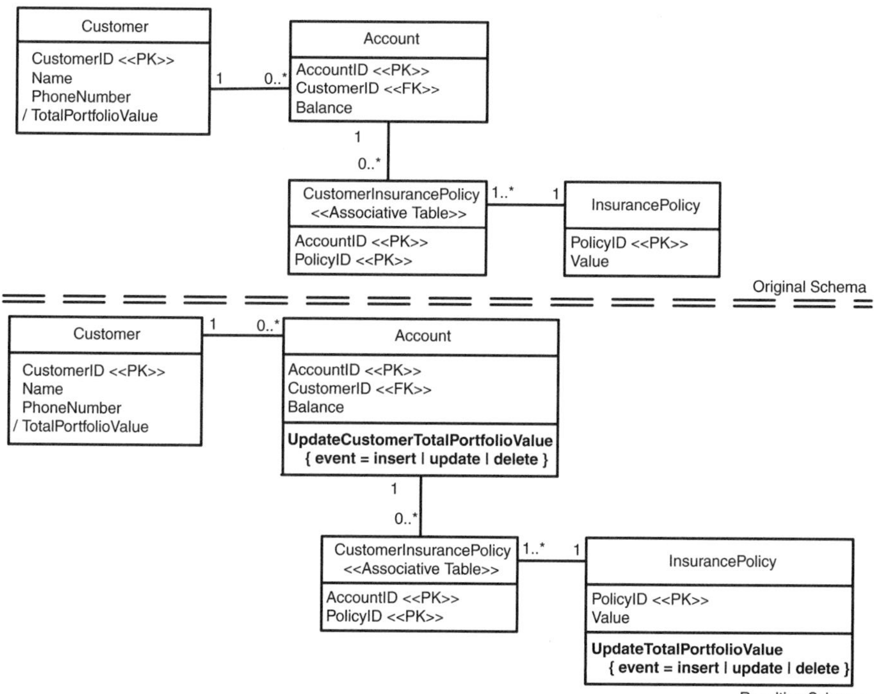

Figure 8.2 Adding a trigger to calculate Customer.TotalPortfolioValue.

Motivation

The primary reason you would apply *Add Trigger For Calculated Column* is to ensure that the value contained in the column is updated properly whenever the source data changes. This should be done by the database so that all the applications are not required to do so.

Potential Tradeoffs

When a calculated column is based on complex algorithms, or simply on data located in several places, your trigger will implement a lot of business logic. This may lead to inconsistency with similar business logic implemented within your applications.

The source data used by the trigger might be updated within the scope of a transaction. If the trigger fails, the transaction fails, too, causing it to be rolled back. This will likely be perceived as an undesirable side effect by external programs.

When a calculated column is based on data from the same table, it may not be possible to use a trigger to do the update because many database products do not allow this.

Schema Update Mechanics

Applying *Add Trigger For Calculated Column* can be complicated because of data dependencies of the calculated column. You will need to do the following:

1. **Determine whether triggers can be used to update the calculated column.** In Figure 8.2, the *TotalPortfolioValue* column is calculated. You know that because of the forward slash (/) in front of the name, a UML convention. When *TotalPortfolioValue* and the source data is in the same table, you likely cannot use triggers to update the data value.

2. **Identify the source data.** You have to identify the source data, and how it should be used, to determine the value of the calculated column.

3. **Identify the table to contain the column.** You have to identify which table should include the calculated column if it does not already exist. To do this, ask yourself which business entity the calculated column describes best. For example, a customer's credit risk indicator is most applicable to the *Customer* entity.

4. **Add the column.** If the column does not exist, add it via the **ALTER TABLE ADD COLUMN** command. Use *Introduce New Column* (page 301).

5. **Add the trigger(s).** You need to add a trigger to each table that contains source data pertinent to calculating the value. In this case, the source data for *TotalPortfolioValue* exists in the *Account* and *InsurancePolicy* tables. Therefore, we need a trigger for each table, *UpdateCustomerTotalPortfolioValue* and *UpdateTotalPortfolioValue*, respectively.

The following code shows you how to add the two triggers:

```
-Update the TotalPortfolioValue with the trigger.
CREATE OR REPLACE TRIGGER
UpdateCustomerTotalPortfolioValue
  AFTER UPDATE OR INSERT OR DELETE
  ON Account
  REFERENCING OLD AS OLD NEW AS NEW
  FOR EACH ROW
  DECLARE
    BEGIN
      UpdateCustomerWithPortfolioValue;
    END;
  END;
/

CREATE OR REPLACE TRIGGER
UpdateCustomerTotalPortfolioValue
  AFTER UPDATE OR INSERT OR DELETE
  ON InsurancePolicy
  REFERENCING OLD AS OLD NEW AS NEW
  FOR EACH ROW
  DECLARE
    BEGIN
      UpdateCustomerWithPortfolioValue;
    END;
  END;
/
```

Data-Migration Mechanics

There is no data to be migrated per se, although the value of *Customer.-TotalPortfolioValue* must be populated based on the calculation. This is typically done once in batch via one or more scripts. In our example, we have to update the *Customer.TotalPortfolioValue* for all the existing rows in the *Customer* table with the sum of *Account.Balance* and *Policy.Value* for each customer:


```
UPDATE Customer SET TotalPortfolioValue =
  (SELECT SUM(Account.Balance) + SUM(Policy.Balance)
    FROM Account, CustomerInsurancePolicy,
    InsurancePolicy
    WHERE
    Account.AccountID =
    CustomerInsurancePolicy.AccountID
    AND CustomerInsurancePolicy.PolicyID=Policy.PolicyID
    AND Account.CustomerID=Customer.CustomerID
  );
```

Access Program Update Mechanics

You need to identify all the places in external applications where this calculation is currently performed and then rework that code to work with *TotalPortfolioValue*—this typically entails removing the calculation code and replacing it with a read to the database. You may discover that the calculation is performed differently in various applications, either because of a bug or because of a different situation, and need to negotiate the appropriate calculation with the business.

Drop Foreign Key Constraint

Remove a foreign key constraint from an existing table so that a relationship to another table is no longer enforced by the database.

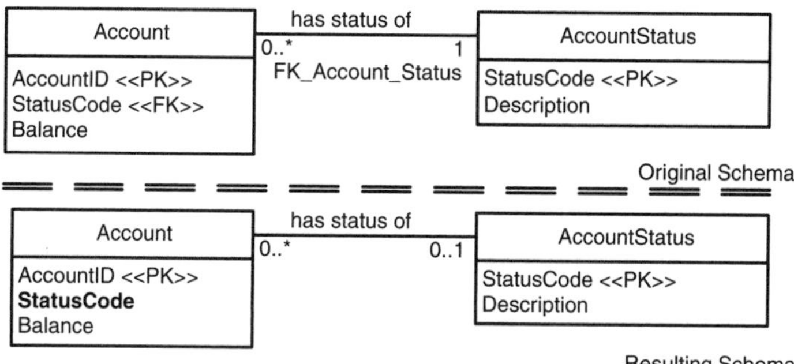

Figure 8.3 Dropping a foreign key constraint from the Account table.

Motivation

The primary reason to apply *Drop Foreign Key Constraint* is to no longer enforce data dependencies at the database level—instead, data integrity is enforced by external applications. This is particularly important when the performance cost of enforcing RI by the database cannot be sustained by the database anymore and/or when the RI rules vary between applications.

Potential Tradeoffs

The fundamental tradeoff is performance versus quality: Foreign key constraints ensure the validity of the data at the database level at the cost of the constraint being enforced each time the source data is updated. When you apply *Drop Foreign Key*, your applications will be at risk of introducing invalid data if they do not validate the data before writing to the database.

Schema Update Mechanics

To drop a foreign key constraint, you must either apply the **ALTER TABLE DROP CONSTRAINT** command or you can just apply the **ALTER TABLE DISABLE CONSTRAINT** command. The advantage of that latter approach is that it ensures that the relationship is documented even though the constraint is not enforced. The following code depicts the two ways by which you can drop the foreign key constraint between *Account.StatusCode* and *AccountStatus.StatusCode* in Figure 8.3. The first way just drops the constraint; the other one disables it and thereby documents the need for it. We recommend the second approach:

```
ALTER TABLE Account DROP CONSTRAINT FK_Account_Status;
ALTER TABLE Account DISABLE CONSTRAINT FK_Account_Status;
```

Data-Migration Mechanics

There is no data to migrate for this database refactoring.

Access Program Update Mechanics

You must identify and then update any external programs that modify the data column(s) on which the foreign key constraint was defined. There are two issues to look for in the external programs. First, individual applications need to be updated to ensure that appropriate RI rules are still being enforced. The rules could vary, but in general, you need to add logic to each application to ensure that a row exists in *AccountStatus* whenever it is referenced in *Account*. The implication is that you will either need to determine that the row already exists—if *AccountStatus* is small, you might consider caching it in memory—and be prepared to add a new row to the table. The second issue concerns exception handling. Because the database will no longer throw RI exceptions pertaining to this foreign key constraint, you will need to rework any external program code appropriately.

Introduce Cascading Delete

The database automatically deletes the appropriate "child records" when a "parent record" is deleted.

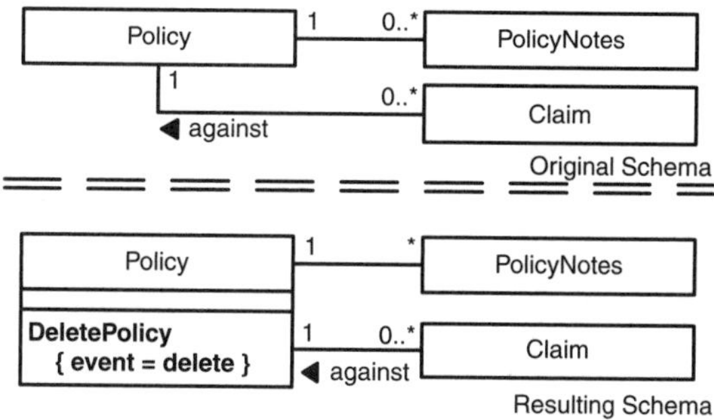

Figure 8.4 Introducing a cascading delete on Policy.

Note that an alternative to deleting child records is just to remove the reference to the parent record within the children records. This option can only be used when the foreign key column(s) in the child tables allows null values, although this alternative may lead to lots of orphaned rows.

Motivation

The primary reason you would apply *Introduce Cascading Delete* is to preserve the referential integrity of your data by ensuring that related rows are appropriately deleted when a parent row is deleted.

Potential Tradeoffs

There are three potential tradeoffs with this refactoring:

- **Deadlock.** When you implement cascading deletes, you must avoid cyclic dependencies; otherwise, deadlock may occur. Modern databases detect deadlocks and will roll back the transaction that caused the deadlock.
- **Accidental mass deletion.** You need to be very careful when applying this refactoring. For example, it may theoretically make sense that if you delete a row in your *CorporateDivision*, then all rows corresponding to that

division in your *Employee* table should also be deleted. However, you could easily delete thousands of employee records when someone inadvertently deletes a record representing a large division.

- **Duplicated functionality.** Persistence frameworks such as Hibernate (www.hibernate.org) and Oracle's Toplink (www.oracle.com) automate relationship management between objects; therefore, you may be duplicating functionality when you apply this refactoring.

Schema Update Mechanics

To apply *Introduce Cascading Delete*, you need to do the following:

1. **Identify what is to be deleted.** You need to identify the "children" of a row that should be deleted when the parent row is deleted. For example, when you delete an order, you should also delete all the order items associated with that order. This activity is recursive; the child rows in turn may have children that also need to be deleted, motivating you to apply *Introduce Cascading Delete* for them, too. We do not recommend applying this refactoring all at once; instead, it is better to apply this refactoring to one set of tables at a time, fully implementing and testing it before moving on to the next. Small changes are easier to implement than large changes.

2. **Choose cascading mechanism.** You can implement cascading deletes either with triggers or with referential integrity constraints with the **DELETE CASCADE** option. (Not all database vendors may support this option.)

3. **Implement the cascading delete.** With the first approach, you write a trigger that deletes all the children of the parent row when it is deleted. This option is best suited when you want to have fine-grained control over what gets deleted when the parent row is deleted. The downside is that you must write code to implement this functionality. You may also introduce deadlock situations when you have not thought through the interrelationships between multiple triggers being executed at the same time. With the second approach, you define RI constraints with the **DELETE CASCADE** option turned on, of the **ALTER TABLE MODIFY CONSTRAINT** SQL command. When you choose this option, you must define referential constraints on the database, which could be a huge task if you do not already have referential constraints defined (because you would need to apply the *Add Foreign Key* refactoring [page 204] to pretty much all the relationships in the database). The primary advantage with this option is that you do not have to write any new code because the database

automatically takes care of deleting the child rows. The challenge with this approach is that it can be very hard to debug.

Figure 8.4 depicts how to *Introduce Cascade Delete* to the *Policy* table using the trigger method. The *DeletePolicy* trigger, the code is shown below, deletes any rows from the *PolicyNotes* or *Claim* tables that are related to the row in the *Policy* table that is being deleted:

```
-Create trigger to delete the PolicyNotes and Claim.
CREATE OR REPLACE TRIGGER DeletePolicy
AFTER DELETE ON Policy
FOR EACH ROW
DECLARE
BEGIN
  DeletePolicyNotes();
  DeletePolicyClaims();
END;
/
```

The following code shows you how to implement *Introduce Cascade Delete* using RI constraints with the **DELETE CASCADE** option:

```
ALTER TABLE POLICYNOTES ADD CONSTRAINT
FK_DELETEPOLICYNOTES
FOREIGN KEY (POLICYID)
REFERENCES POLICY (POLICYID)
ON DELETE CASCADE
ENABLE
;

ALTER TABLE CLAIMS ADD CONSTRAINT FK_DELETEPOLICYCLAIM
FOREIGN KEY (POLICYID)
REFERENCES POLICY (POLICYID)
ON DELETE CASCADE
ENABLE
;
```


Data-Migration Mechanics

There is no data to migrate with this database refactoring.

Access Program Update Mechanics

When you apply this refactoring, you must remove any application code that currently implements the delete children functionality. One challenge will be that some applications implement the deletion whereas others do not—perhaps one application deletes *OrderItem* rows when the corresponding *Order* row is deleted, but another application does not. Implementing the cascading delete within the database may inadvertently impact, perhaps for the better, the second application. The point is that you need to be very careful; you should not assume that all applications implement the same RI rules, regardless of how "obvious" it is to you that they should.

You will also need to handle any new errors returned by the database when the cascading delete does not work. The following code shows how you would change your application code before and after *Introduce Cascade Delete* is applied:

```
//Before code
private void deletePolicy (Policy policyToDelete) {
  Iterator policyNotes =
  policyToDelete.getPolicyNotes().iterator();
  for (Iterator iterator = policyNotes;
  iterator.hasNext();)
{
    PolicyNote policyNote = (PolicyNote) iterator.next();
    DB.remove(policyNote);
}
  DB.remove(policyToDelete);
}

//After code
private void deletePolicy (Policy policyToDelete) {
DB.remove(policyToDelete);
}
```

If you are using any of the O-R mapping tools, you will have to change the mapping file so that you can specify the cascade option in the mapping, as shown here:


```
//After mapping
<hibernate-mapping>
  <class name="Policy" table="POLICY">
  ......
  <one-to-many name="policyNotes"
              class="PolicyNotes"
              cascade="all-delete-orphan"
  />
  ......
  </class>
</hibernate-mapping>
```

Introduce Hard Delete

Remove an existing column that indicates that a row has been deleted (this is called a *soft delete* or *logical delete*) and instead actually delete the row from the application (for example, do a hard delete). This refactoring is the opposite of *Introduce Soft Delete* (page 222).

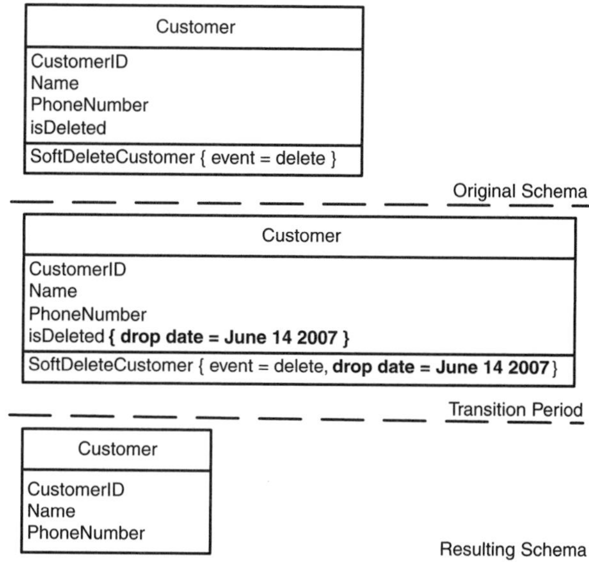

Figure 8.5 Introducing a hard delete for Customer.

Motivation

The primary reason to apply *Introduce Hard Delete* is to reduce the size of your tables, resulting in better performance and simpler querying because you no longer have to check to see whether a row is marked as deleted.

Potential Tradeoffs

The only disadvantage of this refactoring is the loss of historical data, although you can use *Introduce Trigger For History* (page 227) if required.

Schema Update Mechanics

As Figure 8.5 implies, to apply *Introduce Hard Delete* you first need to remove the identifying column. You must remove the deletion indicator column—see the *Drop Column* refactoring (page 72)—which, in this case, is the *Customer.isDeleted* column. Next you remove any code, usually trigger code (although sometimes application code), that updates the *Customer.isDeleted* column. There may be code that sets the initial value to FALSE in the case of a Boolean indicator, or to a predetermined date in the case of a date/timestamp. This logic is typically implemented with a default value column constraint that would be automatically dropped along with the column. There may also be trigger code that sets the value to TRUE, or to the current date/time, when there is an attempt to delete the row. Most likely, you will only need to drop the trigger. The following code shows you how to remove the *Customer.isDeleted* column:

```
ALTER TABLE Customer DROP COLUMN isDeleted;
```

Data-Migration Mechanics

You have to delete all the data rows in the *Customer* where *isDeleted* is set to TRUE, because these are the rows that have been logically deleted. Before you delete these rows, you need to update, and possibly delete, all the data that references the logically deleted data. This is typically done once in batch via one or more scripts. You should also consider archiving all the rows marked for deletion so that you can back out of this refactoring if need be. The following code shows you how to delete the rows from *Customer* table where the *Customer.isDeleted* flag is set to TRUE:


```
-Delete customers marked for delete
DELETE FROM Customer WHERE isDeleted = TRUE;
```

Access Program Update Mechanics

When you apply the *Introduce Hard Delete* refactoring, you must change external programs accessing the data in two ways. First, SELECT statements must not reference the *Customer.isDeleted* column. Second, all logical deletion code must be updated:

```
//Before code
public void customerDelete(Long customerIdToDelete)
throws Exception {
  PreparedStatement stmt = null;
```

```
  try {
    stmt =  DB.prepare("UPDATE Customer "+
             "SET isDeleted = ? "+
             "WHERE CustomerID =  ?");
    stmt.setLong(1, Boolean.TRUE);
    stmt.setLong(2, customerIdToDelete);
    stmt.execute();
  } catch (SQLException SQLexc){
    DB.HandleDBException(SQLexc);
  }
  finally {DB.cleanup(stmt);}
}

//After code
public void customerDelete(Long customerIdToDelete)
  throws Exception {
  PreparedStatement stmt = null;
  try {
    stmt =  DB.prepare("DELETE FROM Customer "+
                   "WHERE CustomerID =  ?");
    stmt.setLong(1, customerIdToDelete);
    stmt.execute();
  } catch (SQLException SQLexc){
    DB.HandleDBException(SQLexc);
  }
  finally {DB.cleanup(stmt);}
}
```

Introduce Soft Delete

Introduce a flag to an existing table that indicates that a row has been deleted (this is called a *soft/logical delete*) instead of actually deleting the row (a hard delete). This refactoring is the opposite of *Introduce Hard Delete* (page 219).

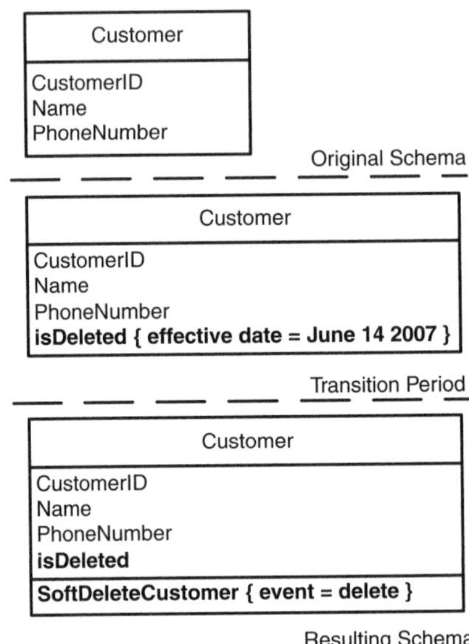

Figure 8.6 Introducing a soft delete to Customer.

Motivation

The primary reason to apply *Introduce Soft Delete* is to preserve all application data, typically for historical means.

Potential Tradeoffs

Performance is potentially impacted for two reasons. First, the database must store all the rows that have been marked as deleted. This could lead to significantly more disk space usage and reduced query performance. Second, applications must now do the additional work of distinguishing between deleted and nondeleted rows, decreasing performance while potentially increasing code complexity.

Schema Update Mechanics

As Figure 8.6 implies, to apply *Introduce Soft Delete*, you will need to do the following:

1. **Introduce the identifying column.** You must introduce a new column to *Customer*—see the *Introduce New Column* transformation (page 301)—that marks the row as deleted or not. This column is usually either a Boolean field that contains the value TRUE when the row is deleted and FALSE otherwise or a date/timestamp indicating when the row was deleted. In our example, we are introducing the Boolean column *isDeleted*. This column should not allow NULL values. (See the *Make Column Non-Nullable* refactoring on page 189.)
2. **Determine how to update the flag.** The *Customer.isDeleted* column can be updated either by your application(s) or within the database using triggers. We prefer the trigger-based approach because it is simple and it avoids the risk that the applications will not update the column properly.
3. **Develop deletion code.** The code must be written and tested to update the deletion indicator column appropriately upon "deletion" of a row. In the case of a Boolean column set to the value to TRUE, in the case of a date/timestamp, set it to the current date and time.
4. **Develop insertion code.** You have to set the deletion indicator column appropriately upon an insert, FALSE in the case of a Boolean column and a predetermined date (for example, the January 1, 5000) for a date/timestamp. This could be easily implemented by using the *Introduce Default Value* refactoring (page 186) or via a trigger.

The following code shows you how to add the *Customer.isDeleted* column and assign it a default value of FALSE:

```
ALTER TABLE Customer ADD isDeleted BOOLEAN;
ALTER TABLE Customer MODIFY isDeleted DEFAULT FALSE;
```

The following code shows you how to create a trigger that intercepts the **DELETE** SQL command and assigns the *Customer.isDeleted* flag to TRUE. The code copies the data row before deletion, updates the deletion indicator, and then inserts the row back into the table after the original is removed:

```
--Create a array to store the deleted Customers
CREATE OR REPLACE PACKAGE SoftDeleteCustomerPKG
```

```
AS
  TYPE ARRAY IS TABLE OF Customer%ROWTYPE INDEX BY
  BINARY_INTEGER;
  oldvals  ARRAY;
  empty    ARRAY;
END;
/

--Initialize the array
CREATE OR REPLACE TRIGGER SoftDeleteCustomerBefore
BEFORE DELETE ON Customer
BEGIN
  SoftDeleteCustomerPKG.oldvals :=
  SoftDeleteCustomerPKG.empty;
END;
/

--Capture the deleted rows
CREATE OR REPLACE TRIGGER
SoftDeleteCustomerStore
BEFORE DELETE ON Customer
FOR EACH ROW
DECLARE
  i NUMBER DEFAULT SoftDeleteCustomerPKG.oldvals.COUNT+1;
BEGIN
  SoftDeleteCustomerPKG.oldvals(i).CustomerID :=
  :old.CustomerID;
  deleteCustomer.oldvals(i).Name := :old.Name;
  deleteCustomer.oldvals(i).PhoneNumber :=
  :old.PhoneNumber;
END;
/

--Insert the customers back with the isdeleted flag set to true.
CREATE OR REPLACE TRIGGER SoftDeleteCustomerAdd
AFTER DELETE ON Customer
DECLARE
BEGIN
  FOR i IN 1 .. SoftDeleteCustomerPKG.oldvals.COUNT LOOP
    insert into Customer(CustomerID,Name,PhoneNumber,isDeleted)
    values( deleteCustomer.oldvals(i).CustomerID,
      deleteCustomer.oldvals(i).Name,
      deleteCustomer.oldvals(i).PhoneNumber,
      TRUE);
  END LOOP;
END;
/
```

Data-Migration Mechanics

There is no data to be migrated per se, although the value of *Customer.isDeleted* must be set to the appropriate default value within all rows when this refactoring is implemented. This is typically done once in batch via one or more scripts.

Access Program Update Mechanics

When you apply the *Introduce Soft Delete* refactoring, you must change external programs accessing the data. First, you must change read queries now to ensure that data read from the database has not been marked as deleted. Applications must add a **WHERE** clause to all **SELECT** queries, such as **WHERE isDeleted = FALSE.** Instead of changing all the read queries, you can use *Encapsulate Table With View* refactoring (page 243) so that the view returns rows from *Customer* where *isDeleted* is not TRUE. Another option is to apply the *Add Read Method* refactoring (page 240) so that the appropriate **WHERE** clause is implemented in one place.

Second, you must change deletion methods. All external programs must change physical deletes to updates that update *Customer.isDeleted* instead of physically removing the row. For example, **DELETE FROM Customer WHERE PKColumn = nnn** will change to **UPDATE Customer SET isDeleted = TRUE WHERE PKColumn = nnn.** Alternatively, as noted earlier, you can introduce a delete trigger that prevents the deletion and updates *Customer.isDeleted* to TRUE.

The following code shows you how to set the initial value of the *Customer.isDeleted* column:

```
UPDATE Customer SET
  isDeleted = FALSE WHERE isDeleted IS NULL;
```


The following code depicts the read method for a simple *Customer* object before and after *Introduce Soft Delete* refactoring is introduced:

```
// Before code
stmt.prepare(
"SELECT CustomerId, Name, PhoneNumber " +
"FROM Customer" +
"WHERE " +
"  CustomerId = ?");
stmt.setLong(1,customer.getCustomerID);
stmt.execute();
ResultSet rs = stmt.executeQuery();
```

```
// After code
stmt.prepare(
"SELECT CustomerId, Name, PhoneNumber " +
"FROM Customer" +
"WHERE " +
"  CustomerId = ? "+
"  AND isDeleted = ?");
stmt.setLong(1,customer.getCustomerID);
stmt.setBoolean(2,false);
stmt.execute();
ResultSet rs = stmt.executeQuery();
```

The before and after code snippet shows you how the delete method changes after *Introduce Soft Delete* refactoring is introduced:

```
//Before code
stmt.prepare("DELETE FROM Customer WHERE CustomerID=?");
stmt.setLong(1, customer.getCustomerID);
:stmt.executeUpdate();

//After code
stmt.prepare("UPDATE Customer SET isDeleted = ?"+
            "WHERE CustomerID=?");
stmt.setBoolean(1, true);
stmt.setLong(2, customer.getCustomerID);
stmt.executeUpdate();
```

Introduce Trigger For History

Introduce a new trigger to capture data changes for historical or audit purposes.

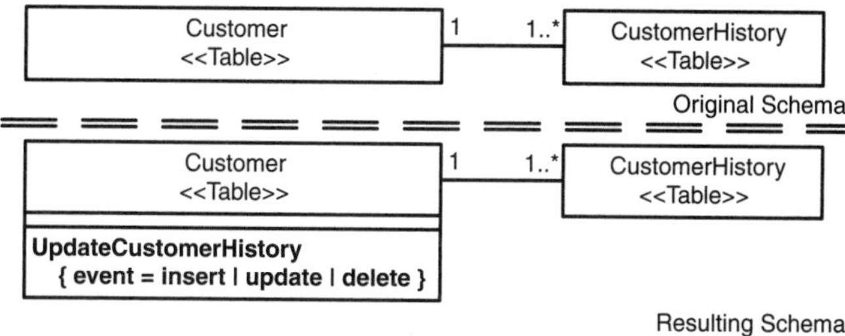

Figure 8.7 Introducing a history trigger for Customer.

Motivation

The primary reason you would apply *Introduce Trigger For History* is to delegate the tracking of data changes to the database itself. This strategy ensures that if any application modifies critical source data, the change will be tracked or audited.

Potential Tradeoffs

The primary trade-off is performance related—the addition of the trigger will increase the time it takes to update rows in *Customer* of Figure 8.7.

Furthermore, you may be forced to update your applications to pass user context information so that the database can record who made the change.

Schema Update Mechanics

To apply *Introduce Trigger for History*, you need to do the following:

1. **Determine actions to collect history for.** Although it is possible to insert, update, and delete data in *Customer*, you may not need to track all the changes. For example, perhaps you are only interested in tracking updates and deletions but not original insertions.

2. **Determine what columns to collect history for.** You have to identify the columns in *Customer* against which you are interested in tracking changes to. For example, perhaps you only want to track changes to the *PhoneNumber* column but nothing else.

3. **Determine how to record the historical data.** You have two basic choices: First, you could have a generic table that tracks all the historical data changes within your database, or you could introduce a corresponding history table for each table that you want to record history for. The single-table approach will not scale very well, although is appropriate for smaller databases.

4. **Introduce the history table.** If the history table does not yet exist, create it via the **CREATE TABLE** command.

5. **Introduce the trigger(s).** Introduce the appropriate trigger(s) via the **CREATE OR REPLACE TRIGGER** command. This could be achieved by just having a trigger that captures the original image of the row and inserting it into the *CustomerHistory* table. A second strategy is to compare the before and after values of the pertinent columns and store descriptions of the changes into *CustomerHistory.*

The following code shows you how to add the *CustomerHistory* table and how to update it via the *UpdateCustomerHistory* trigger. We are capturing the change in every column on the *Customer* table and recording them in *CustomerHistory*:

```
--Create the CustomerHistory table
CREATE TABLE CustomerHistory
(
  CustomerID NUMBER,
  OldName VARCHAR2(32),
  NewName VARCHAR2(32),
  ChangedBy NUMBER,
  ChangedOn DATE
);

--Auditing trigger for table Customer
CREATE OR REPLACE TRIGGER
UpdateCustomerHistory
AFTER INSERT OR UPDATE OR DELETE
ON Customer
REFERENCING OLD AS OLD NEW AS NEW
FOR EACH ROW
DECLARE
BEGIN
--Handle Updating of Rows
```

```
  IF UPDATING THEN
    IF NOT (NVL(:OLD.Name = :NEW.Name,FALSE) OR
    (:OLD.Name IS NULL AND :NEW.Name IS NULL)) THEN
     CreateCustomerHistoryRow( :NEW.CustomerId,
     :NEW.Name, :OLD.Name, User);
    END IF;
  END IF;

--Handle Deleting of Records
  IF DELETING THEN
    IF (:OLD.Name IS NOT NULL) THEN
      CreateCustomerHistoryRow (:OLD.CustomerId,:OLD.Name,NULL,User);
    END IF;
  END IF;

  IF INSERTING THEN
    IF (:NEW.Name IS NOT NULL) THEN
      CreateCustomerHistoryRow(:NEW.CustomerId, :NEW.Name,NULL,User);
    END IF;
  END IF;
END;
/
```

Data-Migration Mechanics

Data migration is typically not required for this database refactoring. However, if you want to track insertions, you may decide to create a history record for each existing row within *Customer*. This works well when *Customer* includes a column recording the original creation date; otherwise, you will need to generate a value for the insertion date. (The easiest thing to do is to use the current date.)

Access Program Update Mechanics

When you apply *Introduce Trigger for History*, you need to do the following:

1. **Stop application generation of history.** When you add triggers to collect historical information, you need to identify any existing logic in external applications where the code is creating historical information and then rework it.

2. **Update presentation code.** If external programs currently display application-generated history, they will need to be reworked to use the information contained in *CustomerHistory*.

3. **Provide user context to database.** If you want the database trigger to record which user made the change to the data, you must provide a user context. Some applications, in particular those built using Web or n-tier technologies, may not be providing this information and will need to be updated to do so. Alternatively, you could just supply a default value for the user context when it is not provided.

Although it would not be part of the refactoring itself, a related schema transformation would be to modify the table design to add columns to record who modified the record and when it was done. A common strategy is to add columns such as *UserCreated*, *CreationDate*, *UserLastModified*, and *LastModifiedDate* to main tables (see *Introduce New Column* on page 301). The two user columns would be a user ID that could be used as a foreign key to a user details table. You may also need to add the user details table (see *Add Lookup Table* on page 153).

Chapter 9

Architectural Refactorings

Architectural refactorings are changes that improve the overall manner in which external programs interact with a database. The architectural refactorings are as follows:

- Add CRUD Methods
- Add Mirror Table
- Add Read Method
- Encapsulate Table With View
- Introduce Calculation Method
- Introduce Index
- Introduce Read-Only Table
- Migrate Method From Database
- Migrate Method To Database
- Replace Method(s) With View
- Replace View With Method(s)
- Use Official Data Source

Add CRUD Methods

Introduce four stored procedures (methods) to implement the creation, retrieval, update, and deletion (CRUD) of the data representing a business entity. After these stored procedures are in place, access to the source tables is restricted to just these procedures and administrators.

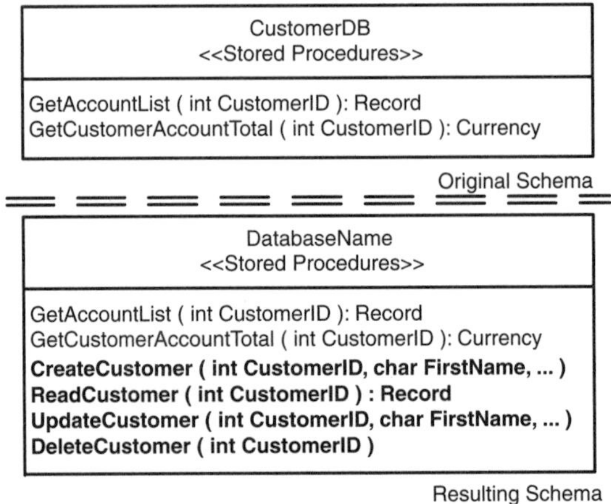

Figure 9.1 Adding Customer CRUD methods.

Motivation

There are several reasons to apply *Add CRUD Methods*:

- **Encapsulate data access.** Stored procedures are a common way to encapsulate access to your database, albeit not as effective as persistence frameworks (see Chapter 1, "Evolutionary Database Development").
- **Decouple application code from database tables.** Stored procedures are an effective way to decouple applications from database tables. They enable you to change database tables without changing application code.
- **Implement entity-based security access control (SAC).** Instead of directly accessing source tables, applications instead invoke the relevant stored procedures. CRUD stored procedures provide a way to implement an entity-level approach to SAC. Database products typically enable data

SAC at the table, column, and sometimes row levels. But, when the data for complex business entities such as *Customer* are stored in several tables, SAC, at the entity level, can become quite complicated if you restrict yourself to data-oriented SAC. Luckily, most database products also implement method SAC, and thus you can implement entity-level SAC via CRUD methods.

Potential Tradeoffs

The primary advantage of encapsulating database access in this manner is that it makes it easier to refactor your table schema. When you implement common schema refactorings such as *Rename Table* (page 113), *Move Column* (page 103), and *Split Column* (page 140), you should only have to refactor the corresponding CRUD methods that access them (assuming that no other external program directly accesses the table schema).

Unfortunately, this approach to database encapsulation comes at a cost. Methods (stored procedures, stored functions, and triggers) are specific to database vendors—Oracle methods are not easily portable to Sybase, for example. Furthermore, there is no guarantee that the methods that work in one version of a database will be easy to port to a newer version, so you may be increasing your upgrade burden, too. Another issue is lack of flexibility. What happens if you want to access a portion of a business entity? Do you really want to work with all the entity's data each time or perhaps introduce CRUD methods for that subentity? What happens if you need data that crosses entities, perhaps for a report? Do you invoke several stored procedures to read each business entity that you require and then select the data you require, or do you apply *Add Read Method* (page 240) to retrieve the data specifically required by the report?

Schema Update Mechanics

To update the database schema, you must do the following:

1. **Identify the business data.** You need to identify the business entity, such as *Customer* of Figure 9.1, for which you want to implement the CRUD methods. After you know what entity you are encapsulating access to, you need to identify the source data within the database for that entity.

2. **Write the stored procedures.** You need to write at least four stored procedures, one to create the entity, one to read it based on its primary key, one to update the entity, and one to delete it. Additional stored procedures to

retrieve the entity via means other than the primary key can be added by applying the *Add Read Method* (page 240) database refactoring.

3. **Test the stored procedures.** One of the best ways to work is to take a Test-Driven Development (TDD) approach; see Chapter 1, "Evolutionary Database Development."

Figure 9.1 depicts how to introduce the CRUD methods for the *Customer* entity. The code for *ReadCustomer* is shown here. The code for the other stored procedures is self-explanatory:

```
CREATE OR REPLACE PACKAGE CustomerCRUD AS
    TYPE customerType IS REF CURSOR RETURN
    Customer%ROWTYPE;
    PROCEDURE ReadCustomer
      (readCustomerId IN NUMBER,customers OUT
      customerType);
    PROCEDURE CreateCustomer(....);
    PROCEDURE UpdateCustomer(....);
    PROCEDURE DeleteCustomer(....);
    END CustomerCRUD;
    /

    CREATE OR REPLACE PACKAGE BODY CustomerCRUD AS

    PROCEDURE ReadCustomer
      (readCustomerId IN NUMBER,customerReturn OUT
      customerType) IS
    BEGIN
    OPEN refCustomer FOR
      SELECT * FROM Customer WHERE CustomerID =
      readCustomerId;
    END ReadCustomer;

    END CustomerCRUD;
/
```


Set Naming Conventions

CRUD methods should follow a common naming convention to improve their readability. We prefer the *CreateCustomer, ReadCustomer, UpdateCustomer*, and *DeleteCustomer* format shown in Figure 9.1—although *CustomerCreate, CustomerRead, CustomerUpdate*, and *CustomerDelete* also make sense. Choose one approach and stick to it.

Data-Migration Mechanics

There is no data to migrate for this database refactoring.

Access Program Update Mechanics

When you introduce the CRUD methods, you need to identify all the places in external applications where the entity is currently used and then refactor that code to invoke the new stored procedures as appropriate. You may discover that the individual programs require different subsets of the data, or another way to look at it is that some programs require just a little bit more data than others. You may discover that you need to apply *Add CRUD Methods* for several entities simultaneously, potentially a major change.

The first code example shows how the *Customer* Java class originally submitted hard-coded SQL to the database to retrieve the appropriate data. The second code example shows how it would be refactored to invoke the stored procedure:

```
// Before code
stmt.prepare(
  "SELECT FirstName, Surname, PhoneNumber FROM
  Customer " +
    "WHERE CustomerId=?");
stmt.setLong(1,customerId);
stmt.execute();
ResultSet rs = stmt.executeQuery();

//After code
stmt = conn.prepareCall("begin ? := ReadCustomer(?); end;");
stmt.registerOutParameter(1, OracleTypes.CURSOR);
stmt.setLong(2, customerId);
stmt.execute();
ResultSet rs = stmt.getObject(1);
```

Add Mirror Table

Create a mirror table, an exact duplicate of an existing table in one database, in another database.

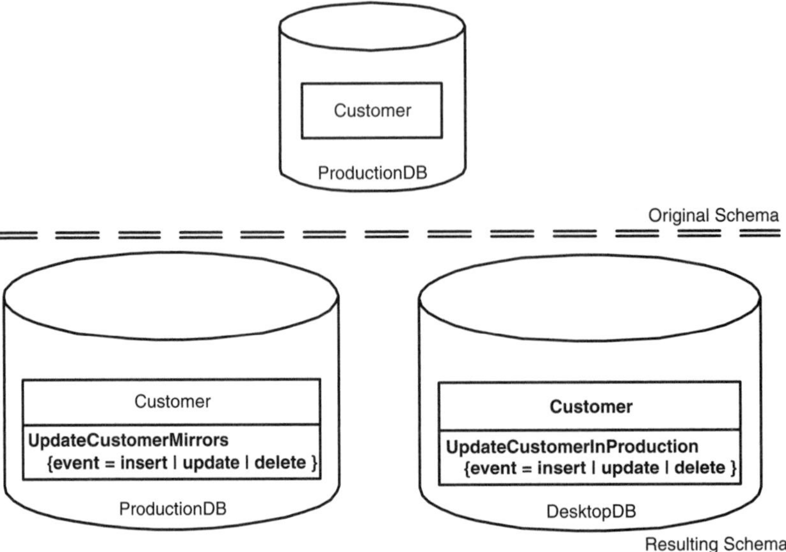

Figure 9.2 Adding a Customer mirror table.

Motivation

There are several reasons why you may want to apply *Add Mirror Table*:

- **Improve query performance.** Querying a given set of tables may be slow due to the database being in a remote location; therefore, a prepopulated table on a local server may improve overall performance.
- **Create redundant data.** Many applications query data in real time from other databases. A table containing this data in your local database reduces your dependency on these other database(s), providing a buffer for when they go down or are taken down for maintenance.
- **Replace redundant reads.** Several external programs, or stored procedures for that matter, often implement the same retrieval query. These queries to the remote database could be replaced by a mirror table on the local database that replicates with the remote database.

Potential Tradeoffs

The primary challenge when introducing a mirror table is "stale data." Stale data occurs when one table is updated but not the other; remember, either the source or the mirror table could potentially be updated. This problem increases as more mirrors of *Customer* are created in other databases. As you see in Figure 9.2, you need to implement some sort of synchronization strategy.

Schema Update Mechanics

As depicted in Figure 9.2, to update the database schema, when you perform *Add Mirror Table* you must do the following:

1. **Determine the location.** You must decide where the mirrored table, *Customer*, will reside—in this case, we will be mirroring it in *DesktopDB*.
2. **Introduce the mirror table.** Create *DesktopDB.Customer* in the other database using the **CREATE TABLE** command of SQL.
3. **Determine synchronization strategy.** The real-time approach of Figure 9.2 should be taken when your end users require up-to-date information, the synchronization of data.
4. **Allow updates.** If you want to allow updates to *DesktopDB.Customer*, you must provide a way to synchronize the data from *DesktopDB.Customer* to the *Customer.* An updatable *DesktopDB.Customer* is known as a *peer-to-peer mirror*; it is also known as a *master/slave mirror*.

The following code depicts the DDL to introduce the *DesktopDB.Customer* table:

```
CREATE TABLE Customer (
  CustomerID  NUMBER NOT NULL,
  Name  VARCHAR(40),
  PhoneNumber VARCHAR2(40),
  CONSTRAINT PKCustomer
    PRIMARY KEY (CustomerID)
);

COMMENT ON Customer 'Mirror table of Customer on Remote Location"
```


Data-Migration Mechanics

You must initially copy all the relevant source data into the mirror table, and then apply your synchronization strategy (real-time update or use database replication). There are several implementation strategies you can apply for your synchronization strategy:

1. **Periodic refresh.** Use a scheduled job that synchronizes your *Customer* and *DesktopDB.Customer* table. The job must be able to deal with data changes on both the tables and be able to update data both ways. Periodic refreshes are usually better when you are building data warehouses and data marts.

2. **Database replication.** Database products provide a feature where you can set up tables to be replicated both ways called multimaster replication. The database keeps both the tables synchronized. Generally speaking, you would use this approach when you want to have the *Customer* and *DesktopDB .Customer* updatable by the users. If your database product provides this feature, it is advisable to use this feature over using custom-coded solutions.

3. **Use trigger-based synchronization.** Create triggers on the *Customer* so that source data changes are propagated to the *DesktopDB.Customer* and create triggers on the *DesktopDB.Customer* so that changes to the table are propagated to *Customer*. This technique enables you to custom code the data synchronization, which is desirable when you have complex data objects that need to be synchronized; however, you must write all the triggers, which could be time consuming.

The following code depicts how to synchronize data in *ProductionDB.Customer* table and *DesktopDB.Customer* using triggers:

```
CREATE OR REPLACE TRIGGER
  UpdateCustomerMirror
  AFTER UPDATE OR INSERT OR DELETE
  ON Customer
  REFERENCING OLD AS OLD NEW AS NEW
  FOR EACH ROW
    DECLARE
      BEGIN
        IF DELETING THEN
          DeleteCustomerMirror;
        END IF;
        IF (UPDATING OR INSERTING) THEN
          UpdateCustomerMirror;
        END IF;
      END;
  END;
  /

CREATE OR REPLACE TRIGGER
  UpdateCustomer
```

```
  AFTER UPDATE OR INSERT OR DELETE
  ON CustomerMirror
  REFERENCING OLD AS OLD NEW AS NEW
  FOR EACH ROW
  DECLARE
  BEGIN
    IF DELETING THEN
      DeleteCustomer;
    END IF;
    IF (UPDATING OR INSERTING) THEN
      UpdateCustomer;
    END IF;
  END;
END;
/
```

Access Program Update Mechanics

You will have already analyzed why you are introducing this *DesktopDB .Customer*. For example, if you are going to mirror *Customer* on your remote database for easy access on the local database, you must make sure that the application connects to this local database when it wants to query the *Customer* table instead of the production database. You can also set up alternate connection properties that enable you to use *DesktopDB* or *ProductionDB* to query your data, as you see in the following code:

```
// Before code
stmt = remoteDB.prepare("select
CustomerID,Name,PhoneNumber FROM Customer WHERE
CustomerID = ?");
stmt.setLong(1, customerID);
stmt.execute();
ResultSet rs = stmt.executeQuery();

//After code
stmt = localDB.prepare("select
CustomerID,Name,PhoneNumber FROM Customer WHERE
CustomerID = ?");
stmt.setLong(1, customerID);
stmt.execute();
ResultSet rs = stmt.executeQuery();
```

Add Read Method

Introduce a method, in this case a stored procedure, to implement the retrieval of the data representing zero or more business entities from the database.

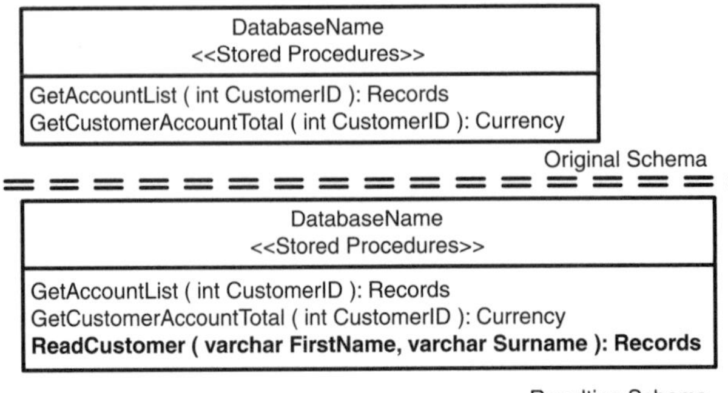

Figure 9.3 Adding a Customer read method.

Motivation

The primary reason to apply *Add Read Method* is to encapsulate the logic required to retrieve specific data from the database in accordance with defined criteria. The method, often a stored procedure, might be required to replace one or more SELECT statements implemented in your application and/or reporting code. Another common motivation is to implement a consistent search strategy for a given business entity.

Sometimes this refactoring is applied to support the *Introduce Soft Delete* (page 222) or *Introduce Hard Delete* (page 219) refactorings. When either of these refactorings is applied, the way in which data is deleted changes—either you mark a row as deleted or you physically delete the data, respectively. A change in strategy such as this may require a multitude of changes to be implemented within your applications to ensure that retrievals are performed correctly. By encapsulating the data retrieval in a stored procedure, and then invoking that stored procedure appropriately, it is much easier to implement these two refactorings because the requisite retrieval logic only needs to be reworked in one place (the stored procedure).

Potential Tradeoffs

The primary advantage of encapsulating retrieval logic in this manner, often in combination with *Add CRUD Methods* (page 232), is that it makes it easier to refactor your table schema. Unfortunately, this approach to database encapsulation comes at a cost. Stored procedures are specific to database vendors, reducing your potential for portability, and may decrease your overall performance if they are written poorly.

Schema Update Mechanics

To update the database schema, you must do the following:

1. **Identify the data.** You need to identify the data you want to retrieve, which may come from several tables.
2. **Identify the criteria.** How do you want to specify the subset of data to retrieve? For example, would you like to be able to retrieve information for bank accounts whose balance is over a specific amount, or which have been opened at a specific branch, or which have been accessed during a specific period of time, or for a combination thereof. Note that the criteria may or may not involve the primary key.
3. **Write and test the stored procedure.** We are firm believers in writing a full, 100 percent regression test suite for your stored procedures. Better yet, we recommend a Test-Driven Development (TDD) approach where you write a test before writing a little bit of code within your stored procedures (Astels 2003; Beck 2003).

Figure 9.3 shows how to introduce a read stored procedure for the *Customer* entity that takes as parameters a first and last name. The code for the *ReadCustomer* stored procedure is shown below. It is written assuming that it would get parameters passed to it such as S% and Ambler and return all the people with the surname Ambler whose first name begins with the letter *S*.


```
PROCEDURE ReadCustomer
  (
  firstNameToFind IN VARCHAR,
  lastNameToFind IN VARCHAR,
  customerRecords OUT CustomerREF
) IS
BEGIN
OPEN refCustomer FOR
```

```
  SELECT * FROM Customer WHERE
  Customer.FirstName = firstNameToFind
  AND Customer.LastName = lastNameToFind;
END ReadCustomer;
/
```

Data-Migration Mechanics

There is no data to migrate for this database refactoring.

Access Program Update Mechanics

When you introduce the stored procedure, you need to identify all the places in external applications where the data is read and then refactor that code to invoke the new stored procedure appropriately. You may discover that the individual programs require different subsets of the data, and therefore you may need to apply *Add Read Method* several times, one for each major collection of data elements.

In the following code, applications would submit **SELECT** statements to the database to retrieve customer information; but after the refactoring, they just invoke the stored procedure:

```
// Before code
stmt.prepare(
  "SELECT * FROM Customer " +
    "WHERE Customer.FirstName=? AND
    Customer.LastName=?");
stmt.setString(1,firstNameToFind);
stmt.setString(2,lastNameToFind);
stmt.execute();
ResultSet rs = stmt.executeQuery();

//After code
stmt = conn.prepareCall("begin ? := ReadCustomer(?,?,?); end;");
stmt.registerOutParameter(1, OracleTypes.CURSOR);
stmt.setString(2, firstNameToFind);
stmt.setString(3,lastNameToFind);
stmt.execute();
ResultSet rs = stmt.getObject(1);
while (rs.next()) {
  getCustomerInformation(rs);
}
```

Encapsulate Table With View

Wrap access to an existing table with a view.

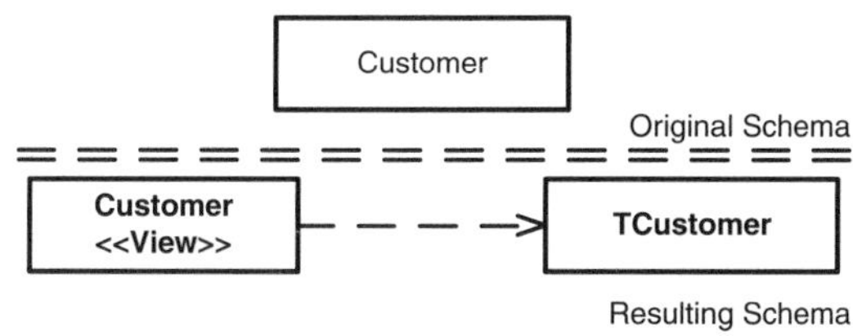

Figure 9.4 Encapsulating the TCustomer table with a view.

Motivation

There are two reasons to apply *Encapsulate Table With View*. First, to implement a façade around an existing table that you intend to later refactor. By writing applications to access source data through views instead of directly through tables, you reduce the direct coupling to the table, making it easier to refactor. For example, you may want to encapsulate access to a table via a view first before you apply refactorings such as *Rename Column* (page 109) or *Drop Column* (page 72).

Second, you may want to put a security access control (SAC) strategy in place for your database. You can do this by encapsulating access to a table via several views, and then restricting access to the table and the various views appropriately. Few users, if any, would have direct access to the source table; users would instead be granted access rights to one or more views. The first step of this process is to encapsulate access to the original table with a view, and then you introduce new views as appropriate.

Potential Tradeoffs

This refactoring, as shown in Figure 9.4, will only work when your database supports the same level of access through views as it does to tables. For example, if *Customer* is updated by an external program, your database must support updatable views. If it does not, you should consider the refactoring *Add CRUD Method* (page 232) to encapsulate access to this table instead.

Schema Update Mechanics

As you can see in Figure 9.4, this refactoring is straightforward. The first step is to rename the existing table, in this case to *TCustomer*. The second step is to introduce a view with the name of the original table, in this case *Customer*. From the point of view of the external programs that access the table, nothing has really changed. They simply access the source data through the view, which to them appears to be the original table.

One way to rename the *Customer* table is to use the **RENAME TO** clause of the **ALTER TABLE** SQL command, as shown below. If your database does not support this clause, you must create *TCustomer*, copy the data from *Customer*, and then drop the *Customer* table. An example of this approach is provided with the *Rename Table* refactoring (page 113). Regardless of how you rename the table, the next step is to add the view via the **CREATE VIEW** command:

```
ALTER TABLE Customer RENAME TO TCustomer;

CREATE VIEW Customer AS
  SELECT * FROM TCustomer;
```

Data-Migration Mechanics

There is no data to migrate for this database refactoring.

Access Program Update Mechanics

You should not have to update any access programs because the view is identical in structure to the original table.

Introduce Calculation Method

Introduce a new method, typically a stored function, that implements a calculation that uses data stored within the database.

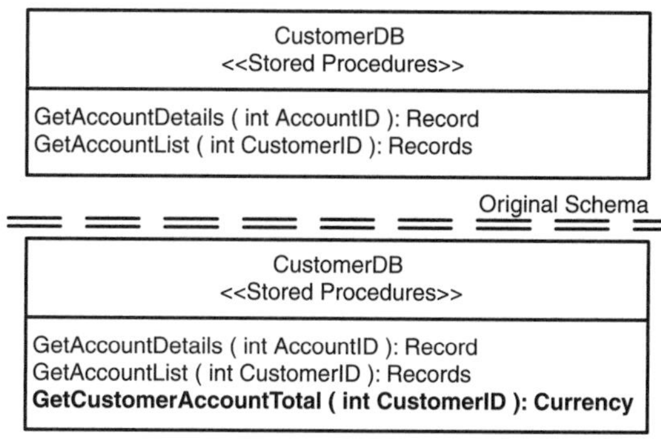

Figure 9.5 Introducing a calculation method for Customer.

Motivation

There are several reasons to apply *Introduce Calculation Method*:

- **To improve application performance.** You can improve overall performance by implementing a calculation that requires significant amounts of data within the database and then responding with just the answer. This avoids shipping the required data across the network to do the calculation.
- **To implement a common, reusable calculation.** A calculation may be implemented by several existing methods. Therefore, it makes sense to extract that calculation into a single database method that is invoked by the others.
- **To support *Introduce Calculated Column* (page 81).** You can implement the logic required to calculate the value of the column in a stored function.
- **To replace a calculated column.** You may choose to replace a calculated column with a stored procedure that you invoke instead. To remove the column, apply the *Drop Column* (page 72) refactoring.

Potential Tradeoffs

When too much logic is implemented within your database, it can become a performance bottleneck if the database has not been architected to handle the load. You need to either ensure that your database is scalable or limit the amount of functionality that you implement in it.

Schema Update Mechanics

To update the database schema, you must write and then test the stored procedure. If existing stored procedures implement this logic, they should be refactored to invoke this stored procedure. The following code shows how to introduce the stored function *GetCustomerAccountTotal* to the *CustomerDB* database:

```
CREATE OR REPLACE FUNCTION getCustomerAccountTotal
(CustomerID IN NUMBER) RETURN NUMBER IS
customerTotal NUMBER;
  BEGIN
    SELECT SUM(Amount) INTO customerTotal FROM Policy
      WHERE PolicyCustomerId=CustomerID;
        RETURN customerTotal;
      EXCEPTION WHEN no_data_found THEN
        RETURN 0;
  END;
END;
/
```

Data-Migration Mechanics

There is no data to migrate for this database refactoring.

Access Program Update Mechanics

When you introduce the calculation method, you need to identify all the places in external applications where this calculation is currently implemented and then refactor the code to appropriately invoke the new stored procedure. The following code shows how the calculation used to be performed as a Java operation, but afterward the operation simply invokes the appropriate stored function:

```
//Before code
private BigDecimal getCustomerTotalBalance() {
BigDecimal customerTotalBalance = new BigDecimal(0);
```

```
for (Iterator iterator =
customer.getPolicies().iterator(); iterator.hasNext();)
{
  Policy policy = (Policy) iterator.next();
  customerTotalBalance.add(policy.getBalance());
}
return customerTotalBalance;
}

//After code
private BigDecimal getCustomerTotalBalance() {
  BigDecimal customerTotalBalance = new BigDecimal(0);
  stmt = connection.prepareCall("{call
  getCustomerAccountTotal(?)}");
  stmt.registerOutParameter(1, Types.NUMBER);
  stmt.setString(1, customer.getId);
  stmt.execute();
  customerTotalBalance = stmt.getBigDecimal(1);
  return customerTotalBalance;
}
```

You may discover that the calculation is implemented in slightly different ways in various applications; perhaps the business rule has changed over time but the application was not updated, or perhaps there is a valid reason for the differences. Regardless, you need to negotiate any changes with the appropriate project stakeholders.

Introduce Index

Introduce a new index of either unique or nonunique type.

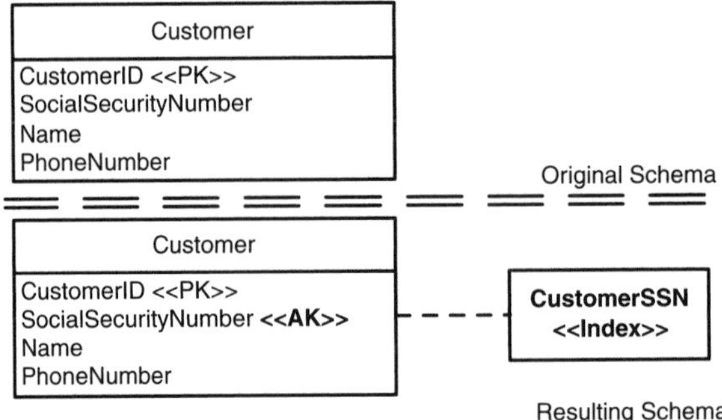

Figure 9.6 Introducing an index for the Customer table.

Motivation

The reason why you want to introduce an index to a table is to increase query performance on your database reads. You may also need to introduce an index to create a primary key for a table, or to support a foreign key to another table, when applying *Consolidate Key Strategy* (page 168).

Potential Tradeoffs

Too many indexes on a table will degrade performance when you update, insert into, or delete from the table. Many times you may want to introduce a unique index but will not be able to because the existing data contains duplicate values, forcing you to remove the duplicates before applying this refactoring.

Schema Update Mechanics

Applying *Introduce Index* can be complicated because of data dependencies, potentially requiring updates to both data and application code. You need to do the following:

1. **Determine type of index.** You have to decide whether you need a unique or nonunique index, which is usually determined by the business rules surrounding the data attributes and your usage of the data. For example,

in the United States, individuals are assigned unique Social Security Numbers (SSNs). Within most companies, customers are assigned unique customer numbers. But, your telephone number may not be unique (several people may share a single number). Therefore, both *SSN* and *CustomerNumber* would potentially be valid columns to define a unique index for, but *TelephoneNumber* would likely require a nonunique index.

2. **Add a new index.** In the example of Figure 9.6, a new index based on *SocialSecurityNumber* needs to be introduced for *Customer*, using the **CREATE INDEX** command of SQL.

3. **Provide more disk space.** When you use the *Introduce Index* refactoring, you must plan for more disk space usage, so you may need to allocate more disk space.

Data-Migration Mechanics

There is no data to be migrated per se, although the value of *Customer.SocialSecurityNumber* must be checked for duplicate values if you are introducing a unique index. Duplicate values must be addressed by either updating them or by deciding to use a nonunique index. The following code determines whether we have duplicate values in the *Customer.SocialSecurityNumber* column:

```
--Find any duplicate values in customer.socialsecuritynumber.
SELECT SocialSecurityNumber,COUNT(SocialSecurityNumber)
  FROM Customer
  GROUP BY SocialSecurityNumber
  HAVING COUNT(SocialSecurityNumber)>1;
```

If you find any duplicate values, you will have to change them before you can apply *Introduce Index*. The following code shows a way to do so: First, you use the *Customer.CustomerID* as an anchor to find duplicate rows, and then you replace the duplicate values by apply the *Update Data* refactoring (page 310):


```
--Create a temp table of the duplicates
CREATE TABLE temp_customer
AS
  SELECT * FROM Customer parent
  WHERE CustomerID != (SELECT MAX(CustomerID)
    FROM Customer child
    WHERE parent.SocialSecurityNumber =
    child.SocialSecurityNumber);
```

```
--Now create the Unique Index
CREATE UNIQUE INDEX Customer_Name_UNQ
  ON Customer(SocialSecurityNumber)
;
```

Access Program Update Mechanics

To update access programs, you need to first analyze the dependencies to determine which external programs access data in *Customer*. First, these external programs must be able to manage database exceptions that are thrown by the database in case they generate duplicate values. Second, you should change your queries to make use of this new index to get better performance of data retrieval. Some database products enable you to specify what index to use while retrieving rows from the database through the use of hints, an example of which follows:

```
SELECT /*+ INDEX(Customer_Name_UNQ) */
CustomerID,
SocialSecurityNumber
FROM Customer
WHERE
  SocialSecurityNumber = 'XXX-XXX-XXX';
```

Introduce Read-Only Table

Create a read-only data store based on existing tables in the database. There are two ways to implement this refactoring: as a table populated in real time or as a table populated in batch.

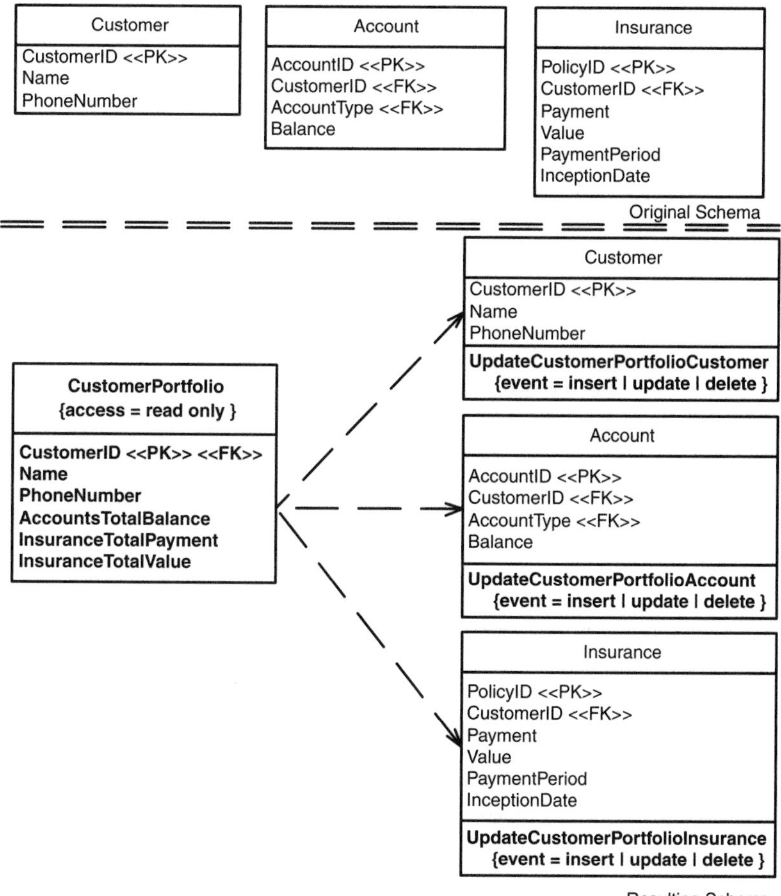

Figure 9.7 Introducing the read-only table CustomerPortfolio.

Motivation

There are several reasons why you may want to apply *Introduce Read-Only Table*:

- **Improve query performance.** Querying a given set of tables may be very slow because of the requisite joins; therefore, a prepopulated table may improve overall performance.

- **Summarize data for reporting.** Many reports require summary data, which can be prepopulated into a read-only table and then used many times over.
- **Create redundant data.** Many applications query data in real time from other databases. A read-only table containing this data in your local database reduces your dependency on these other database(s), providing a buffer for when they go down or are taken down for maintenance.
- **Replace redundant reads.** Several external programs, or stored procedures for that matter, often implement the same retrieval query. These queries can be replaced by a common read-only table or a new view; see *Introduce View* (page 306).
- **Data security.** A read-only table enables end users to query the data but not update it.
- **Improve database readability.** If you have a highly normalized database, it is usually difficult for users to navigate through all the tables to get to the required information. By introducing read-only tables that capture common, denormalized data structures, you make your database schema easier to understand because people can start by focusing just on the denormalized tables.

Potential Tradeoffs

The primary challenge with introducing a read-only table is "stale data," data that does not represent the current state of the source where it was populated from. For example, you could pull data from a remote system to populate a local table, and immediately after doing so, the source data gets updated. The users of the read-only table need to understand both the timeliness of the copied data as well as the volatility of the source data to determine whether the read-only table is acceptable to them.

Schema Update Mechanics

As depicted in Figure 9.7, to update the database schema when you perform *Introduce Read-Only Table*, you must first introduce the new table. You must decide on the structure of the read-only table that you want to introduce and then can create it using the **CREATE TABLE** command. Next, determine a population strategy. A real-time approach should be taken when your end users require up-to-date information; the join to create the read-only table is relatively simple, and the data can therefore be safely updated; and the resulting table is small, thus allowing for adequate performance. A batch approach should be taken when the real-time approach is not appropriate.

Figure 9.7 shows an example where the *CustomerPortfolio* table is a read-only table based on the *Customer, Account*, and *Insurance* tables that summarizes the business that we do with each customer. This provides an easier way for end users to do ad-hoc queries that analyze the customer information. The following code depicts the DDL to introduce the *CustomerPortfolio* table:

```
CREATE TABLE CustomerPortfolio (
  CustomerID NUMBER NOT NULL,
  Name VARCHAR(40),
  PhoneNumber VARCHAR2(40),
  AccountsTotalBalance NUMBER,
  InsuranceTotalPayment NUMBER,
  InsuranceTotalValue NUMBER,
  CONSTRAINT PKCustomerPortfolio
    PRIMARY KEY (CustomerID)
);
```

There are several implementation strategies. First, you could trust developers to do the right thing and simply mark the table as read-only via a comment. Second, you could implement triggers which throw an error on insertion, update, or deletion. Third, you could restrict access to the table via your security access control (SAC) strategy. Fourth, apply *Encapsulate Table With View* (page 243) and make the view read-only.

Data-Migration Mechanics

You must initially copy all the relevant source data into the read-only table, and then apply your population strategy (real-time update or periodic batch update). There are several implementation strategies you can apply for your population strategy:

1. **Periodic refresh.** Use a scheduled job that refreshes your read-only table. The job may refresh all the data in the read-only table or it may just update the changes since the last refresh. Note that the amount of time taken to refresh the data should be less than the scheduled interval time of the refresh. This technique is particularly suited for data warehouse kind of environments, where data is generally summarized and used the next day. Hence, stale data can be tolerated; also, this approach provides you with an easier way to synchronize the data.

2. **Materialized views.** Some database products provide a feature where a view is no longer just a query; instead, it is actually a table based on a

query. The database keeps this materialized view current based on the options you choose when you create it. This technique enables you to use the database's built-in features to refresh the data in the materialized view, with the major downside being the complexity of the view SQL. When the view SQL gets more complicated, the database products tend not to support automated synchronization of the view.

3. **Use trigger-based synchronization.** Create triggers on the source tables so that source data changes are propagated to the read-only table. This technique enables you to custom code the data synchronization, which is desirable when you have complex data objects that need to be synchronized; however, you must write all of the triggers, which could be time consuming.
4. **Use real-time application updates.** You can change your application so that it updates the read-only table, making the data current. This can only work when you know all the applications that are writing data to your source database tables. This technique allows for the application to update the read-only table, and hence its always kept current, and you can make sure that the data is not used by the application. The downside of the technique is you must write your information twice, first to the original table and second to the denormalized read-only table; this could lead to duplication and hence bugs.

The following code depicts how to populate data in *CustomerPortfolio* table for the first time:

```
INSERT INTO CustomerPortfolio
  SELECT Customer.CustomerID,
    Customer.Name,
    Customer.PhoneNumber,
    SUM(Account.Balance),
    SUM(Insurance.Payment),
    SUM(Insurance.Value)
  FROM
    Customer,Account,Insurance
  WHERE
    Customer.CustomerID=Account.CustomerID
    AND Customer.CustomerID=Insurance.CustomerID
  GROUP BY
    Customer.CustomerID,
    Customer.Name,
    Customer.PhoneNumber;
```

The following code depicts how to synchronize data from the source tables of *Customer*, *Account*, and *Insurance*. Because the source tables are updatable but *CustomerPortfolio* is not, we only need one-way updates:

```
CREATE OR REPLACE TRIGGER
UpdateCustomerPortfolioCustomer
  AFTER UPDATE OR INSERT OR DELETE
  ON Customer
  REFERENCING OLD AS OLD NEW AS NEW
  FOR EACH ROW
  DECLARE
  BEGIN
    IF DELETING THEN
      DeleteCustomerPortfolio;
    END IF;
    IF (UPDATING OR INSERTING) THEN
      UpdateCustomerPortfolio;
    END IF;
  END;
END;
/

CREATE OR REPLACE TRIGGER
UpdateCustomerPortfolioAccount
  AFTER UPDATE OR INSERT OR DELETE
  ON Account
  REFERENCING OLD AS OLD NEW AS NEW
  FOR EACH ROW
  DECLARE
  BEGIN
    UpdateCustomerPortfolioForAccount;
  END;
END;
/

CREATE OR REPLACE TRIGGER
UpdateCustomerPortfolioInsurance
  AFTER UPDATE OR INSERT OR DELETE
  ON Insurance
  REFERENCING OLD AS OLD NEW AS NEW
  FOR EACH ROW
  DECLARE
  BEGIN
    UpdateCustomerPortfolioForInsurance;
  END;
END;
/
```

Access Program Update Mechanics

You will have already analyzed why you are introducing this read-only table. For example, in Figure 9.7, if you are going to use *CustomerPortfolio* inside the application, you must make sure that the application uses this for read-only purposes. If you are providing *CustomerPortfolio* as a summarized table for integration to some other application, you must keep the data updated in *CustomerPortfolio*. When you decide to use data from *CustomerPortfolio*, you must change all the places where you currently access the source tables and rework them to use *CustomerPortfolio* instead.

You may also want to show your end users how recent the data is by displaying the value of the *CustomerPortfolio.LastUpdatedTime* column. Furthermore, if batch reports require up-to-date data, the batch job will need to be reworked to first refresh *CustomerPortfolio* and then run the reports:

```
// Before code
stmt.prepare(
"SELECT Customer.CustomerId, " +
"  Customer.Name, " +
"  Customer.PhoneNumber, " +
"  SUM(Account.Balance) AccountsTotalBalance, " +
"  SUM(Insurance.Payment) InsuranceTotalPayment, " +
"  SUM(Insurance.Value) InsuranceTotalPayment " +
"FROM Customer, Account, Insurance " +
"WHERE " +
"  Customer.CustomerId = Account.CustomerId " +
"  AND Customer.CustomerId = Insurance.CustomerId " +
"  AND Customer.CustomerId = ?");
stmt.setLong(1,customer.getCustomerID);
stmt.execute();
ResultSet rs = stmt.executeQuery();
```

```
// After code
stmt.prepare(
"SELECT CustomerId, " +
"  Name, " +
"  PhoneNumber, " +
"  AccountsTotalBalance, " +
"  InsuranceTotalPayment, " +
"  InsuranceTotalPayment " +
"FROM CustomerPortfolio " +
"WHERE CustomerId = ?");
stmt.setLong(1,customer.getCustomerID);
stmt.execute();
ResultSet rs = stmt.executeQuery();
```

Migrate Method From Database

Rehost an existing database method (a stored procedure, stored function, or trigger) in the application(s) that currently invoke it.

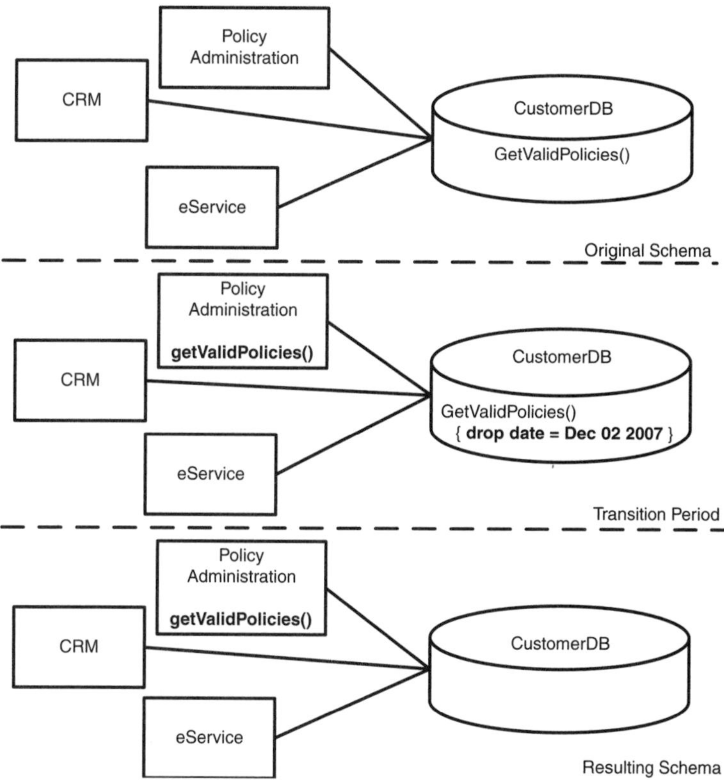

Figure 9.8 Migrating policy retrieval code into the policy administration application.

Motivation

There are four reasons why you may want to apply *Migrate Method From Database*:

- **To support variability.** When the method was originally implemented in the database, the business logic was consistent, or at least was thought to be consistent, between applications. Over time, the application requirements evolved, and now different logic is required in the individual applications.

- **To increase portability.** Database method languages are specific to individual database vendors. By implementing logic outside of the database, perhaps in a shared component or Web service, you will make it easy to port to a new database.
- **To increase scalability.** Although it is possible to scale databases through the use of grid technology, the fact still remains that you can also scale via other means such through the addition of additional application servers. Your enterprise architectural strategy may be to scale your systems via nondatabase means; and if the method is proving to be a bottleneck, you will want to migrate it out of the database.
- **To increase maintainability.** The development tools for leading programming languages such as Java, C#, and Visual Basic are often much more sophisticated than the tools for database programming languages. Better tools—and, of course, better development practices—will make your code easier and therefore less expensive to maintain. Also, by programming in a single language, you reduce the programming skill requirements for project team members—it is easier to find someone with C# experience than it is to find someone with C# and Oracle PLSQL experience.

Potential Tradeoffs

There are several trade-offs associated with this refactoring:

- **Reduced reusability.** Relational databases are a lowest common denominator technology. Virtually any application technology can access them, and therefore implementing shared logic within a relational database offers the greatest chance for reusability.
- **Performance degradation.** There is the potential for decreased performance, particularly if the method accesses significant amounts of data, which would need to get transmitted to the method before it could get processed.

Schema Update Mechanics

As depicted in Figure 9.8, the change to the database schema is straightforward—you just mark the method to be removed, and then after the transition period has ended, you physically remove the method from the database. In this example, the *GetValidPolicies* stored procedure was migrated from *CustomerDB* to the policies administration application. This was done for several reasons: Only one application required that business logic, the network traffic remained the same regardless of where the functionality was performed, and the project team wanted to improve the maintainability of their application. It is interesting to note that the name of the method changed slightly to reflect the naming conventions of the programming language.

Data-Migration Mechanics

There is no data to migrate with this database refactoring.

Access Program Update Mechanics

The method must be developed and tested within the appropriate application(s). You need to search your program code for invocations of the existing method, and then replace that code with the corresponding function call. The following code example shows how application code will be developed to replace functionality provided by the method:

```
//Before code
stmt.prepareCall("begin ? := getValidPolicies(); end;");
stmt.registerOutParameter(1, OracleTypes.CURSOR);
stmt.execute();
ResultSet rs = stmt.getObject(1);
List validPolicies = new ArrayList();
Policy policy = new Policy();
while (rs.next()) {
  policy.setPolicyId(rs.getLong(1));
  policy.setCustomerID(rs.getLong(2));
  policy.setActivationDate(rs.getDate(3));
  policy.setExpirationDate(rs.getDate(4));
  validPolicies.add(policy);
}
return validPolicies;

//After code
stmt.prepare(
  "SELECT PolicyId, CustomerId, "+
  "ActivationDate, ExpirationDate " +
  "FROM Policy" +
  "WHERE ActivationDate < TRUNC(SYSDATE) AND "+
  "ExpirationDate IS NOT NULL AND "+
  "ExpirationDate > TRUNC(SYSDATE)");
ResultSet rs = stmt.execute();
List validPolicies = new ArrayList();
Policy policy = new Policy();
while (rs.next()) {
```

```
    policy.setPolicyId(rs.getLong("PolicyId"));
    policy.setCustomerID(rs.getLong("CustomerId"));
    policy.setActivationDate(rs.getDate
    ("ActivationDate"));
    policy.setExpirationDate(rs.getDate
    ("ExpirationDate"));
    validPolicies.add(policy);
  }
  return validPolicies;
```

Migrate Method To Database

Rehost existing application logic in the database.

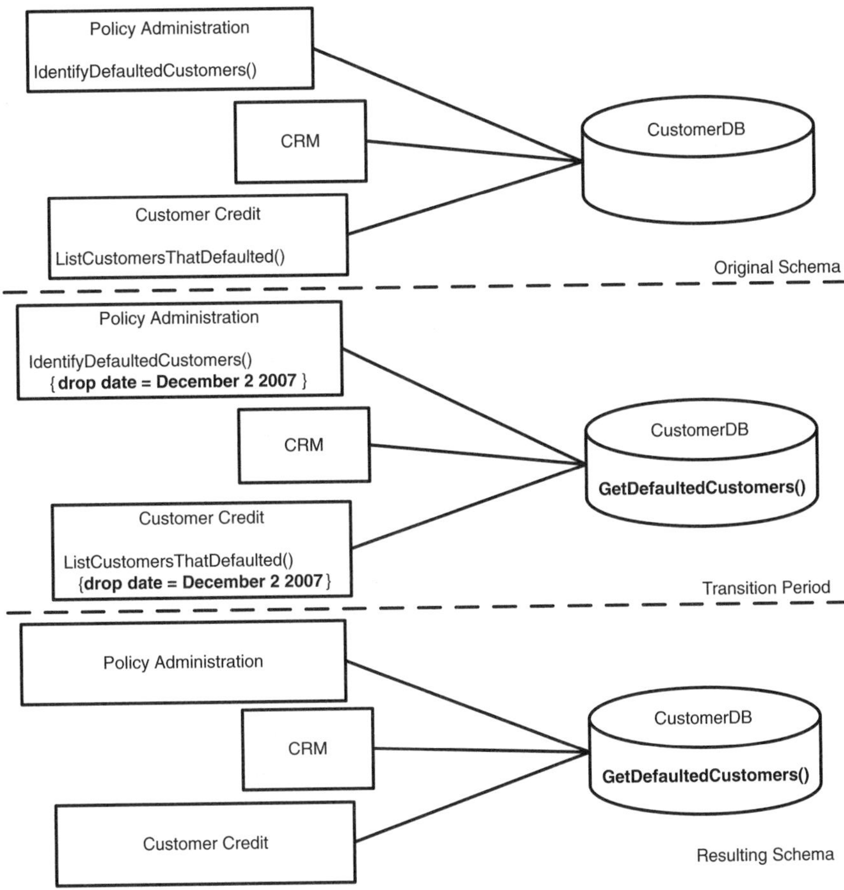

Figure 9.9 Migrating application logic to the database.

Motivation

There are three reasons why you may want to apply *Migrate Method To Database*:

- **To support reuse.** Virtually any application technology can access relational databases, and therefore implementing shared logic as database methods (stored procedures, functions, or triggers) within a relational database offers the greatest chance for reusability.

- **To increase scalability.** It is possible to scale databases through the use of grid technology; therefore, your enterprise architecture may direct you to host all data-oriented logic within your database.
- **To improve performance.** There is the potential for improved performance, particularly if the stored procedure will process significant amounts of data, because the processing will happen closer to the database, which results in a reduced result set being transmitted across the network.

Potential Tradeoffs

The primary drawback to this refactoring is the decreased portability of database methods, code that is specific to the individual database vendor. This problem is often overblown by purists—it is not common for organizations to switch database vendors, perhaps because the vendors have their existing client base locked in or perhaps because it simply is not worth the expense any more.

Schema Update Mechanics

As depicted in Figure 9.9, the change to the database schema is straightforward—you just develop and test the stored procedure. In this example, the logic is to identify a list of defaulted customers, those who are behind on their payments. This logic is implemented in two places, the *Policy Administration* and the *Customer Credit* applications. Each application named the operation differently, *IdentifyDefaultedCustomers()* and *ListCustomersThatDefaulted()*, respectively, although both are replaced by *CustomerDB.GetDefaultedCustomers()*.

Data-Migration Mechanics

There is no data to migrate with this database refactoring.

Access Program Update Mechanics

The method logic must be removed from any application implementing it, and the stored procedure invoked instead. The easiest way to accomplish this is to simply invoke the stored procedure from the existing application method(s). You will likely discover that individual applications have named this method differently, or they may have even designed it differently. For example, one application may implement the business logic as a single large function, whereas another one may implement it as several, smaller functions.

Similarly, you may discover that different applications implement the method in different ways, either because the code no longer reflects the actual requirements (if it ever did) or because the individual applications had good reason to implement the logic differently. For example, the *DetermineVacationDays(Year)* operation provides a list of dates for which employees get paid vacations. This operation is implemented in several applications, but upon examination of the code, it is implemented in different manners. The various versions were written at different times, the rules have changed since some of the older versions were written, and the rules vary by country, state, and sometimes even city. At this point, you would either need to decide to leave the various versions alone (for example, live with the differences), fix the existing application methods, or write a stored procedure(s) in the database that implements the correct version of the logic.

The following code sample shows how the application logic was moved to the database and how the application now uses the stored procedure to get a list of defaulted customers. The example does not show the code for the creation of the stored procedure:

```
//Before code
stmt.prepare(
  "SELECT CustomerId, "+
  "PaymentAmount" +
  "FROM Transactions" +
  "WHERE LastPaymentdate < TRUNC(SYSDATE-90) AND "+
  "PaymentAmount > 30 ");
ResultSet rs = stmt.execute();
List defaulters = new ArrayList();
DefaultedCustomer defaulted  = new DefaultedCustomer();
while (rs.next()) {
  defaulted.setCustomerID(rs.getLong("CustomerId"));
  defaulted.setAmount(rs.getBigDecimal
  ("PaymentAmount"));
  defaulters.add(defaulted);
}
return defaulters;

//After code
stmt.prepareCall("begin ? := getDefaultedCustomers(); end;");
stmt.registerOutParameter(1, OracleTypes.CURSOR);
```

```
stmt.execute();
ResultSet rs = stmt.getObject(1);
List defaulters = new ArrayList();
DefaultedCustomer defaulted  = new DefaultedCustomer();
while (rs.next()) {
  defaulted.setCustomerID(rs.getLong(1));
  defaulted.setAmount(rs.getBigDecimal(2));
  defaulters.add(defaulted);
}
return defaulters;
```

Replace Method(s) With View

Create a view based on one or more existing database methods (stored procedures, stored functions, or triggers) within the database.

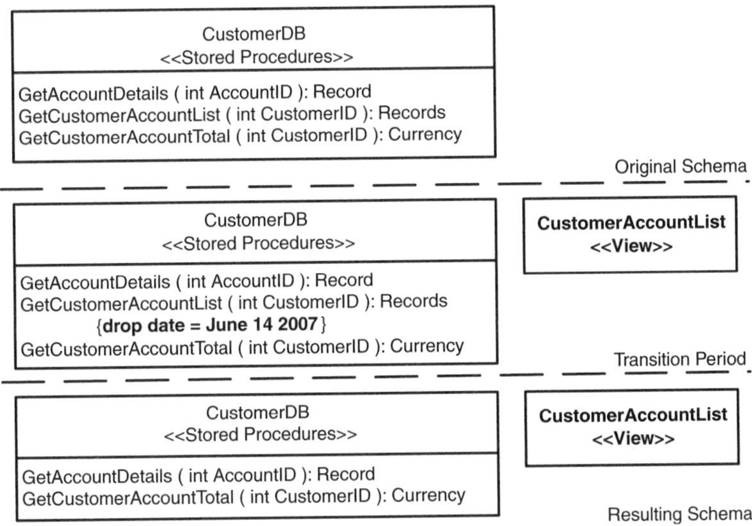

Figure 9.10 Introducing the CustomerAccountList view.

Motivation

There are three basic reasons why you may want to apply *Replace Method(s) With View*:

- **Ease of use.** You may have adopted new tools, in particular reporting tools, that work with views much easier than with methods.
- **Reduce maintenance.** Many people find view definitions easier to maintain than methods.
- **Increase portability.** You can increase the portability of your database schema. Database method languages are specific to individual database vendors, whereas view definitions can be written so that they are SQL standards compliant.

Potential Tradeoffs

This refactoring can typically be applied only to relatively simple methods that implement logic that could also be implemented by a view definition. The implication is that this refactoring limits your architectural flexibility. Furthermore, if your database does not support updatable views, you are limited to replacing only retrieval-oriented methods. Performance and scalability are rarely impacted because all the work still occurs within the database.

Schema Update Mechanics

To update the database schema, you must first introduce the view via the *Introduce View* refactoring (page 306). You must then mark the method for removal, and then eventually remove it after the transition period expires via the **DROP PROCEDURE** command. Figure 9.10 depicts an example where the *Get CustomerAccountList* stored procedure is replaced with the *Customer AccountList* view. The following code depicts the DDL to do so:

```
CREATE VIEW CustomerAccountList (
  CustomerID      NUMBER NOT NULL,
  CustomerName    VARCHAR(40),
  CustomerPhone   VARCHAR2(40),
  AccountNumber   VARCHAR(14),
  AccountBalance  NUMBER,
) AS
SELECT
  Customer.CustomerID,
  Customer.Name,
  Customer.PhoneNumber,
  Account.AccountNumber,
  Account.Balance
FROM Customer,Account
WHERE Customer.CustomerID=Account.CustomerID
;

-- Run this code after June 14 2007
DROP PROCEDURE GetCustomerAccountList
```


Data-Migration Mechanics

There is no data to migrate with this database refactoring.

Access Program Update Mechanics

You need to refactor the access programs to work through the view instead of invoking the stored procedure. The error codes thrown by the database will change when using a view, so you may need to rework your error handling code. The following code shows how an application would be changed to call the view rather than the stored procedure:

```
//Before code
stmt.prepareCall("begin ? := getCustomerAccountList(?); end;");
stmt.registerOutParameter(1, OracleTypes.CURSOR);
stmt.setInt(1,customerId);
stmt.execute();
ResultSet rs = stmt.getObject(1);
List customerAccounts = new ArrayList();
while (rs.next()) {
  customerAccounts.add(populateAccount(rs));
}
return customerAccounts;

//After code
stmt.prepare(
  "SELECT CustomerID, CustomerName, "+
  "CustomerPhone, AccountNumber, AccountBalance " +
  "FROM CustomerAccountList " +
  "WHERE CustomerId = ? ");
stmt.setLong(1,customerId);
ResultSet rs = stmt.executeQuery();
List customerAccounts = new ArrayList();
while (rs.next()) {
  customerAccounts.add(populateAccount(rs));
}
return customerAccounts;
```

Replace View With Method(s)

Replace an existing view with one or more existing methods (stored procedures, stored functions, or triggers) within the database.

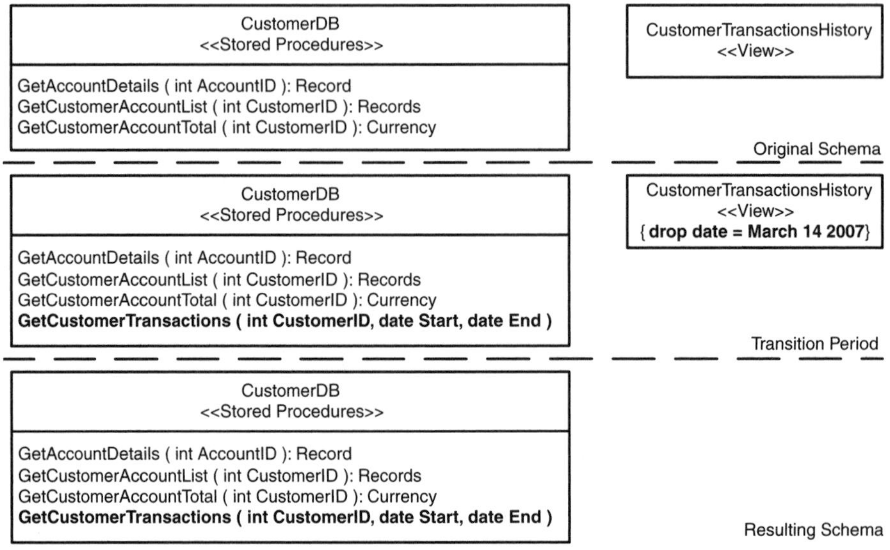

Figure 9.11 Introducing the GetCustomerTransactions stored procedure.

Motivation

Replace View With Method(s)

There are two fundamental reasons why you may want to apply *Replace View With Method(s)*. First, it is possible to implement more complex logic with methods than with views, so this refactoring would be the first step in that direction. Second, methods can update data tables. Some databases do not support updatable views, or if they do, it is often limited to a single table. By moving from a view-based encapsulation strategy to a method-based one, your database architecture becomes more flexible.

Potential Tradeoffs

There are several potential problems with this refactoring. First, reporting tools usually do not work well with methods, but they do with views. Second, there is a potential decrease in portability because database method languages

are specific to individual database vendors. Third, maintainability may decrease because many people prefer to work with views rather than methods (and vice versa). Luckily, performance and scalability are rarely impacted because all the work still occurs within the database.

Schema Update Mechanics

To update the database schema, you must first introduce the appropriate method(s) required to replace the view. You must then mark the view for removal, and then eventually remove it after the transition period expires using the *Drop View* (page 79) refactoring.

Figure 9.11 depicts an example where the *CustomerTransactionsHistory* view is replaced with the *GetCustomerTransactions* stored procedure. The following code depicts the code to introduce the method and to drop the view:

```
CREATE OR REPLACE PROCEDURE GetCustomerTransactions
{
  P_CustomerID IN NUMBER
  P_Start IN DATE
  P_End IN DATE
}
IS
BEGIN
  SELECT *
  FROM Transaction
  WHERE Transaction.CustomerID = P_CustomerID
  AND Transaction.PostingDate BETWEEN P_Start AND P_End;
END;

--On March 14 2007
DROP VIEW CustomerTransactionsHistory;
```

Data-Migration Mechanics

There is no data to migrate with this database refactoring.

Access Program Update Mechanics

You need to refactor the access programs to work through the method(s) rather than the view. The error codes thrown by the database will change when using methods, so you may need to rework your error handling code.

When you replace the *CustomerTransactionsHistory* view with the *GetCustomerTransactions* stored procedure view, your code needs to change as shown here:

```
//Before code
stmt.prepare(
  "SELECT * " +
  "FROM CustomerTransactionsHistory " +
  "WHERE CustomerId = ? "+
  "AND TransactionDate BETWEEN ? AND ? ");
stmt.setLong(1,customerId);
stmt.setDate(2,startDate);
stmt.setDate(3,endDate);
ResultSet rs = stmt.executeQuery();
List customerTransactions = new ArrayList();
while (rs.next()) {
  customerTransactions.add(populateTransactions(rs));
}
return customerTransactions;

//After code
stmt.prepareCall("begin ? :=
getCustomerTransactions(?,?,?); end;");
stmt.registerOutParameter(1, OracleTypes.CURSOR);
stmt.setInt(1,customerId);
stmt.setDate(2,startDate);
stmt.setDate(3,endDate);
stmt.execute();
ResultSet rs = stmt.getObject(1);
List customerTransactions = new ArrayList();
while (rs.next()) {
  customerTransactions.add(populateAccount(rs));
}
return customerTransactions;
```

Use Official Data Source

Use the official data source for a given entity, instead of the current one which you are using.

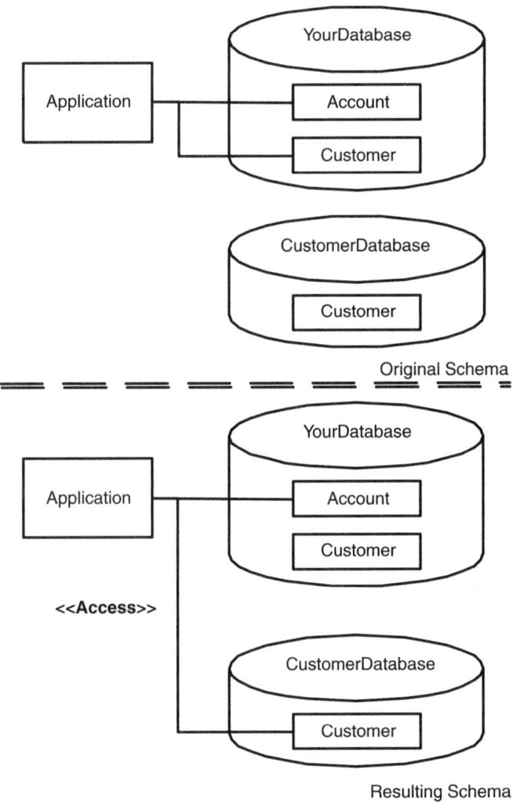

Figure 9.12 Directly accessing the official customer data from the Customer database.

Motivation

The primary reason to apply *Use Official Data Source* is to use the correct version of the data for a given table or tables. When the same data is stored in several places, you run the risk of inconsistency and lack of availability. For example, assume that you have multiple databases in your enterprise, one of which, the CRM database, is the official source of customer information.

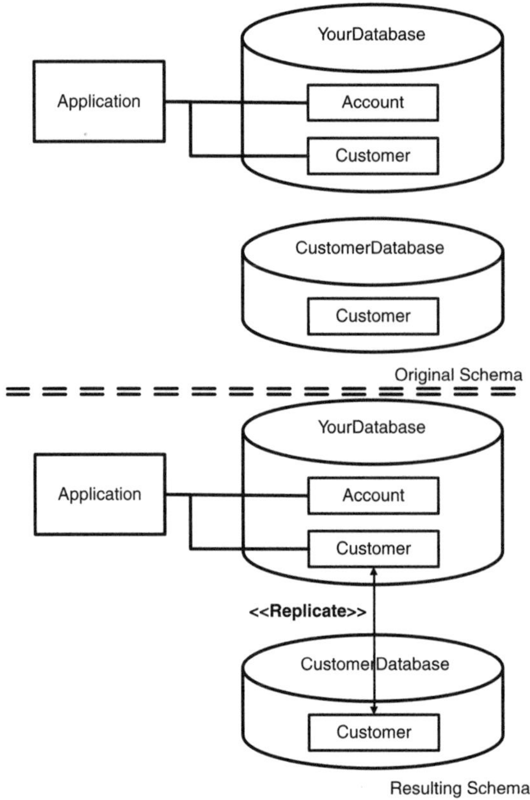

Figure 9.13 Using official customer data via a replication strategy.

If your application is using its own Customer table, you may not be working with all the customer data available within your organization. Worse yet, your application could record a new customer but their information is not made available to the CRM database, and therefore it is not available to the other applications within your organization.

Potential Tradeoffs

The primary tradeoff is the cost of refactoring all the references to the table in your local database to now use the official database tables. If the key strategy of the official data source is different from what your table is using, you may want to first apply *Consolidate Key Strategy* (page 168) so that the identifiers used in your database reflect that of the official data source. Furthermore, the semantics and timeliness of the official source data may not be identical to that of the data you are currently using. You may need to apply refactorings such as *Apply Standard Codes* (page 157), *Apply Standard Type* (page 162), and *Introduce Common Format* (page 183) to convert your existing data over to something that conforms to the official data source.

Schema Update Mechanics

To update the schema, you must do the following:

1. **Identify the official data source.** You have to identify the official data source, which will often be in an external database that is outside the scope of your control. Worse yet, there could be several "official sources," which you either need to pick from or consolidate appropriately for your situation. You need to negotiate agreement with both your project stakeholder(s) and the owners of the data source that your application should be accessing.

2. **Choose an implementation strategy.** You have two choices: to either rework your application(s) to directly access the official data source (the strategy depicted in Figure 9.12) or to replicate the source data with your existing table (the strategy depicted in Figure 9.13). When the official data source is in another database, the replication strategy scales better than the direct access strategy because your application will potentially be only coupled to a single database.

3. **Direct access strategy.** You change your application such that the application now directly accesses *CustomerDatabase*. Note that this may require a different database connection than what is currently used, or the invocation of a web service or transaction. Following this strategy, you must be able to handle transactions across different databases.

4. **Replication strategy.** You can set up replication between *YourDatabase* and *CustomerDatabase* so that you replicate all the tables that you require. If you want to have updatable tables in *YourDatabase*, you must use multimaster replication. Following this strategy, you should not have to change your application code as long as both the schema and the semantics of your source data remains the same. If changes are required to your schema, such as renaming tables or, worse yet, the semantics of the official data are different from that of your current data, you will likely require change to your external programs.

5. **Remove tables that are not used anymore.** When you choose to directly access the official source data, you no longer have any use for the tables in the *YourDatabase*. You should use *Drop Table* (page 77) refactoring to remove those tables.

Data-Migration Mechanics

There is no data to migrate for this refactoring if the data semantics of the official *YourDatabase* and the local *YourDatabase* are the same. If they are not the same, you need to either consider backing out of this refactoring, following a replication strategy where you convert the different values back and forth, or refactoring your application(s) to accept the data semantics of the official source. Unless the data is semantically similar, or you get very lucky and find a way to safely convert the data back and forth, it is unlikely that a replication strategy will work for you.

Access Program Update Mechanics

The way that you change external programs varies depending on your implementation strategy. If you use the direct access strategy, the programs must now connect to and work with the official data source, *CustomerDatabase*. With the replication strategy, you must create replication scripts between the appropriate tables in *YourDatabase* and *CustomerDatabase*. When the table(s) in *YourDatabase* match the table(s) in *CustomerDatabase*, the programs should not need to be changed. Otherwise, you either have to adopt the schema and semantics of the official data source, and then refactor your application(s) appropriately, or you need to figure out a way to implement the replication in such a way that the schema in *YourDatabase* is not changed. One way to do that is to implement scripts that convert the data back and forth, which is often difficult to accomplish in practice because the mappings are rarely one to one. Another way, equally difficult, is to replace the source table(s) in *YourDatabase* with the appropriate ones from *CustomerDatabase*, and then apply the *Encapsulate Table With View* refactoring (page 243) so that the existing applications can still work with "the old schema." These new view(s) would need to implement the same conversion logic as the previously mentioned scripts.

The following code shows how to change your application to work with the official data source by using the *crmDB* connection instead:

```
// Before code
stmt = DB.prepare("select CustomerID,Name,PhoneNumber "+
  "FROM Customer WHERE CustomerID = ?");
stmt.setLong(1, customerID);
stmt.execute();
ResultSet rs = stmt.executeQuery();

// After code
stmt = crmDB.prepare("select CustomerID,Name,PhoneNumber "+
  "FROM Customer WHERE CustomerID = ?");
stmt.setLong(1, customerID);
stmt.execute();
ResultSet rs = stmt.executeQuery();
```

Chapter 10

Method Refactorings

This chapter summarizes the code refactorings that we have found applicable to stored procedures, stored functions, and triggers. For the sake of simplicity, we refer to these three types of functionality simply as *methods*, the term that Martin Fowler used in *Refactoring* (Fowler 1999). As the name suggests, a method refactoring is a change to a stored procedure that improves its quality. Our goal is to present an overview of these refactorings. You can find detailed descriptions in *Refactoring*, the seminal work on the subject.

We differentiate between two categories of method refactorings, those that change the interface of the database offered to external programs and those that modify the internals of a method. For example, the refactoring *Add Parameter* (page 278) would change the interface of a method, whereas *Consolidate Conditional Expression* (page 283) does not. (It replaces a complex comparison with an invocation to a new method that implements just the comparison.) We distinguish between the two categories because refactorings that change the interface will require external programs to be refactored, whereas those that only modify the internals of a method do not.

10.1 Interface Changing Refactorings

Each of these refactorings includes a transition period to provide development teams sufficient time to update external programs that invoke the methods. Part of the refactoring is to rework the original version of the method(s) to invoke the new version(s) appropriately, and then after the transition period, the old version is invoked accordingly.

10.1.1 Add Parameter

As the name suggests, this refactoring adds a new parameter to an existing method. In Figure 10.1, you see an example where *MiddleName* was added as a third parameter to *ReadCustomer*. The safest way to add a parameter is to add it to the end of parameter list; that way, when you refactor the invocations of the method, you do not run the risk of reordering the parameters improperly. If you later decide that the parameters appear in the wrong order, you can apply the *Reorder Parameters* refactoring (page 281).

10.1.2 Parameterize Method

Sometimes two or more methods do basically the same thing. For example, in Figure 10.2, the *GetAmericanCustomers*, *GetCanadianCustomers*, and *GetBrazilianCustomers* stored procedures produce a list of American, Canadian, and Brazilian customers, respectively. Although these separate procedures have the advantage of being specific, thereby ensuring that the right queries are being invoked on the database, they are more difficult to maintain than a single stored procedure. These stored procedures are replaced with the *GetCustomerByCountry* stored procedure, which takes a country identifier as a parameter. There is now less code to maintain as a result, and it is easy to add support for new countries just by adding new country codes.

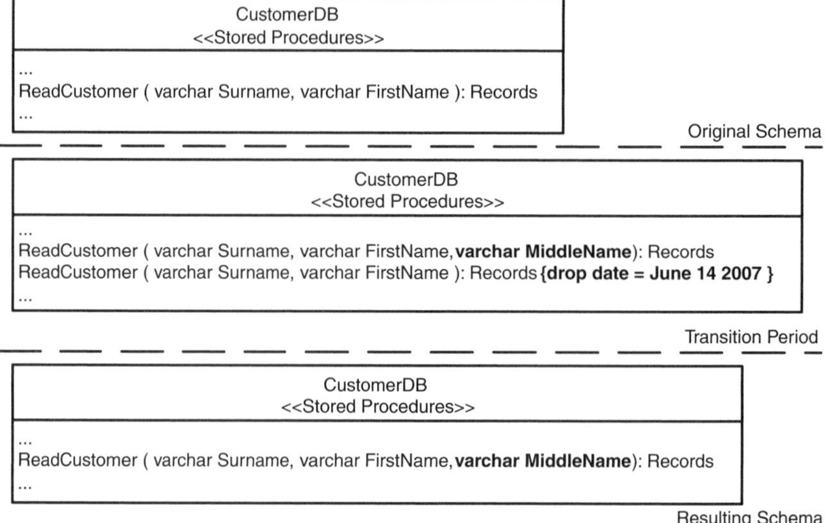

Figure 10.1 Adding a parameter.

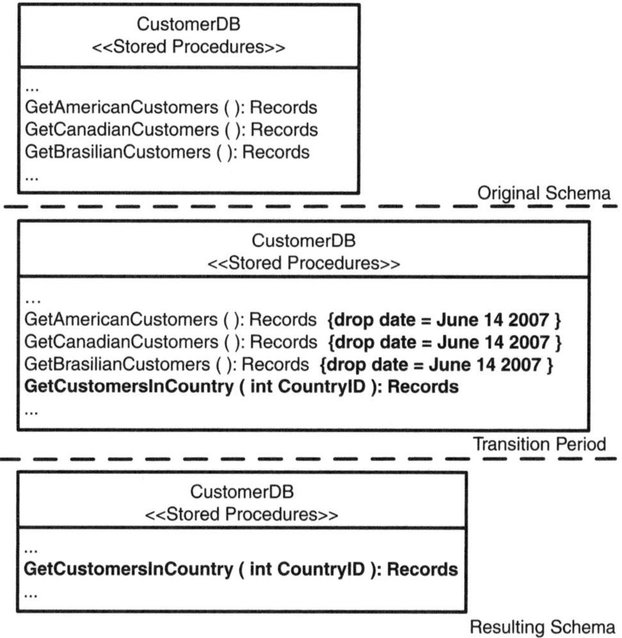

Figure 10.2 Parameterizing a stored procedure.

10.1.3 Remove Parameter

Sometimes a method includes an extra parameter, perhaps because it was originally included in the belief that it would be needed in the future, or perhaps because the business changed and it is no longer required, or perhaps the parameter value can be obtained via another manner, such as reading it from a lookup table. In Figure 10.3, you see that *GetAccountList* has an extraneous *AsOfDate* parameter that is removed to reflect the actual usage of the stored procedure.

10.1.4 Rename Method

Sometimes a method is poorly named, or it simply does not follow your corporate naming conventions. For example, in Figure 10.4, the *GetAccountList* stored procedure is renamed to *GetAccountsForCustomer* to reflect your standard naming conventions.

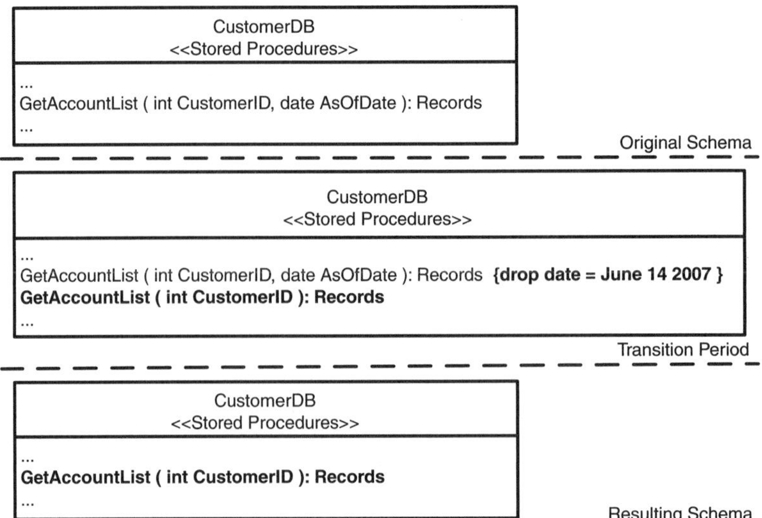

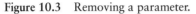

Figure 10.3 Removing a parameter.

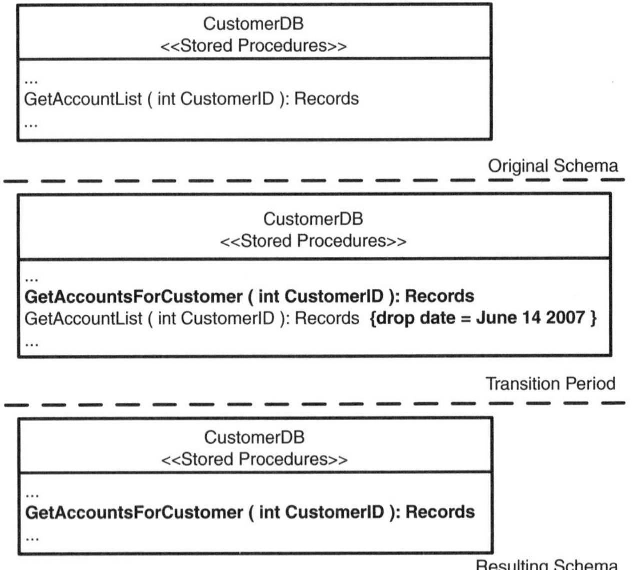

Figure 10.4 Renaming a stored procedure.

10.1.5 Reorder Parameters

It is common to discover that the ordering of the parameters of a method does not make sense, perhaps because new parameters have been added in the wrong order via *Add Parameter* (page 278) or simply because the ordering does not reflect the current business needs. Regardless, you can make a stored procedure easier to understand by ordering its parameters appropriately (see Figure 10.5).

As you see in Figure 10.6, the parameters of *GetCustomers* were reordered to reflect common business ordering conventions. Note that this is a highly risky example—you cannot have a transition period in this case because the types of all three parameters are identical, and therefore you cannot simply override the method. The implication is that you could reorder the parameters but forget to reorder them in external code that invokes the method—the method would still run, but with the wrong values for the parameters, a tricky defect to find without good test cases. Had the parameters been of different types, external applications that had not been refactored to pass the parameters in the new order would break, and it would be very easy to find the affected code as a result.

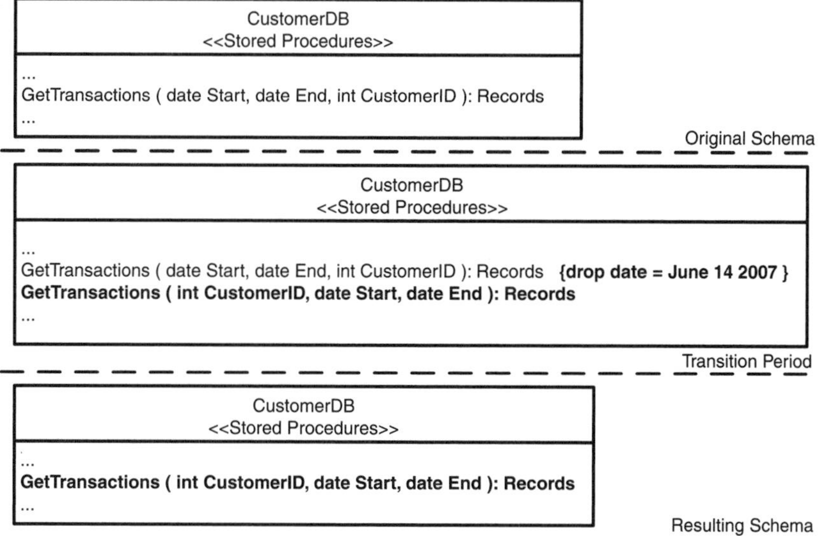

Figure 10.5 Reordering the parameters of a method.

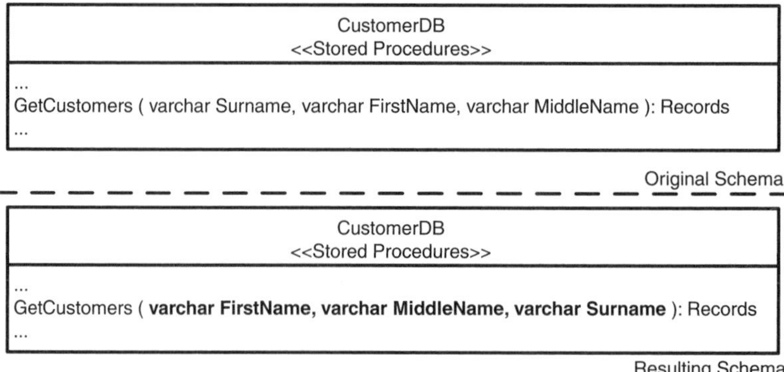

Figure 10.6 Reordering the parameters of a method without a transition period.

10.1.6 Replace Parameter with Explicit Methods

Sometimes you will have a single method doing one of several things, based on the value of a parameter being passed to it. For example, in Figure 10.7, you see that *GetAccountValue*, which is basically a generic getter that returns the value of a column within a row, is replaced with the more specific *GetAccountBalance*, *GetAccountCustomerID*, and *GetAccountOpeningDate* stored procedures.

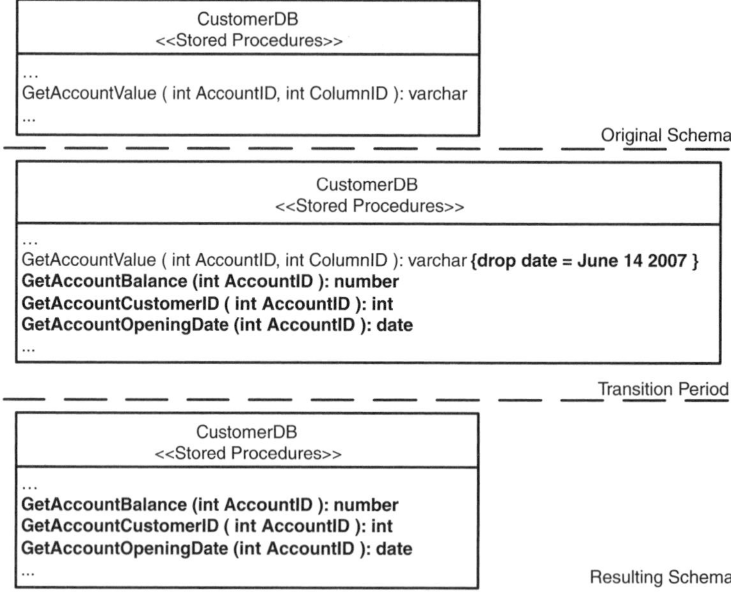

Figure 10.7 Replacing a parameter with explicit stored procedures.

10.2 Internal Refactorings

Internal refactorings improve the quality of the implementation of a method without changing its interface.

10.2.1 Consolidate Conditional Expression

Within the logic of a method, you often have a series of conditional tests that produce the same result. You should refactor your code to combine those conditionals to make your code clearer, as you see in the following example, in which the three conditionals are combined into one. This refactoring also sets you up to apply *Extract Method* (page 285) to create a method that implements the conditional:

```
-- Before code

CREATE OR REPLACE FUNCTION GetAccountAverageBalance
 ( inAccountID IN NUMBER)
 RETURN NUMBER;
AS
 averageBalance := 0;
BEGIN
 IF inAccountID = 10000 THEN
  RETURN 0;
 END IF;
 IF inAccountID = 123456 THEN
  RETURN 0;
 END IF;
 IF inAccountID = 987654 THEN
  RETURN 0;
 END IF;
 -- Code to calculate the average balance
 RETURN averageBalance;
END;

-- After code

CREATE OR REPLACE FUNCTION GetAccountAverageBalance
 ( inAccountID IN NUMBER)
 RETURN NUMBER;
AS
 averageBalance := 0;
BEGIN
 IF inAccountID = 10000 || inAccountID = 123456 || inAccountID = 987654 THEN
  RETURN 0;
 END IF;
```

```
 -- Code to calculate the average balance
  RETURN averageBalance;
END;
```

10.2.2 Decompose Conditional

You have a conditional **IF-THEN-ELSE** expression that is complex and therefore difficult to understand. Replace the *condition*, *then part*, and *else part* with invocations to methods that implement the logic of the expression. In the first version of the following code, the logic to determine which interest rate to apply is determined based on whether the value of *inBalance* is below, within, or over a certain threshold. In the second version, the code is simplified by the addition of calls to *BalanceIsSufficient*, *CalculateLowInterest*, and *CalculateHighInterest*. (These functions are not shown.)

```
-- Before code

CREATE OR REPLACE FUNCTION CalculateInterest
 ( inBalance IN NUMBER )
 RETURN NUMBER;
AS
 lowBalance NUMBER;
 highBalance NUMBER;
 lowInterestRate NUMBER;
 highInterestRate NUMBER;
BEGIN

 lowBalance := GetLowBalance();
 highBalance := GetHighBalance();
 lowInterestRate := GetLowInterestRate();
 highInterestRate := GetHighInterestRate();

 IF inBalance < lowBalance THEN
  RETURN 0;
 END IF

 IF inBalance >= lowBalance && inBalance <= highBalance THEN
  RETURN inBalance * lowInterestRate;
 ELSE
  RETURN inBalance * highInterestRate;
 END IF;
END;

-- After code

CREATE OR REPLACE FUNCTION CalculateInterest
 ( inBalance IN NUMBER )
 RETURN NUMBER;
```

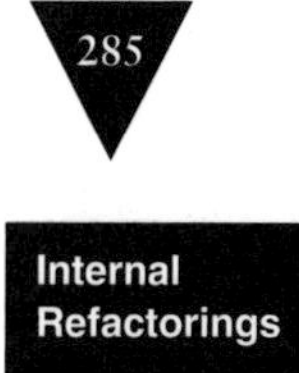


```
AS
BEGIN

 IF BalanceIsInsufficient( inBalance ) THEN
  RETURN 0;
 END IF

 IF IsLowInterestBalance( inBalance ) THEN
  RETURN CalculateLowInterest( inBalance );
 ELSE
  RETURN CalculateHighInterest( inBalance );
 END IF;
END;
```

10.2.3 Extract Method

Within an existing method, you have a code fragment that could be grouped together and extracted into its own method whose name explains what it does. The code fragment is usually duplicated elsewhere and/or or implements meaningful functionality; therefore, you can apply this refactoring to simplify your code. Short, well-named operations are easier to understand and therefore to maintain, and they are more likely to be reused. As you can see in the following code, the first version is simplified by replacing the logic to determine the starting daily balance with an invocation of the *GetDailyBalance* stored function. In the final version of the code, we have applied this refactoring several times more to further simplify the code. A side effect of applying this refactoring is that your high-level, public stored procedures will read like well-commented, highly literate code:

```
-- Initial version of the code

CREATE OR REPLACE FUNCTION CalculateAccountInterest
 ( inAccountID IN NUMBER,
 inStart IN DATE,
 inEnd IN DATE )
 RETURN NUMBER;
AS
 medianBalance NUMBER;
 startBalance NUMBER;
 endBalance NUMBER;
 interest := 0;
BEGIN
 BEGIN
  -- Determine the starting balance
  SELECT Balance INTO startBalance
   FROM DailyEndBalance
   WHERE AccountID = inAccountID && PostingDate = inStart;
```

```
  EXCEPTION WHEN NO_DATA_FOUND THEN
   startBalance := 0;

  -- Determine the ending balance
  SELECT Balance INTO endBalance
   FROM DailyEndBalance
   WHERE AccountID = inAccountID && PostingDate = inEnd;
  EXCEPTION WHEN NO_DATA_FOUND THEN
   endBalance := 0;
  END;
  medianBalance := ( startBalance + endBalance ) / 2;
  IF medianBalance < 0 THEN
   medianBalance := 0;
             END IF;
            IF medianBalance >= 500 THEN
   interest := medianBalance * 0.01;
  END IF;
 RETURN interest;
END;

-- Intermediate version of the code

CREATE OR REPLACE Function CalculateAccountInterest
 ( inAccountID IN NUMBER,
 inStart IN DATE,
 inEnd IN DATE )
 RETURN NUMBER;
AS
 medianBalance NUMBER;
 startBalance NUMBER;
 endBalance NUMBER;
 interest := 0;
BEGIN
 startBalance := GetDailyEndBalance ( inAccountID, inStart );

 BEGIN
   -- Determine the ending balance
  SELECT Balance INTO endBalance
   FROM DailyEndBalance
   WHERE AccountID = inAccountID && PostingDate = inEnd;
  EXCEPTION WHEN NO_DATA_FOUND THEN
   endBalance := 0;
 END;
 medianBalance := ( startBalance + endBalance ) / 2;
 IF medianBalance < 0 THEN
  medianBalance := 0;
 END IF;

 IF medianBalance >= 500 THEN
  interest := medianBalance * 0.01;
 END IF;
```

```
 RETURN interest;
END;

CREATE OR REPLACE Function GetDailyBalance
 ( inAccountID IN NUMBER,
 inDate IN DATE )
 RETURN NUMBER;
AS
 endbalance NUMBER;
BEGIN
 BEGIN
   SELECT Balance INTO endBalance
   FROM DailyEndBalance
   WHERE AccountID = inAccountID < PostingDate = inDate;
  EXCEPTION WHEN NO_DATA_FOUND THEN
   endBalance := 0;
 END;
 RETURN endBalance;
END;

-- Final version of the code

CREATE OR REPLACE FUNCTION CalculateAccountInterest
( inAccountID IN NUMBER,
 inStart IN DATE,
 inEnd IN DATE )
 RETURN NUMBER;
AS
 medianBalance NUMBER;
 startBalance NUMBER;
 endBalance NUMBER;
BEGIN
 startBalance := GetDailyEndBalance ( inAccountID, inStart );
 endBalance:= GetDailyEndBalance ( inAccountID, inEnd );
 medianBalance := CalculateMedianBalance ( startBalance, endBalance );
 RETURN CalculateInterest ( medianBalance );
END;

-- Code for GetDailyEndBalance, CalculateMedianBalance, & CalculateInterest goes here
```

10.2.4 Introduce Variable

Your method code contains a complicated expression that is difficult to read. You can introduce well-named variables in your code that are used to implement portions of the expression and then are composed to form the original expression, thereby making the method easier to understand. This refactoring is the equivalent of Martin Fowler's *Introduce Explaining Variable* (Fowler 1999). After speaking with him, he suggested that we use the simpler name; in

Internal Refactorings

hindsight, he realized that he should have originally called this refactoring *Introduce Variable*, and most tool vendors also use the simpler name:

```
-- Before code

CREATE OR REPLACE FUNCTION DetermineAccountStatus
 ( inAccountID IN NUMBER,
  inStart IN DATE,
  inEnd IN DATE )
 RETURN VARCHAR;
AS
      lastAccessedDate DATE;
BEGIN
 -- Some code to calculate lastAccessDate

 IF ( inDate < lastAccessDate && outdate > lastAccessDate )
  && ( inAccountID > 10000 )
  && ( inAccountID != 123456 && inAcountID != 987654) THEN
  -- do something
 END IF;
 -- do another thing
END;

-- After code

CREATE OR REPLACE FUNCTION DetermineAccountStatus
 ( inAccountID IN NUMBER,
  inStart IN DATE,
  inEnd IN DATE )
 RETURN VARCHAR;
AS
 lastAccessedDate DATE;
 isBetweenDates BOOLEAN;
 isValidAccountID BOOLEAN;
 isNotTestAccount BOOLEAN
BEGIN
 -- Some code to calculate lastAccessDate
 isBetweenDates := inDate < lastAccessDate && outdate > lastAccessDate;
 isValidAccountID := inAccountID > 100000;
 isNotTestAccount := inAccountID != 123456 && inAcountID != 987654;
 IF isBetweenDates && isValidAccountID &&
 isNotTestAccount THEN
  -- do something
 END IF;
 -- do another thing
END;
```

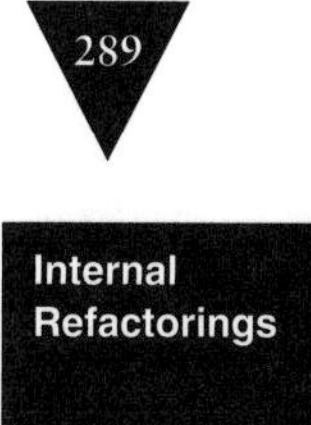

10.2.5 Remove Control Flag

You have a variable acting as a control flag to break out of a control construct such as a loop. You can simplify your code by replacing the use of the control flag by examining the expression within the control construct. As you see in the following example, when you remove the *controlFlag* logic, the code is simplified:

```
-- Before code

DECLARE
 controlFlag := 0;
 anotherVariable := 0;
BEGIN
 WHILE controlFlag = 0 LOOP
  -- Do something
  IF anotherVariable > 20 THEN
   controlFlag = 1;
  ELSE
   -- Do something else
  END IF;
 END LOOP;
END;

-- After code

DECLARE
 anotherVariable := 0;
BEGIN
 WHILE anotherVariable <= 20 LOOP
  -- Do something
  -- Do something else
 END LOOP;
END;
```

10.2.6 Remove Middle Man

Sometimes a method just acts as a pass through, or middle man, for other methods. This can happen when a stored procedure is renamed and then a stored procedure is introduced with the original name, which merely calls the stored procedure with the new name. It can also happen when you realize that you have two stored procedures that do the same thing; so, as you can see, one of them was rewritten to simply invoke the other. Regardless, when you see code

Internal Refactorings

such as the following example, you should refactor whatever invokes *AProcedure* to now invoke *AnotherProcedure* (thus allowing you to drop *AProcedure*):

```
CREATE OR REPLACE PROCEDURE AProcedure
 parameter1 IN NUMBER;
 ...
 parameterN IN VARCHAR;
AS
BEGIN
 EXECUTE AnotherProcedure ( parameter1, ..., parameterN );
END;
```

10.2.7 Rename Parameter

It is common to discover that an existing parameter name is difficult to understand—either the parameter name made sense at the time and its usage has changed over time or it was simply misnamed to begin with. This is a rather simple refactoring to implement; you merely change the parameter name in the original source code.

10.2.8 Replace Literal with Table Lookup

You have hard-coded a literal number that has a particular meaning in the code of a method, making it difficult to maintain. A better approach is to store the value in a table, and then retrieve it as needed from the table. (This table could be cached to improve performance.) In the following code, the minimum balance of $500 is retrieved in the new version of the code from a single row table called *CorporateBusinessConstants* used to store such values. (We could have also implemented a multirow table with a limited number of columns, one for each type, in which to store the data.) The code is then further improved by applying this refactoring again to obtain the value for the interest rate. We also apply *Extract Method* (page 285) to consolidate the logic of obtaining the values from the lookup table. This refactoring is the database version of the *Replace Magic Number With Symbolic Constant* (Fowler 1999) code refactoring:

```
-- Initial version of the code

CREATE OR REPLACE FUNCTION CalculateInterest
 ( inBalance IN NUMBER )
 RETURN NUMBER;
AS
 interest := 0;
BEGIN
```

```
 IF inBalance >= 500 THEN
  interest := medianBalance * 0.01;
 END IF;
 RETURN interest;
END;

-- Intermediate version of the code

CREATE OR REPLACE FUNCTION CalculateInterest
 ( inBalance IN NUMBER )
 RETURN NUMBER;
AS
 interest := 0;
 minimumBalance NUMBER;
BEGIN
 BEGIN
  SELECT MinimumBalanceForInterest INTO minimumBalance
   FROM CorporateBusinessConstants
   WHERE RowNumber = 1;
  EXCEPTION WHEN NO_DATA_FOUND THEN
   minimumBalance := 0;
 END;
 IF inBalance >= minimumBalance THEN
  interest := medianBalance * 0.01;
 END IF;
 RETURN interest;
END;

-- Final version of the code

CREATE OR REPLACE FUNCTION CalculateInterest
 ( inBalance IN NUMBER )
 RETURN NUMBER;
AS
 interest := 0;
 minimumBalance NUMBER;
 interestRate NUMBER;
BEGIN

 minimumBalance := GetMinimumBalance();
 interestRate := GetInterestRate();

 IF inBalance >= minimumBalance THEN
  interest := medianBalance * interestRate;
 END IF;
 RETURN interest;
END;
```

10.2.9 Replace Nested Conditional with Guard Clauses

Nested conditional statements can be difficult to understand. In the following example, the nested **IF** statements were replaced with a series of separate **IF** statements to improve the readability of the code:

```
-- Before code

BEGIN
 IF condition1 THEN
  -- do something 1
 ELSE
  IF condition2 THEN
   -- do something 2
  ELSE
   IF condition3 THEN
    -- do something 3
   END IF;
  END IF;
 END IF;
END;

-- After code

BEGIN
 IF condition1 THEN
  -- do something 1
  RETURN;
 END IF;
 IF condition2 THEN
  -- do something 2
  RETURN;
 END IF;
 IF condition3 THEN
  -- do something 3
  RETURN;
 END IF;
END;
```

10.2.10 Split Temporary Variable

You have a temporary variable being used for one or more purposes within your method. This has likely prevented you from giving it a meaningful name, or perhaps it has a meaningful name for one purpose but not the other. The solution is to introduce a temporary variable for each purpose, as you see in the following code, which uses *aTemporaryVariable* as a repository for the converted imperial values into metric values:

```
-- Before code

DECLARE
 aTemporaryVariable := 0;
 farenheitTemperature := 0;
 lengthInInches := 0;
BEGIN
 -- retrieve farenheitTemperature
 aTemporaryVariable := (farenheitTemperature-32 ) * 5 / 9;
 -- do something
 -- retrieve lengthInInches
 aTemporaryVariable := lengthInInches * 2.54;
 -- do something
END;

-- After code

DECLARE
 celciusTemperature := 0;
 farenheitTemperature := 0;
 lenghtInCentimeters := 0;
 lengthInInches := 0;
BEGIN
 -- retrieve farenheitTemperature
 celciusTemperature := (farenheitTemperature-32 ) * 5 / 9;
 -- do something
 -- retrieve lengthInInches
 lenghtInCentimeters := lengthInInches * 2.54;
 -- do something
END;
```

10.2.11 Substitute Algorithm

If you find a clearer way to write the logic of an algorithm implemented as a method, you should do it. If you need to change an existing algorithm, it is often easier to simplify it first and then update it. Because it is hard to rewrite a complicated algorithm, you should first simplify it via other refactorings, such as *Extract Method* (page 285) before applying *Substitute Algorithm*.

Chapter 11

Transformations

Transformations are changes that change the semantics of your database schema by adding new features to it. The transformations described in this chapter are as follows:

- Insert Data
- Introduce New Column
- Introduce New Table
- Introduce View
- Update Data

Insert Data

Insert data into an existing table.

Schema:

AccountType
AccountTypeID <<PK>> Name EffectiveDate

Data Values Before:

AccountType		
AccountTypeID	Name	EffectiveDate
1	Checking	Dec 6 2005
2	Saving	Nov 12 2005
3	Private	Jan 7 2006
4	Money Market	Jun 4 2006
5	Credit	Mar 12 2006

Data Values After:

AccountType		
AccountTypeID	Name	EffectiveDate
1	Checking	Dec 6 2005
2	Saving	Nov 12 2005
3	Private	Jan 7 2006
4	Money Market	Jun 4 2006
5	Credit	Mar 12 2006
6	**Brokerage**	**Feb 1 2007**

Figure 11.1 Inserting a new AccountType.

Motivation

You typically need to apply *Insert Data* as the result of structural changes within your table design. You may need to apply *Insert Data* as the result of the following:

- **Table reorganization.** When you are using *Rename Table* (page 113), *Merge Tables* (page 96), *Split Table* (page 145), or *Drop Table* (page 77) refactorings, you may have to use *Insert Data* to reorganize the data in the existing tables.

- **Provide static lookup data.** All applications need static lookup data—for example, tables listing the states/provinces (for instance, Illinois and Ontario) that you do business in, a list of address types (for instance, home, business, vacation), and a list of account types (for instance, checking, savings, and investment). If your application does not include administrative editing screens for maintaining these lists, you need to insert this data manually.
- **Create test data.** During development, you need known data values inserted into your development database(s) to support your testing efforts.

Potential Tradeoffs

Inserting new data into tables can be tricky, especially when you are going to insert lookup data that is referenced from one or more other tables. For example, assume the *Address* table references data in the *State* table, which you are inserting new data into. The data that you insert into *State* must contain valid values that will appear in *Address*.

Schema Update Mechanics

To update the database schema, you must do the following:

1. **Identify the data to insert.** This includes identifying any dependencies. If this is part of moving data from another table, should the source row be deleted? Is the inserted data new, and if so, have the values been accepted by your project stakeholder(s)?
2. **Identify the data destination.** Which table is the data being inserted into?
3. **Identify the data source.** Is the data coming from another table or is it a manual insert (for example, you are writing a script to create the data)?
4. **Identify transformation needs.** Does the source data need to be translated before it can be inserted into the target table? For example, you may have a list of metric measurements that need to be converted into imperial values before being inserted into a lookup table.

Data-Migration Mechanics

When small amounts of data need to be inserted, you will likely find that a simple SQL script that inserts the source data into the target location is sufficient. For large amounts of data, you need to take a more sophisticated approach, such as using database utilities such as Oracle's SQLLDR or a bulk loader (because of the time it will take to insert the data).

Figure 11.1 shows how we insert a new record into the *AccountType* table representing brokerage accounts. This *AccountType* supports new functionality that needs to first be tested and then moved to production later on. The following code depicts the DML to insert data into the *AccountType* table:

```
INSERT INTO AccountType
(AccountTypeId,Name,EffectiveDate)
VALUES
(6,'Brokerage','Feb 1 2007');
```

Access Program Update Mechanics

When *Insert Data* is applied as the result of another database refactoring, the applications should have been updated to reflect that refactoring. However, when *Insert Data* is applied to support the addition of data within an existing schema, it is possible that external application code will need to be changed. You need to update **WHERE** clauses. For example, in Figure 11.1, we inserted *Brokerage* into the *AccountType* table. You may need to update **SELECT** statements to not read this value when you only want to work with standard banking accounts (everything but brokerage), as you see in the following code. You can also use *Introduce View* (page 306) to create a specific view that the application uses which returns this subset of data:

```
// Before code
stmt.prepare(
  "SELECT * FROM AccountType " +
    "WHERE AccountTypeId NOT IN (?,?)");
stmt.setLong(1,PRIVATEACCOUNT.getId);
stmt.setLong(2,MONEYMARKETACCOUNT.getId);
stmt.execute();
ResultSet standardAccountTypes = stmt.executeQuery();

//After code
stmt.prepare(
  "SELECT * FROM AccountType " +
    "WHERE AccountTypeId NOT IN (?,?,?)");
```

```
stmt.setLong(1,PRIVATEACCOUNT.getId);
stmt.setLong(2,MONEYMARKETACCOUNT.getId);
stmt.setLong(3,BROKERAGE.getId);
stmt.execute();
ResultSet standardAccountTypes = stmt.executeQuery();
```


Similarly, you need to update source code that validates the values of data attributes. For example, you may have code that defines premium accounts as being either of type *Private* or *Money Market* in your application logic. You now have to add *Brokerage* to this list, as you see in the following code:

```
//Before code
public enum PremiumAccountType {
  PRIVATEACCOUNT(new Long(3)),
  MONEYMARKET(new Long(4));

private Long id;
public Long getId() {
  return id;
}

PremiumAccountType(Long value) {
  this.id = value;
}

public static Boolean
  isPremiumAccountType(Long idToFind) {
    for (PremiumAccountType premiumAccountType :
          PremiumAccountType.values()) {
      if (premiumAccountType.id.equals(idToFind))
        return Boolean.TRUE;
      }
       Return Boolean.FALSE
}

//After code
public enum PremiumAccountType {
  PRIVATEACCOUNT(new Long(3)),
  MONEYMARKET(new Long(4)),
  BROKERAGE(new Long(6));

private Long id;
public Long getId() {
  return id;
}

PremiumAccountType(Long value) {
  this.id = value;
}
```

```
public static Boolean
  isPremiumAccountType(Long idToFind) {
    for (PremiumAccountType premiumAccountType :
          PremiumAccountType.values()) {
      if (premiumAccountType.id.equals(idToFind))
        return Boolean.TRUE;
      }
       Return Boolean.FALSE
}
```

Introduce New Column

Introduce a new column in an existing table.

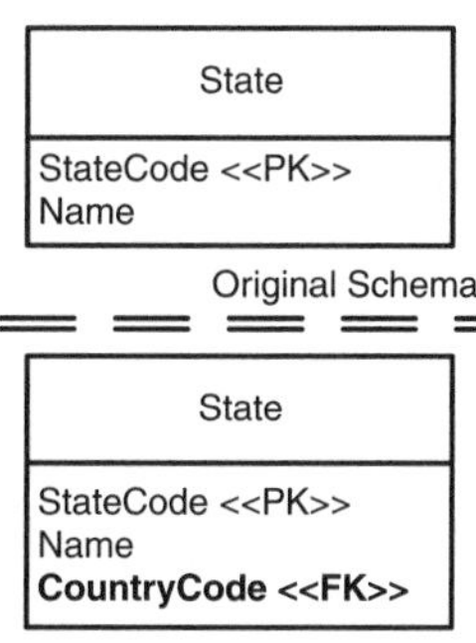

Figure 11.2 Introducing the State.CountryCode column.

Motivation

There are several reasons why you may want to apply the *Introduce New Column* transformation:

- **To persist a new attribute.** A new requirement may necessitate the addition of a new column in your database.
- **Intermediate step of a refactoring.** Many database refactorings, such as *Move Column* (page 103) and *Rename Column* (page 109), include a step in which you introduce a new column into an existing table.

Potential Tradeoffs

You need to ensure that the column does not exist elsewhere; otherwise, you are at risk of increasing referential integrity problems due to greater data redundancy.

Schema Update Mechanics

As depicted in Figure 11.2, to update the database schema you must simply introduce *CountryCode* via the **ADD** clause of the **ALTER TABLE** SQL command. The *State.CountryCode* column is a foreign key reference to the *Country* table (not shown), enabling our application(s) to track states by country. The following code depicts the DDL to introduce the *State.CountryCode* column. To create the referential constraint, apply the *Add Foreign Key Constraint* refactoring (page 204):

```
ALTER TABLE State ADD Country Code VARCHAR2(3) NULL;
```

Data-Migration Mechanics

Although not a data migration per se, a significant primary challenge with this transformation is to populate the column with data values after you have added it to the table. You need to do the following:

1. Work with your project stakeholders to identify the appropriate values.
2. Either manually input the new values into the column or write a script to automatically populate the column (or a combination of the two strategies).
3. Consider applying the refactorings *Introduce Default Value* (page 186) *Drop Non-Nullable* (page 177), or *Make Column Non-Nullable* (page 189), as appropriate, to this new column.

The following code depicts the DML to populate *State.CountryCode* with the initial value of 'USA':

```
UPDATE State SET CountryCode = 'USA'
  WHERE CountryCode IS NULL;
```

Access Program Update Mechanics

The update mechanics are simple because all you must do is use the new column in your application(s) to work with the new column. In the following code, we show an example of how hibernate OR mapping meta data would be affected:

```
//Before mapping
<hibernate-mapping>
<class name="State" table="STATE">
  <id name="id" column="StateCode"></id>
  <property name="name"/>
</class>
</hibernate-mapping>
```

```
//After mapping
<hibernate-mapping>
<class name="State" table="STATE">
  <id name="id" column="StateCode"></id>
  <property name="name"/>
  <many-to-one name="country"
              class="Country"
              column="COUNTRYCODE"/>
</class>
</hibernate-mapping>
```

Introduce New Table

Introduce a new table in an existing database.

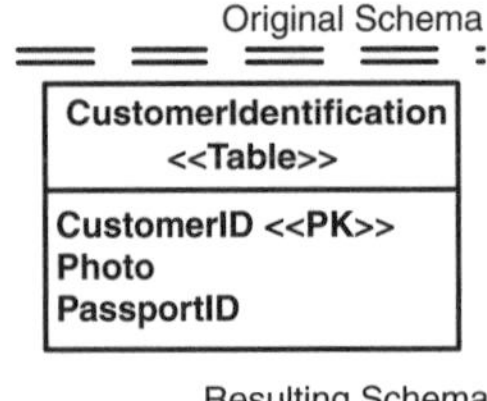

Figure 11.3 Introducing the CustomerIdentification table.

Motivation

There are several reasons why you may want to apply the *Introduce New Table* transformation:

- **To persist a new attribute.** A new requirement may necessitate the addition of a new table in your database.
- **As an intermediate step of a refactoring.** Many database refactorings, such as *Split Table* (page 145) and *Rename Table* (page 113), include a step in which you introduce a new table in place of an existing table.
- **To introduce a new official data source.** It is quite common to discover that similar information is stored in several tables. For example, there may be several sources of customer information, sources that are often out of synchronization with each other and sometimes even contradictory. In this scenario, you must use *Use Official Data Source* (page 271), and then over time apply *Drop Table* (page 77) to the original source tables.
- **Need to back up data.** While implementing some refactorings, such as *Drop Table* (page 77) or *Merge Tables* (page 96), you may need to create a table to hold table data for intermediate usages or for backup purposes.

Potential Tradeoffs

The primary tradeoff is that you need to ensure that the table you want to introduce does not exist elsewhere already. Often, the exact table that you require will not exist, but something close will—you may discover that it is easier to refactor that existing table than it is to add a new table containing redundant information.

Schema Update Mechanics

As depicted in Figure 11.3, to update the database schema you must simply introduce *CustomerIdentification* via the **CREATE TABLE** SQL command. The following code depicts the DDL to introduce the *CustomerIdentification* table. The *CustomerIdentification.CustomerID* column is a foreign key reference to the *Customer* table (not shown), enabling our application(s) to track the various ways to identify individual customers:

```
CREATE TABLE CustomerIdentification(
  CustomerID NUMBER NOT NULL,
  Photo      BLOB,
  PassportID NUMBER,
  CONSTRAINT PK_CustomerIdentification
    PRIMARY KEY (CustomerID)
  );
```

Data-Migration Mechanics

Although not a data migration per se, a significant primary challenge with this transformation is to populate the table with data values after you have added it to the database. You need to do the following:

1. Work with your project stakeholders to identify the appropriate values.
2. Either manually input the new values into the table or write a script to automatically populate the table (or a combination of the two strategies).
3. Consider applying the *Insert Data* transformation (page 296).

Access Program Update Mechanics

Ideally, the update mechanics are straightforward because all you should have to do is use the new table in your application(s) to work with the new table. However, when you are introducing a new table as a replacement for several other tables, you will often discover that your new table has a slightly different schema, and worse yet implements slightly different data semantics, than the existing tables. When this is the case, you need to refactor the access programs to work with the new version.

Introduce View

Create a view based on existing tables in the database.

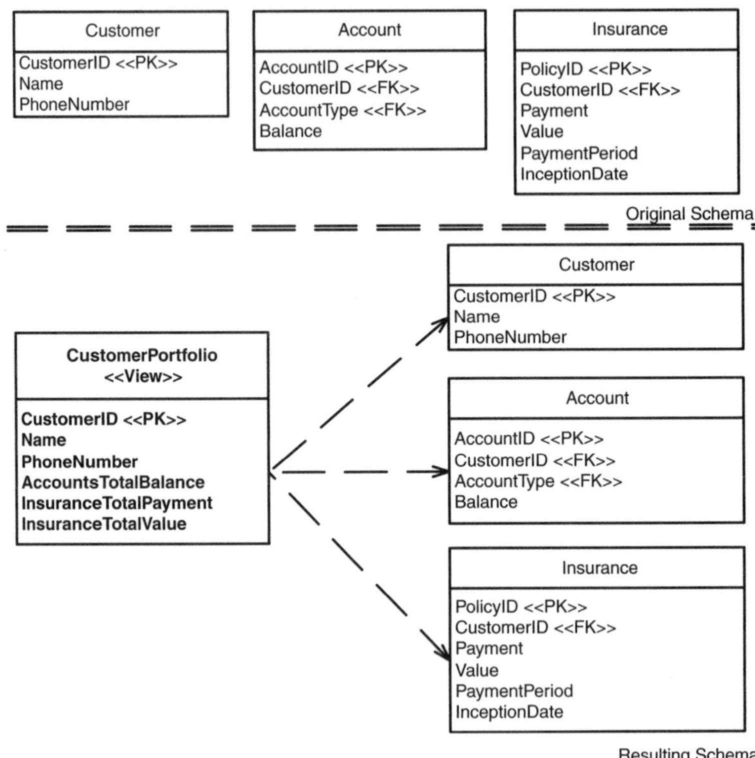

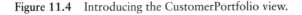

Figure 11.4 Introducing the CustomerPortfolio view.

Motivation

There are several reasons why you may want to apply *Introduce View*:

- **Summarize data for reporting.** Many reports require summary data, which can be generated via the view definition.
- **Replace redundant reads.** Several external programs, or stored procedures for that matter, often implement the same retrieval query. These queries can be replaced by a common read-only table or view.

- **Data security.** A view can be used to provide end users with read access to data but not update privileges.
- **Encapsulate access to a table.** Some organizations choose to encapsulate access to tables by defining updateable views that external programs access instead of the source tables. This enables the organization to easily perform database refactorings such as *Rename Column* (page 109) or *Rename Table* (page 113) without impacting the external applications, because views add an encapsulation layer between your tables and your application.
- **Reduce SQL duplication.** When you have complex SQL queries in an application, it is common to discover that parts of the SQL are duplicated in many places. When this is the case, you should introduce views to extract out the duplicate SQL, as shown in the example section.

Potential Tradeoffs

There are two primary challenges with introducing a view. First, the performance of the joins defined by the view may not be acceptable to your end users, requiring a different approach such as the refactoring *Introduce Read-Only Table* (page 251). Second, the addition of a new view increases the coupling within your database schema—as you can see in Figure 11.4, the view definition depends on the table schema(s) definitions.

Schema Update Mechanics

To update the database schema when you perform *Introduce View*, you must simply introduce the view via the **CREATE VIEW** command. Figure 11.4 depicts an example where the *CustomerPortfolio* view is based on the *Customer, Account,* and *Insurance* tables to summarize the business that we do with each customer. This provides an easier way for end users to do ad-hoc queries. The following code depicts the DDL to introduce the *CustomerPortfolio* view:

```
CREATE VIEW CustomerPortfolio (
  CustomerID
  Name
  PhoneNumber
  AccountsTotalBalance
  InsuranceTotalPayment
  InsuranceTotalValue
) AS SELECT
  Customer.CustomerID,
```

Introduce View

```
  Customer.Name,
  Customer.PhoneNumber,
  SUM(Account.Balance),
  SUM(Insurance.Payment),
  SUM(Insurance.Value)
  FROM
    Customer,Account,Insurance
  WHERE
    Customer.CustomerID=Account.CustomerID
    AND Customer.CustomerID=Insurance.CustomerID
;
```

Data-Migration Mechanics

There is no data to migrate with this database refactoring.

Access Program Update Mechanics

The update mechanics depend on the situation. If you are introducing the view to replace common SQL retrieval code within access programs, you must refactor that code accordingly to use the new view instead. If you are introducing the view for reporting purposes, new reports should be written to take advantage of that view. For programs accessing the view, the view looks like a read-only table.

When SQL code in your application is duplicated, there is a greater potential for bugs because when you change the SQL in one place, you must make similar changes to all of the duplicates. For example, let's consider instances of application SQL code:

```
SELECT Customer.CustomerID, SUM(Insurance.Payment), SUM(Insurance.Value)
FROM Customer, Insurance
WHERE
  Customer.CustomerID=Insurance.CustomerID
  AND Customer.Status = 'ACTIVE'
  AND Customer.InBusinessSince <= TodaysDateLastYear
GROUP BY Customer.CustomerID
;

SELECT Customer.CustomerID, SUM(Account.Balance)
FROM Customer, Account
WHERE
  Customer.CustomerID=Account.CustomerID
  AND Customer.Status = 'ACTIVE'
  AND Customer.InBusinessSince <= TodaysDateLastYear
GROUP BY Customer.CustomerID
```

As you can see in the preceding two code examples, the part to select an active customer is duplicated. We can create a view that extracts this duplicated SQL into the view and you can use the view in these SQLs, so that when the SQL to select an active customer changes, you do not have to change it multiple times:

```
CREATE OR REPLACE VIEW ActiveCustomer
SELECT Customer.CustomerID
FROM Customer
WHERE
  Customer.Status = 'ACTIVE'
  AND Customer.InBusinessSince <= TodaysDateLastYear
;

SELECT ActiveCustomer.CustomerID,
SUM(Insurance.Payment), SUM(Insurance.Value)
FROM ActiveCustomer, Insurance
WHERE ActiveCustomer.CustomerID=Insurance.CustomerID
GROUP BY ActiveCustomer.CustomerID
;

SELECT ActiveCustomer.CustomerID, SUM(Account.Balance)
FROM ActiveCustomer, Account
WHERE ActiveCustomer.CustomerID=Account.CustomerID
GROUP BY ActiveCustomer.CustomerID
;
```

Update Data

Update data within an existing table.

Schema:

AccountType
AccountTypeID <<PK>> Name EffectiveDate

Data Values Before:

AccountType		
AccountTypeID	Name	EffectiveDate
1	Checking	Dec 6 2005
2	Saving	Nov 12 2005
3	Private	Jan 7 2006
4	Money Market	Jun 4 2006
5	Credit	Mar 12 2006

Data Values After:

AccountType		
AccountTypeID	Name	EffectiveDate
1	**Chequing**	**Sep 29 2006**
2	Saving	Nov 12 2005
3	**Private Banking**	**Sep 29 2006**
4	Money Market	Jun 4 2006
5	Credit	Mar 12 2006

Figure 11.5 Updating the AccountType table with new names.

Motivation

You may need to apply *Update Data* as the result of the following:

- **Table reorganization.** When you apply *Rename Table* (page 113), *Rename Column* (page 109), *Move Column* (page 103), *Split Table* (page 145), *Split Column* (page 140), *Merge Tables* (page 96), or *Merge Columns* (page 92), you may have to apply *Update Data* to reorganize the data in the existing tables.
- **Provide data where none existed.** When applying transformations such as *Introduce New Column* (page 301), you may need to provide data for the newly added column in your existing production databases. For example,

if you added a *Country* column to the *Address* table, you would need to populate it with appropriate values.

- **Change reference data.** When business rules change, there is a need to change some of the reference/lookup data. For example, you need to change the *AccountType.Name* value to 'Private Banking' from 'Private' due to a change in business terminology.
- **Support a column change.** Refactorings such as *Apply Standard Codes* (page 157) and *Apply Standard Types* (page 162) often require an update to the values stored in the column. The first refactoring often consolidates the values being used within a column—for example "US", "USA", and "U.S." are consolidated to the single value of "USA". The second refactoring often requires a conversion of data values, from numeric to character for example.
- **Fix transactional data.** Because of defects in a deployed application or database, you may get invalid results that need to be changed as part of fixing the defect(s). For example, an application may have populated incorrect interest amount in the *Charges* table for a customer, based on data in the *InterestRate* table; as part of fixing this defect, you must update the *InterestRate* table and the *Charges* table to reflect the correct value.

Potential Tradeoffs

Updating data in tables can prove tricky, especially when you are going to update reference data. For example, assume the *Account* table references data in the *AccountType* table. The data that you update in *AccountType* must contain values that make sense for the data contained with *Account*. When you are updating data, you must ensure that you are updating only, and all of, the correct rows.

Schema Update Mechanics

The database schema does not change with this transformation.

Data-Migration Mechanics

When small amounts of data need to be updated, you will likely find that a simple SQL script that updates the target table(s) is sufficient. For large amounts of data to be updated, you need to take a more sophisticated approach, such as using an extract-transform-load (ETL) tool, particularly when the data is being derived based on complex algorithms from existing table data. Important issues to consider include the following:

- Is the source data being provided from existing application tables, or is the data being provided by your business users?
- Have the values been accepted by your project stakeholder(s)?
- Which rows need to be updated?
- Which columns of those rows?
- What dependencies exist?

Figure 11.5 depicts how we update in the *AccountType* table representing brokerage accounts. This *AccountType* supports new naming convention that needs to first be tested and then deployed into production later on. The following code depicts the DML to update data in the *AccountType* table:

```
UPDATE AccountType SET Name = 'Chequing'
  WHERE AccountTypeID=1;

UPDATE AccountType SET Name = 'Private Banking'
  WHERE AccountTypeID=3;
```

Access Program Update Mechanics

When *Update Data* is applied as the result of another database refactoring, the external programs should have been updated to reflect that refactoring. When *Update Data* is applied to support the change of data within an existing schema, it is possible that external code will need to be changed. First, you may need to update **SELECT** statements to have the correct values in the **WHERE** clause. For example, assume you update values into the *AccountType* table for the row where *AccountType.Name* is "Private" and is now defined as "Private Banking".

Similarly, you may need to update source code that validates the values of data attributes. For example, you may have code that tries to validate whether the *AccountType* is "Private". Now that code needs to change, and it needs to validate whether the *AccountType* is "Private Banking" in your logic.

The following view definition shows how the affected parts of the application need to change when the "Private" account type is changed to "Private Banking":

```
//Before view
CREATE OR REPLACE VIEW PrivateAccounts AS
SELECT
  Account.AccountId,
  Account.CustomerId,
  Account.StartDate,
  Account.Balance,
  Account.isPrimary
FROM
  Account, AccountType
WHERE
  Account.AccountTypeId = AccountType.AccountTypeId
  AND AccountType.Name = 'Private'
;

//After view
CREATE OR REPLACE VIEW PrivateAccounts AS
SELECT
  Account.AccountId,
  Account.CustomerId,
  Account.StartDate,
  Account.Balance,
  Account.isPrimary
FROM
  Account, AccountType
WHERE
  Account.AccountTypeId = AccountType.AccountTypeId
  AND AccountType.Name = 'Private Banking'
;
```

Appendix

The UML Data Modeling Notation

This appendix overviews the physical data modeling notation used throughout the book. We have used a subset of the notation described in the Unified Modeling Language (UML) profile originally presented in *Agile Database Techniques* (Ambler 2003) and now maintained online at www.agiledata.org/essays/umlDataModelingProfile.html.

Figure A.1 describes the basic notation for tables within a database schema. Tables are represented as boxes with one, two, or three sections. The first section, the one containing the table name, is mandatory. The other two are optional, the second one listing the columns of the table, and the third one listing the triggers

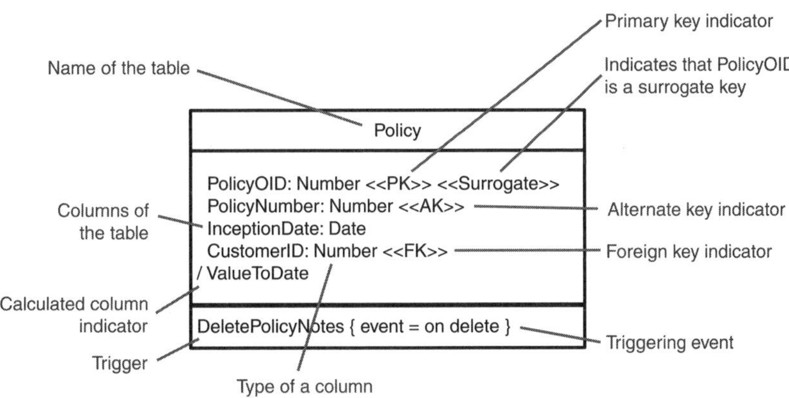

Figure A.1 Notation for modeling tables.

associated with the table (if any). In the column list, only the names are mandatory; throughout this book, for the sake of simplicity, we often list the names but not the types of the columns. When a column is part of a key, it is followed by one or more UML stereotypes, described in Table A.1.

It is possible to indicate more information pertaining to keys, as you can see in Figure A.2. The *PolicyNotes* table has three keys: a primary key made up of the *PolicyNumber* and *NoteNumber* columns, the first alternate key made up of the *PolicyOID* and *NoteNumber* columns, and the second alternate key *PolicyNoteOID* column. When a key is composite—in other words, it is made up of several columns—it can be important to indicate the order of the columns

Table A.1 *Stereotypes for Keys*

Stereotype	Usage
PK	Indicates that the column is part of the primary key for the table.
FK	Indicates that the column is part of a foreign key to another table.
AK	Indicates that the column is part of an alternate key, sometimes called a secondary key.
Natural	Indicates that the key is a natural property of the entity (for example, Policy) stored within the table. This stereotype is rarely assigned—if a key column is not labeled as a surrogate, it is assumed to be natural.
Surrogate	Indicates that the key is artificial (not natural).

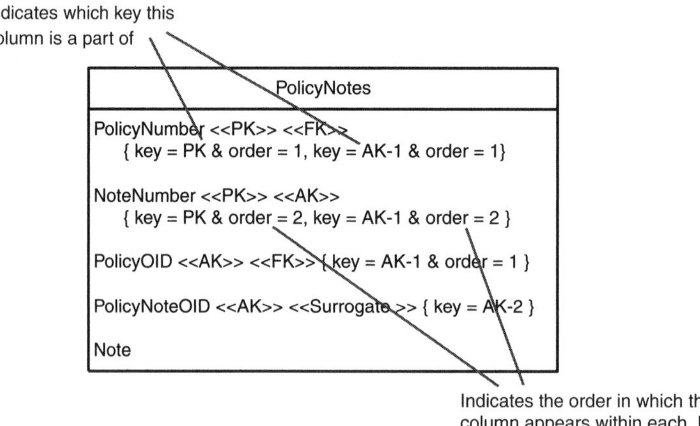

Figure A.2 Notation for modeling the details of keys.

within the key so that the corresponding indices are defined properly. Order is shown via the *order* named value. For example, we can see that the *PolicyNumber* column is the first column within the primary key and that *NoteNumber* is the second column. Because it adds clutter to your diagrams, you should indicate the order of columns only when necessary.

Relationships, often called associations, are modeled as solid lines between two tables. In Figure A.3, you would say that a customer may own zero or more policies, and that a policy is owned by a single customer. The arrowhead beside the *owns* label on the relationship between *Customer* and *Account* indicates the direction in which to read the relationship; this is an optional symbol to be used only when it is not clear which way to read it. Common convention is to write a label so that it makes sense when read from left to right, or top to bottom, as the case may be (Ambler 2005b). We know that customers may own zero or more policies—because of the multiplicity indicator of *0..** on the relationship line beside the *Policy* table—and that any given policy is owned by only one customer (as indicated by the other multiplicity indicator). Table A.2 summarizes the various multiplicity indicators.

In Figure A.3, we would also say that a customer accesses zero or more accounts and that an account is accessed by one or more customers. Although there is a many-to-many association between the customer and account entities, we cannot natively implement this in a relational database, hence the addition of the *CustomerAccount* associative table to maintain the relationship. Furthermore, an order item is part of a single order, and an order is made up of one or

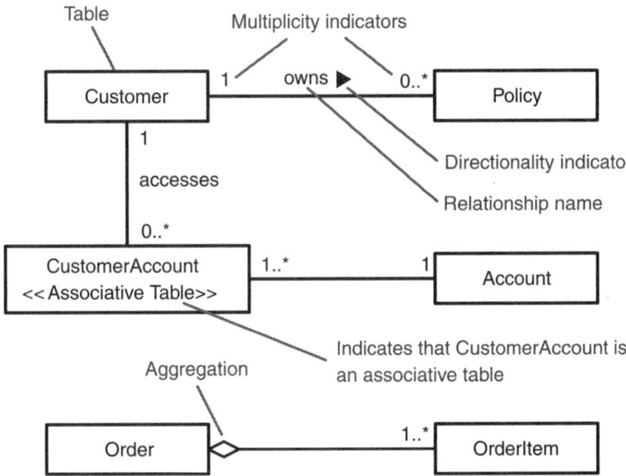

Figure A.3 Notation for modeling relationships.

more order items. The diamond on the end of the line indicates that the relationship between *Order* and *OrderItem* is one of aggregation, also called a "part of" association. When the multiplicity is not indicated beside the diamond, a *1* is assumed. Figure A.4 presents several more examples of relationships between tables and how to read them.

Table A.2 *UML Multiplicities*

Multiplicity	Meaning
0..1	Zero or one
1	One only
0..*	Zero or more
1..*	One or more
*	One or more
n	Only n (where n > 1)
0..n	Zero to n (where n > 1)
1..n	One to n (where n > 1)

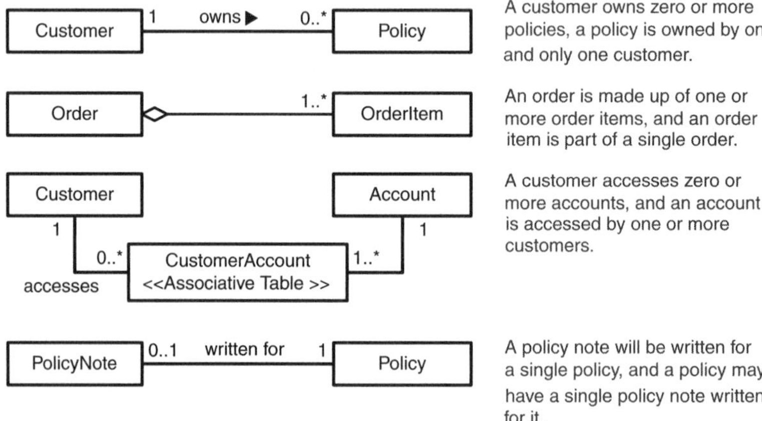
Customer
1
owns ▶
0..*
Policy
A customer owns zero or more policies, a policy is owned by one and only one customer.
Order
1..*
OrderItem
An order is made up of one or more order items, and an order item is part of a single order.
Customer
Account
1
1
0..*
CustomerAccount
<<Associative Table >>
1..*
accesses
A customer accesses zero or more accounts, and an account is accessed by one or more customers.
PolicyNote
0..1
written for
1
Policy
A policy note will be written for a single policy, and a policy may have a single policy note written for it.

Figure A.4 Examples of relationships.

Figure A.5 overviews the notation for several other common database concepts:

- **Stored procedures.** Stored procedures are presented in a two-section rectangle. The top section indicates the name of the database and the stereotype of *Stored Procedures*. The bottom section lists the signatures of the stored procedures (or functions) within the database.
- **Indices.** An index is modeled as a box with the name of the index, the stereotype *Index*, and dependency relationships pointing to the column(s) upon which the index is based.
- **Views.** A view is depicted as a two-section rectangle. The top section indicates the name of the view and the stereotype *View*. The bottom section, which is optional, lists the columns contained within the view.

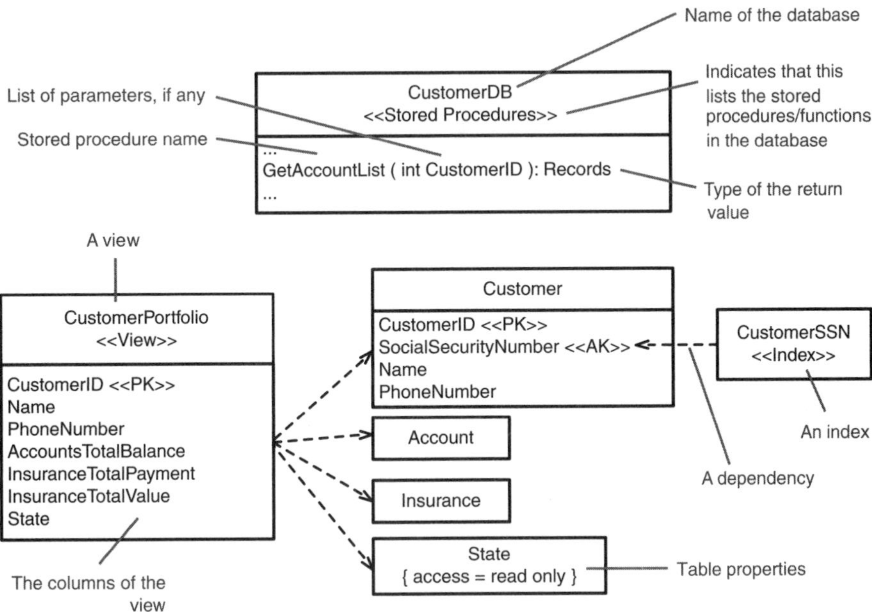

Figure A.5 Notation for modeling stored procedures, views, and indices.

Glossary

This glossary describes the major terms as we have used them within the context of this book.

Agile Data (AD) method A collection of philosophies and roles for defining how data-oriented development activities can be applied in an agile manner.

Agile Model-Driven Development (AMDD) A highly iterative approach to development in which you create agile models before you write source code.

Agile Modeling (AM) A chaordic, practices-based methodology that describes how to be effective at modeling and documentation.

Agile software development An evolutionary and highly collaborative approach to development in which the focus is on delivering high-quality, tested software that meets the highest-priority needs of its stakeholders on a regular basis.

Agile Unified Process (AUP) An instantiation of the Unified Process (UP) that applies common agile practices such as database refactoring, Test-Driven Development, and Agile Model-Driven Development.

Architectural refactoring A change that improves the overall manner in which external programs interact with a database.

Artifact A document, model, file, diagram, or other item that is produced, modified, or used during the development, operation, or support of a system.

Behavioral semantics The meaning of the functionality implemented within your database.

Code smell A common category of problem in your source code that indicates the need to refactor it.

Conceptual/domain model A model that depicts the main business entities and the relationships between them, and optionally the attributes or responsibilities of those entities.

Coupling A measure of the dependence between two items; the more highly coupled two things are, the greater the chance that a change in one will require a change in another.

Crystal A self-adapting family of "human-powered" agile methodologies developed by Alistair Cockburn.

Data access object (DAO) A class that implements the necessary database code to persist a corresponding business class.

Database refactoring (noun) A simple change to a database schema that improves its design while retaining both its behavioral and informational semantics—in other words, you can neither add new functionality nor break existing functionality, nor can you add new data nor change the meaning of existing data.

Database refactoring (verb) The process by which you evolve an existing database schema a small bit at a time to improve the quality of its design without changing its semantics.

Database regression testing A process in which you ensure that the database schema actually works by developing and then regularly running a test suite against it.

Database schema The structural aspects, such as table and view definitions, and the functional aspects, such as database methods, of a database.

Database smell A common problem within a database schema that indicates the potential need to refactor it.

Database transformation A change to your database schema that may or may not change the semantics of the schema. A database refactoring is a kind of database transformation.

Data definition language (DDL) Commands supported by a database that enable the creation, removal, or modification of structures (such as relational tables or classes) within it.

Data manipulation language (DML) Commands supported by a database that enables the access of data within it, including the creation, retrieval, update, and deletion of that data.

Data quality refactoring A change that improves the quality of the information contained within a database.

Demo sandbox A technical environment into which you deploy software to demonstrate it to people outside of your immediate development team.

Deployment window A specific point in time during which it is permissible to deploy a system into production. Often called a release window.

Deprecation period *See* Transition period.

Development sandbox A technical environment in which IT professionals write, test, and build software.

Dynamic System Development Method (DSDM) An agile method that is a formalization of the Rapid Application Development (RAD) methods of the 1980s.

Enterprise Unified Process (EUP) An extension to the Rational Unified Process (RUP) which addresses the cross-project/system needs.

Evolutionary data modeling A process in which you model the data aspects of a system iteratively and incrementally, to ensure that the database schema evolves in step with the application code.

Evolutionary software development An approach in which you work both iteratively and incrementally.

Extract-transform-load (ETL) An approach to moving data from one source to another in which you "cleanse" it during the process.

Extreme Programming (XP) A disciplined and deliberate agile development method that focuses on the critical activities required to build software.

Feature-Driven Development (FDD) An agile development method based on short iterations that is driven by a shared object domain model and features (small requirements).

Incremental software development An approach to software development that organizes a project into several releases instead of one "big-bang" release.

Informational semantics The meaning of the information within the database from the point of view of the users of that information.

Iteration A period of time, often a week or two, during which working software is written. Also called a development cycle.

Iterative software development A nonserial approach to development in which you are likely to do some requirements definition, some modeling, some programming, or some testing on any given day.

Method Within a database, a stored procedure, stored function, or trigger.

Method refactoring A change to a method that improves its quality. Many code refactorings are applicable to database methods.

Model storming A short burst of modeling, often 5 to 15 minutes in duration, in which two or more people work together to explore part of the problem or solution domain. Model storming sessions are immediately followed by coding sessions (often several hours or days in length).

Multi-application database A database that is accessed by several applications, one or more of which are outside the scope of your control.

Object-relational mapping (ORM) The definition of a relationship(s) between the data aspects of an object schema (for example, Java classes) and a relational database schema.

Production environment The technical environment in which end users run one or more systems.

Production phase The portion of the system life cycle where the system is run by its end users.

Project integration sandbox A technical environment where the code of all project team members is compiled and tested.

Rapid Application Development (RAD) An approach to software development that is highly evolutionary in nature that typically involves significant amounts of user interface prototyping.

Rational Unified Process (RUP) A rigorous, four-phase software development process created by IBM Rational that is evolutionary in nature.

Refactoring (noun) A simple change to source code that retains its behavioral semantics: You neither add functionality when you are refactoring nor take it away. A refactoring merely improves the design of your code—nothing more and nothing less.

Refactoring (verb) A programming technique that enables you to evolve your code slowly over time, to take an evolutionary approach to programming.

Referential integrity The assurance that a reference from one entity to another entity is valid. If entity A references entity B, entity B exists. If entity B is removed, all references to entity B must also be removed.

Referential integrity refactoring A change that ensures that a referenced row exists within another table and/or ensures that a row that is no longer needed is removed appropriately.

Regression test suite A collection of tests that are run against a system on a regular basis to validate that it works according to the tests.

Sandbox A fully functioning environment in which a system may be built, tested, and/or run.

Scrum An agile method whose focus is on project management and requirements management. Scrum is often combined with XP.

Serial development An approach in which fairly detailed models are created before implementation is "allowed" to begin. Also known as waterfall development.

Single-application database A database that is accessed by a single application that is "owned" by the same team that owns the database.

Standup meeting A short meeting that is held with team members standing up and giving status reports on tasks they did yesterday and plan to do today, problems they faced, architecture they changed, and other important things that need to be communicated to the team.

Stereotype A UML construct that denotes a common use of a modeling element. Stereotypes are used to extend the UML in a consistent manner.

Structural refactoring A change to the definition of one or more tables or views.

Test-Driven Development (TDD) The combination of TFD and refactoring.

Test-First Development (TFD) An evolutionary approach to development in which you must first write a test that fails before you write new functional code so that the test passes. This is also known as Test-First Programming.

Transaction A single unit of work that either completely succeeds or completely fails. A transaction may be one or more updates to an object, one or more reads, one or more deletes, one or more insertions, or any combination thereof.

Transition period The time during which both the old schema and the new schema are supported in parallel. Also referred to as a deprecation period.

Trigger A database method that is automatically invoked as the result of Data Manipulation Language (DML) activity within a persistence mechanism.

Unified Modeling Language (UML) The definition of a standard modeling language for object-oriented software, including the definition of a modeling notation and the semantics for applying it, as defined by the Object Management Group (OMG).

Waterfall development *See* Serial development.

XUnit A family of unit testing tools, including JUnit for Java, VBUnit for Visual Basic, NUnit for .NET, and OUnit for Oracle.

References and Recommended Reading

Agile Alliance (2001a). *Manifesto for Agile Software Development.* www.agilealliance.com

Agile Alliance (2001b). *Principles: The Agile Alliance.* www.agilealliance.com/principles.html

Ambler, S. W. (2002). *Agile Modeling: Best Practices for the Unified Process and Extreme Programming.* New York: John Wiley & Sons. www.ambysoft.com/agileModeling.html

Ambler, S. W. (2003). *Agile Database Techniques: Effective Strategies for the Agile Software Developer.* New York: John Wiley & Sons. www.ambysoft.com/agileDatabaseTechniques.html

Ambler, S. W. (2004). *The Object Primer, 3rd Edition: Agile Model Driven Development with UML 2.* New York: Cambridge University Press. www.ambysoft.com/theObjectPrimer.html

Ambler, S. W. (2005a). *A UML Profile for Data Modeling.* www.agiledata.org/essays/umlDataModelingProfile.html

Ambler, S. W. (2005b). *The Elements of UML 2.0 Style.* New York: Cambridge University Press. www.ambysoft.com/elementsUMLStyle.html

Ambler, S. W. (2005c). *The Agile Unified Process.* www.ambysoft.com/unifiedprocess/agileUP.html

Astels D. (2003). *Test Driven Development: A Practical Guide.* Upper Saddle River, NJ: Prentice Hall.

Beck, K. (2003). *Test Driven Development: By Example.* Boston: Addison-Wesley.

Boehm, B. W., and Turner, R. (2003). *Balancing Agility and Discipline: A Guide for the Perplexed.* Reading, MA: Addison-Wesley Longman, Inc.

Burry, C., and Mancusi, D. (2004). *How to Plan for Data Migration.* Computerworld. www.computerworld.com/databasetopics/data/story/0,10801,93284,00.html

Celko, J. (1999). *Joe Celko's Data & Databases: Concepts in Practice.* San Francisco: Morgan Kaufmann.

Cockburn, A. (2002). *Agile Software Development.* Reading, MA: Addison-Wesley Longman, Inc.

Date, C. J. (2001). *An Introduction to Database System, 7/e.* Reading, MA: Addison-Wesley Longman, Inc.

Feathers, M. (2004). *Working Effectively with Legacy Code.* Boston: Addison-Wesley.

Fowler, M. (1999). *Refactoring: Improving the Design of Existing Code.* Menlo Park, CA: Addison-Wesley Longman.

Fowler, M., and Sadalage, P. (2003). *Evolutionary Database Design.* martinfowler.com/articles/evodb.html

Halpin, T. A. (2001). *Information Modeling and Relational Databases: From Conceptual Analysis to Logical Design.* San Francisco: Morgan Kaufmann.

Hay, D. C. (1996). *Data Model Patterns: Conventions of Thought.* New York: Dorset House Publishing.

Hay, D. C. (2003). *Requirements Analysis: From Business Views to Architecture.* Upper Saddle River, NJ: Prentice Hall.

Hernandez, M. J., and Viescas, J. L. (2000). *SQL Queries for Mere Mortals: A Hands-on Guide to Data Manipulation in SQL.* Reading, MA: Addison-Wesley.

Kerievsky, J. (2004). *Refactoring to Patterns.* Boston: Addison-Wesley.

Kyte, T. (2005). *Avoiding Mutating Tables.* asktom.oracle.com/~tkyte/Mutate/

Larman, C. (2004). *Agile and Iterative Development: A Manager's Guide.* Boston: Addison-Wesley.

Loshin, D. (2004a). *Issues and Opportunities in Data Quality Management Coordination. DM Review Magazine*, April 2004.

Loshin, D. (2004b). *More on Information Quality ROI.* The Data Administration Newsletter (TDAN.com), July 2004. www.tdan.com/nwt_issue29.htm

Manns, M. L., and Rising, L. (2005). *Fearless Change: Patterns for Introducing New Ideas*. Boston: Pearson Education, Ltd.

Meszaros, G. (2006). *Xunit Test Patterns: Refactoring Test Code*. Boston: Prentice Hall.

Muller, R. J. (1999). *Database Design for Smarties: Using UML for Data Modeling*. San Francisco: Morgan Kaufmann.

Mullins, C. S. (2002). *Database Administration: The Complete Guide to Practices and Procedures*. Reading, MA: Addison-Wesley Longman, Inc.

Pascal, F. (2000). *Practical Issues in Database Management: A Reference for the Thinking Practitioner*. Upper Saddle River, NJ: Addison-Wesley.

Sadalage, P., and Schuh, P. (2002). *The Agile Database: Tutorial Notes*. Paper presented at XP/Agile Universe 2002. Retrieved November 12, 2003 from www.xpuniverse.com

Seiner, R. (2004). *Data Stewardship Performance Measures*. The Data Administration Newsletter, July 2004.
www.tdan.com/i029fe01.htm

Williams, L., and Kessler, R. (2002). *Pair Programming Illuminated*. Boston: Addison-Wesley.

Index

A

B–C

D

F

G–H

I

J–K

L

M

N

O–P

Q–R

T

U

THIS BOOK IS SAFARI ENABLED

INCLUDES FREE 45-DAY ACCESS TO THE ONLINE EDITION

The Safari® Enabled icon on the cover of your favorite technology book means the book is available through Safari Bookshelf. When you buy this book, you get free access to the online edition for 45 days.

Safari Bookshelf is an electronic reference library that lets you easily search thousands of technical books, find code samples, download chapters, and access technical information whenever and wherever you need it.

TO GAIN 45-DAY SAFARI ENABLED ACCESS TO THIS BOOK:

- Go to **http://www.awprofessional.com/safarienabled**
- Complete the brief registration form
- Enter the coupon code found in the front of this book on the "Copyright" page

If you have difficulty registering on Safari Bookshelf or accessing the online edition, please e-mail customer-service@safaribooksonline.com.